the Wilton Way of Cake Decorating

the Wilton Way of Cake Decorating

EDITED BY EUGENE T. AND MARILYNN C. SULLIVAN

WILTON ENTERPRISES, INC., WOODRIDGE, ILLINOIS

Printed and bound in the United States of America

FIRST EDITION

Library of Congress Catalog Card Number: 74-13330
International Standard Book Number: 0-912696-16-8

Library of Congress Cataloging in Publication Data
Sullivan, Marilynn C.

   The Wilton Way of Cake Decorating, Volume Three

    1. Cake decorating. I. Sullivan, Eugene T.,
joint author. II. Wilton Enterprises. III. Title.
TX771.S87   641.8/653   74-13330
ISBN 0-912696-16-8

**MEMBERS OF THE
WILTON BOOK DIVISION STAFF**

CO-EDITORS
Marilynn C. Sullivan
Eugene T. Sullivan

SENIOR DECORATOR
Michael Nitzsche

DECORATORS
Dong Tuy Hoa
Amy Rohr

ART ASSISTANT
Sandra Larson

PRODUCTION ASSISTANT
Ethel LaRoche

STAFF PHOTOGRAPHER
Edward Hois

READERS' EDITOR
Diane Kish

DECORATING CONSULTANT
Norman Wilton

Volume Three of *The Wilton Way of Cake Decorating,* much more than any other book on decorating, goes to the very heart of this fascinating art. It highlights the importance of tubes—the basic tools employed by the decorator.

DECORATING TUBES were among the very first products manufactured by Wilton in the early days of our company. Then, tools for cake decorating were generally only available to bakers and other professionals. To bring the fun and excitement of decorating to everyone, Wilton first produced a few dozen basic tools, and then began teaching people with a desire to be creative how to use them. Most important and needed of all the tools were the tubes.

Now there are thousands of Wilton products available at shops and major stores throughout the country and, indeed, the entire world. Foremost among all these products are still the indispensable decorating tubes. We craft them to function as precisely as possible to assist you in decorating beautiful cakes.

By studying the pages of this book, you'll gain an amazing insight into the magic that each of the 180 tubes can perform. We've also pictured scores of outstanding cakes decorated through the use of the various families of tubes.

I'm proud to present this book to you, and hope it will lead you to even more enjoyable adventures in the rewarding art of cake decorating.

Vincent A. Naccarato

VINCENT A. NACCARATO, PRESIDENT
WILTON ENTERPRISES, INC.

CONTENTS

Section Four: The Leaf Tubes

Section Five: The Ribbon Tubes

Section Six: The Giant Tubes

Section Seven: The Specialty Tubes

Section Eight: Appendix

YOU CAN BE A GOOD DECORATOR by using just one or two dozen tubes for all your cakes, just those familiar to you through habit and experience.

YOU CAN BECOME AN ARTIST in this craft by exploring the full range of all 180 decorating tubes. Each produces its own unique form. Each creates effects no other tube can achieve. After all, cake decorating is just like music. Just a few notes in a limited range are enough to voice a simple melody—but the composer who aspires to works of rare and unusual beauty needs all the notes at his command.

SEVERAL YEARS AGO, we decided to work with all the decorating tubes in depth, to discover the ornate effects each tube was capable of. After just a few months of this fascinating effort we had made so many discoveries that we realized we could only share them with all of you in a really important book. That is how *Volume Three* of *The Wilton Way Of Cake Decorating* began. Now we are proud to offer it to you.

You'll find reading and studying *Volume Three* a real adventure. To make your learning easy, we've grouped the tubes into families. Within each family, each tube will produce an effect somewhat similar to that of other related tubes. Frankly, I was amazed myself at some of our discoveries. Did you know that tubes in each of the seven tube families can pipe realistic icing flowers that no other tube can produce? That a petal tube can pipe beautiful lettering? That a multiple-hole tube can make a delicate, lacy trim five times faster than a round tube?

We didn't stop just with showing borders, flowers, motifs and trims done with each tube. After all, the purpose of decorating is a beautiful cake, so we put all of these lovely forms on hundreds of magnificent new cakes. We hope you'll enjoy viewing them, and that they will inspire you to original masterpieces of your own.

THE ADVENTURE HAS JUST BEGUN. I know that each of you will come to new discoveries, new effects, new beauty as you work with these basic tools, the decorating tubes. These shared discoveries make cake decorating the fascinating art form it has become—ever changing, always beautiful.

NORMAN WILTON, FOUNDER
WILTON ENTERPRISES, INC.

CHAPTER ONE

Petal Tubes Pipe a Garden of Flowers

OF ALL THE TUBE FAMILIES, the petal tubes give decorators the most pleasure. They're just a joy to use—and the results are sheer beauty.

These tubes, quick hand movements and colorful icing pipe delicate petals to form flowers nearly as beautiful as nature's own.

Look through this chapter to renew your acquaintance with this wonder-working tube family. See a sampling of exquisite cakes trimmed with piped flowers—then go on to create blossoming masterpieces of your own.

BELOW: twin oval cakes crowned with bouquets piped with standard petal tubes. For description turn to page 18.

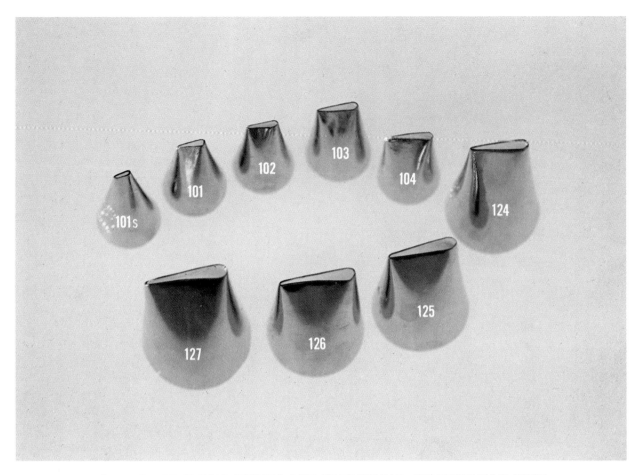

STANDARD PETAL TUBES ARE IDENTICAL, EXCEPT FOR SIZE

Pictured above are the standard petal tubes, the ones you'll use most often to pipe amazingly realistic flowers. Each has a long wedge-shaped opening. The wide end of this opening forms the base of the petal and gives solidity to the flower. The narrow end shapes the thin fragile edge of the petal.

The picture on the facing page shows you the roses and wild roses this family of tubes pipes. Each flower is pictured in actual size. Tubes 101s and 101 pipe flowers small enough for the daintiest petit four. Blossoms piped with tubes 102, 103 and 104 are usually used to trim cakes of moderate size. Tubes 124, 125, 126 and 127 form large and striking flowers to be used alone or in clusters for heroic effects.

For sharpest detail, and for convenience in piping ahead, we recommend royal icing for piping flowers. Flowers made with boiled icing have good detail too, and may be stored for some time—but only royal icing flowers may have spikes piped on their backs to attach firmly to cake sides. Flowers may be piped in buttercream, then air-dried or frozen for cake-top trim only. Experiment with the icing—it may need to be slightly stiffened with confectioners' sugar.

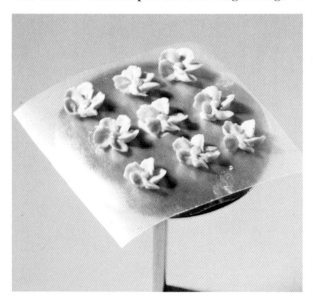

AT LEFT: a shortcut for piping tiny flowers. Attach a 3″ square of wax paper to a number 14 flower nail with a dot of icing. Pipe up to nine or ten little flowers on it.

TUBE 101s

TUBE 101

TUBE 102

TUBE 101s

TUBE 101

TUBE 103

TUBE 102

TUBE 104

TUBE 103

ROSES AND WILD ROSES
IN ACTUAL SIZE
PIPED WITH
STANDARD PETAL TUBES

TUBE 124

TUBE 104

TUBE 125

TUBE 124

TUBE 126

TUBE 125

TUBE 127

TUBE 126

TUBE 127

11

VIOLET
Tube 101

WILD ROSE
Tube 102

SWEET PEA
Tube 104

CALIFORNIA POPPY
Tube 103

DAFFODIL
Tube 104

DAISY
Tube 103

PANSY
Tube 104

ROSE
Tube 103

PETUNIA
Tube 102

MORNING GLORY
Tube 104

CARNATION
Tube 104

NASTURTIUM
Tube 103

Pictured at left are the flowers most favored by cake decorators, in their actual sizes. The same flowers can be made in larger or smaller versions simply by varying the sizes of the standard petal tubes used. The basic petal shapes and methods demonstrated here can be used to form many other beautiful icing flowers—hawthorne, apple blossoms, forget-me-nots, dogwood, iris and primroses. The nasturtium leaf and other rounded leaves are also piped with petal tubes. Most of the flowers are piped on a number 7 nail.

VIOLET. Tiny round petals form a flower of delightful daintiness. Make it in quantity, using the shortcut shown on page 10. For each little flower, hold tube 101 with wide end touching nail, narrow end slightly out. Squeeze and move tube out ½-inch as you turn nail to form a tiny petal. Form two more the same size, then finish with two ¼-inch petals. Pipe tube 1 stamens.

WILD ROSE. Another small and pretty blossom. Touch wide end of tube 103 to nail with narrow end lying almost flat. Squeeze as you move tube out ½-inch and back again, spinning nail and turning hand over slightly to create a petal with cupped edge. Pipe four more petals, overlapping them as you go. Pull out tube 1 stamens.

SWEET PEA. A trio of curved petals to use in graceful clusters. This simple version is piped quickly on a flat surface. Begin with center petal, touching tube 104 to surface with narrow end straight up. Squeeze, raising tube slightly, then relax pressure to bring petal to a point at base. Add two more curving petals at right and left.

CALIFORNIA POPPY. Full, flamboyant petals of brilliant hues. Press foil half-way into a 1¼" lily nail. Touch center of nail with wide end of tube 103, pulling icing over edge, then straight across and back to center for a square, cupped petal. Repeat for four petals. Pull out long tube 1 stamens.

DAFFODIL. Pointed petals surround the center trumpet. Pipe six long petals on flower nail with tube 104. Pinch petals into points with fingers dipped in cornstarch. Add tube 3 coil of string at center and edge top with a tight tube 1 zigzag.

DAISY. Slender white petals radiate around a heart of gold. With tube 103, pipe a dot of icing in middle of nail to center petals. Then touch wide end of tube to outer end of nail and squeeze, moving in to center dot. Decrease pressure so petal narrows slightly at base. Turning nail, repeat for a total of twelve petals. Squeeze a large

tube 5 dot at center. Pick up yellow-tinted sugar on damp finger and touch dot for pollen.

PANSY. One of the prettiest of the ruffled petal flowers. With tube 104, pipe two cupped back petals first, curving widely and overlapping. Then pipe two more, atop first two. For bottom half of flower, squeeze out a single full petal, using a back and forth motion for a ruffled effect. Add a final pair of small cupped petals, using very light pressure. Pipe a tube 1 loop.

ROSE. With this basic technique, you can make many rose varieties—by adding petals for a "cabbage" look, pinching petals at edges. Make a base for the flower by coiling a ribbon of icing into a cone on flower nail with tube 104 (wide end of tube down, narrow end straight up). Add rows of tube 104 overlapping petals, starting with three stand-up petals around base, then a second row of four or five petals curving out slightly and finally, a row of seven petals, turning narrow end of tube over so petals lie almost flat.

PETUNIA. Line a 1⅝" lily nail with foil. Pipe tube 102 petals, beginning at center well and moving to outer edge and over. Increase pressure as you reach outer edge and turn nail to widen and ruffle petal, then decrease as you return to center for a narrow petal base. Repeat for five identical petals, then center with tube 14 green star, topped with tube 1 yellow dots.

MORNING GLORY. A trumpet-shaped bloom with a five-pointed shape. Line a 1⅝" lily nail with foil and coil a tube 104 band of white icing in center well. Change to tube 103 and blue icing and pipe outer edge, increasing pressure in five places to form points. Brush colors smoothly together. Add a star shape and center dot with tube 1.

CARNATION. A fluffy, feminine blossom that looks like a little bouquet. Start with a tube 10 ball. Stiffen icing to give the characteristic ragged edge to petals and fit cone with tube 104. Pipe several upstanding petals in center of ball, then circle them with ruffled petals. As you continue piping rows of petals to cover ball, turn narrow end of tube farther out. Pipe last row of petals at base of flower with tube straight out.

NASTURTIUM. A fragile flower, very similar to the petunia but with petals that are wide at the outer edge and so narrow at the base they are almost separate. Line a 1⅝" flower nail with foil and pipe five petals with tube 103. Center with a tube 6 dot and push in artificial stamens.

Tube 59°

Tube 59

Tube 123

**TEARDROP-SHAPED OPENINGS
ON "LEFT-HANDED" PETAL TUBES
PIPE FURLED PETALS**

Tube 122

Tube 60

Tube 61

Tube 121

Tube 119

**"S"-SHAPED OPENINGS
ON THESE TUBES
PIPE LUSH ROSES**

Tube 97

Tube 116

Tube 118

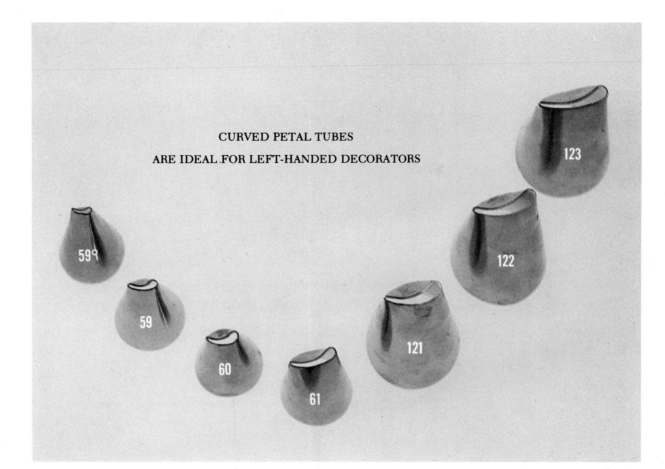

CURVED PETAL TUBES
ARE IDEAL FOR LEFT-HANDED DECORATORS

THE PETAL TUBES
WITH CURVED OPENINGS

Two groups in the petal tube family have curved openings that give petals an automatic, very attractive curl at the edges. Roses have a pretty, full-blown look, rosebuds look just about to open, the petals of wild roses have a lilting curve. Daisies have more pointed petals.

TUBES 59°, 59, 60, 61, 121, 122 AND 123 pipe identical but progressively larger flowers. These tubes have curved teardrop-shaped openings. The curved openings furl the petal edges as you pipe.

The unusual feature of these tubes is that *they are ideal for left-handed decorators.* In contrast to piping with standard petal tubes, turn the flower nail *clockwise* as you pipe the petals, adding one to the left of another. Right-handed decorators, please note.

TUBES 97, 116, 118 AND 119 have openings with double, "S"-shaped curves—wider at one end, narrow at the other. The wide end forms the base of the petal, the same as the standard petal tubes. Using these tubes, roses have a very lush, almost overblown appearance.

THE PETAL TUBES
WITH DOUBLE CURVES

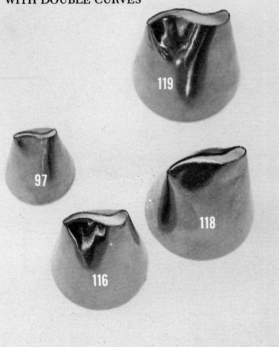

THE FLOWER NAILS . . . EACH LITTLE TURNTABLE HAS A SPECIAL USE

Before beginning to pipe flowers, attach a wax paper square with a dot of icing to the flat nails. Press foil smoothly into the well-shaped nails, and cover dome nails with foil.

The flat "table top" nails, numbers 1, 2, 7, 9, 13 and 14 are used to pipe a wide variety of flowers—the rose, violet, daisy, dogwood and many more. Use the size of nail that best accommodates the tube used—then the outer edge of the nail will guide the circumference of the flower. Nail number 1 pipes small roses made with tube 101s or 101, plus many others—violets, apple blossoms, wild roses. The number 7 nail has the most frequent use and numbers 13 and 14 hold very large flowers or a number of tiny ones. (See page 10.)

The dome nails, numbers 3 and 6, pipe large hollow chrysanthemums and carnations without the use of the icing ball for base. Start petals at the outer edge of the nail and work up toward center. Nail number 3 is also used for piping shaped lattice and lace.

Nail number 4 curves the petals of zinnias and small jonquils. Nail number 5 gives a tilt to daisies and pansies. Use nail number 8 for oriental poppies, or for any flower usually made in a lily nail where a shallower bell-shape is desired. Nail number 12 is the lily nail and helps form many bell-shaped flowers. Tubes 103 and 104 are the ideal sizes for use with this nail.

THE TWO-PIECE LILY NAILS at left have two advantages. By placing a square of foil over the lower half of nail and pressing with the upper half, lining the nail is made fast and automatic. The large range of sizes make it possible to pipe flowers as tiny as a shamrock or very large morning glories or Easter lilies.

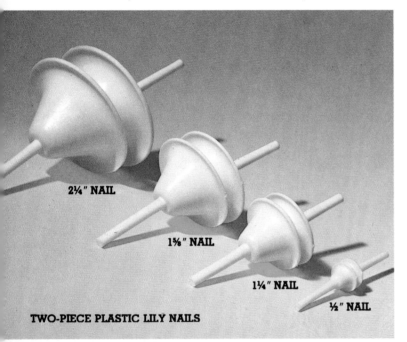

2¼" NAIL

1⅜" NAIL

1¼" NAIL

½" NAIL

TWO-PIECE PLASTIC LILY NAILS

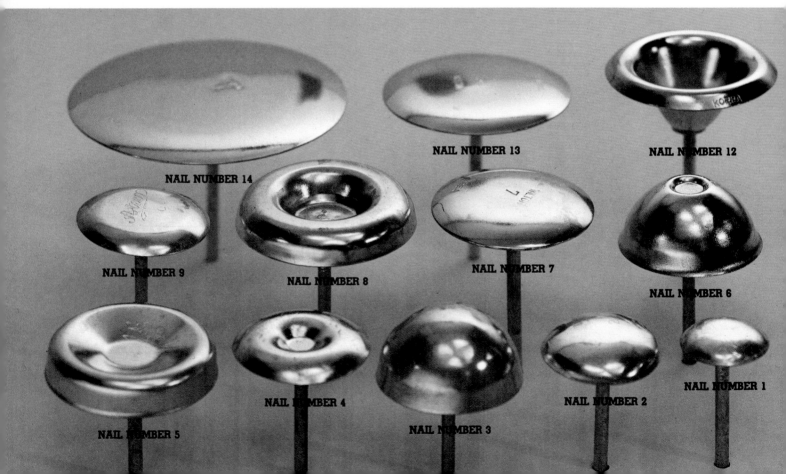

NAIL NUMBER 14

NAIL NUMBER 13

NAIL NUMBER 12

NAIL NUMBER 9

NAIL NUMBER 8

NAIL NUMBER 7

NAIL NUMBER 6

NAIL NUMBER 5

NAIL NUMBER 4

NAIL NUMBER 3

NAIL NUMBER 2

NAIL NUMBER 1

A DAINTY, BLOSSOMING BIRTHDAY CAKE

Clusters of flowers, as pretty as those in an old-fashioned garden, circle this sweet cake for a girl of any age. Curved petal tubes are used to pipe the flowers and give them a special fluffy charm. See these tubes on page 15.

STEP ONE. Pipe the royal icing flowers in advance. Use tube 97 for the roses and buds, pipe daisies with tubes 59 and 97 and add tube 4 centers. Pipe the wild roses with tubes 59 and 59° and add tube 1 stamens. Set flowers aside to dry.

STEP TWO. Prepare the cake. Bake two layers in 10″ round pans, fill and ice smoothly with buttercream. Divide top edge into sixths and mark with a toothpick for flower clusters. Lightly mark a 3″ and a 4″ circle on top center of cake as guide for scallops. Cookie cutters do this quickly.

STEP THREE. Pipe a shell border at base of cake with tube 105, then go back and pipe contrasting strings in grooves of shells with tube 3.

Using marks at top edge as guide, drop six curves of double and triple strings with tube 3 on side of cake to frame flower clusters. Connect each group of strings with triple dropped strings and add double dots at points. Pipe a tube 16 top shell border. Insert taper in center of cake, edge with tube 3 and pipe parallel scallops and dots with same tube.

Mound icing on cake edge at marked points and arrange flowers attaching each with a dot of icing. Finish with tube 65 leaves. Light the candle and serve to 14 guests.

17

One cake for the bride and two for the parents of the bridal couple—a thoughtful touch for a summer wedding to add a special glow of love.

PIPE THE ROYAL ICING FLOWERS in advance. Use tubes 102 and 103 for daisies and add tube 5 centers to each. Use tubes 102, 103 and 104 for wild roses and center all with tube 1. Pipe roses with tubes 103 and 104. For the carnation, use a tube 10 base on a number 7 flower nail and add petals with tube 104. When dry, pipe spikes on the backs of a few roses, carnations and poppies to attach to side of bridal cake. Mount a few smaller flowers on wires for ornament.

RUFFLED SWEET PEA. Use tube 103 and begin with side petals. Use back and forth motions to create a ruffly petal, swinging curves to left and to right. Finish with ruffled center petal.

HIMALAYAN POPPY. Pipe on a flower nail, using tube 104. Form four rounded, slightly ruffled petals, overlapping them. Finish with a cluster of tube 1 dots, add artificial stamens.

THE BRIDAL CAKE

TO PREPARE THE CAKE, bake two two-layer round tiers, 12″ and 16″, each layer 2″ high—and a two-layer oval tier, each layer 1½″ high. Fill, ice and assemble on cake board.

Divide top edge of oval tier into fourteenths. Leaving a 3″ space open on front and back of tier, drop strings to define three curves on each end. Divide top edge of middle tier into twelfths and drop strings to define curves. Using middle tier

RUFFLED SWEET PEA

HIMALAYAN POPPY

as guide, divide top edge of base tier into twelfths, then between each division for a total of 24. Divide side into fourths, leaving a 3″ open space between each. Drop three guidelines for curves in each division.

TRIM BASE TIER. Pipe a tube 7 line of icing around bottom. Over it, pipe a tube 126 pleated ribbon, using a shell motion. Following string guidelines, pipe tube 124 ruffles, then cover with ribbon swags. Pipe scallops from mark to mark on tier top with same tube. Finish with tube 4 dots at scallop points.

TRIM CENTER TIER. Pipe a tube 6 line around base of tier, cover with tube 124 pleated shell-motion ribbon. Use tube 124 to pipe a ruffle, then a ribbon over string guidelines. Pipe a tube 5 top ball border, then cover with a tube 126 ruffle.

TRIM TOP TIER. Pipe a tube 124 ruffle at base of tier, then edge with tube 3 beading. Following guidelines, pipe tube 104 ribbon swags and trim points with pairs of tube 3 beads. Edge tier top with tube 103 ruffled scallops from mark to mark. Edge with tube 3 beading.

ADD FLOWER TRIM. Push in spiked flowers on sides of base tier, and attach more flowers on mounds of icing. Trim middle and top tier with flowers. Paint leaf detail on lovebird ornament with pale green thinned royal icing, dry, and secure to cake top. Secure flowers on mounds of icing around it, and add wired flowers in rear. Trim all bouquets with tube 67 leaves, tube 2 tendrils. Two lower tiers serve 186, top tier serves 30.

THE PARENTS' CAKES, *shown on page 9*

Bake, fill and ice two-layer ovals each 4″ high.

DIVIDE TOP EDGE of each cake in sixteenths and mark. On front and back of ovals, measure a 3″ space and mark about 1″ up from base. Divide remaining spaces at ends of ovals in thirds and mark. Drop string guidelines for curves.

ADD RIBBON BORDERS. Pipe a tube 7 line around base of each cake and top with tube 124 pleated ribbon. Following guidelines, pipe tube 104 ruffles and top with ribbon swags. Trim points with pairs of tube 3 dots. On cake top, pipe tube 103 ribbon scallops from mark to mark. Trim points with tube 3 dots.

FINISH WITH CAKE-TOP BOUQUETS. Pipe sprays of tube 3 stems on cake tops. Arrange flowers on mounds of icing in bouquets. Trim with tube 70 leaves. Each cake serves twelve party guests.

PETAL TUBES CROWN A CARNATION CAKE FOR MOTHER

This gorgeous example of petal tube wizardry will be the center of attention at your Mother's Day celebration—after Mother herself, of course. It features flamboyant trios of pink carnations, rhythmic ribbons of icing for borders and decorative lettering, all produced by the versatile petal tubes.

DECORATE THE CAKE

With flowers made ahead of time, this lovely cake takes little time to complete. Directions for petal tube printing are given below.

STEP ONE. Pipe the royal icing flowers in advance. Make 18 pink carnations, using tube 10 for the base, tube 104 for the petals and the method given on page 13. Set flowers aside to dry. Pipe tube 5 spikes on backs of all flowers. Dry again.

STEP TWO. Prepare the cake. Bake a layer in a 10" round pan, and one in a 10" bevel pan. Finished height should be 4". Fill and ice smoothly with buttercream. Divide cake into twelfths, making divisions on sides at midpoint and on edge of bevel top as a guide for scallops.

STEP THREE. Pipe a row of tube 6 white beads around cake base. Then, starting at side marks, pipe stand-out pink ribbon swags with tube 104, curling a hook of icing first, then swinging down to base just about an inch beyond the next mark. Repeat around cake, then trim with tube 1 white dots to accent design.

Mark lettering pattern on cake top. Pipe lettering with tube 101s. Add frame around lettering with the same tube, then trim with tube 1 white dots. Using division marks as a guide, pipe stand-up scallops with tube 103 around edge of bevel top. Inside scallops pipe tube 1 white dots.

STEP FOUR. Add flower trims. Pipe a trio of stems with tube 3 on cake side within every other curve of border. Trim with tube 65s leaves. Pipe a mound of icing on back of each spiked carnation and push into bevel surface. Complete each spray with a tube 102 ribbon bow.

Cake serves 14 certain-to-be-impressed party guests.

PRINTING WITH PETAL TUBES

Petal tubes can pipe highly decorative lettering that gives real distinction to a cake. Until you gain experience in this technique it is best to use a pattern to guide the piping.

To make your own pattern, print the words you wish to pipe on graph paper. This will make it easy to keep the letters on a straight line and of uniform height.

Do not make the printing too small—the ribbon-like strokes made by petal tubes take space. A height of ½" is minimum.

To practice, tape your pattern to a stiff board and tape wax paper over it. Use tube 101s. For straight strokes like those in "M", hold the tube with its entire width just touching surface, and pull straight down, using light pressure. For curves, begin with wide end of tube on inner side of curve. Hold tube as flat as possible on cake. For a horizontal stroke as on "t", pull the tube straight across. Add curved serifs on the ends of a letter after you have completed it.

Turn to pages 48 and 49 to see other examples of this attractive printing with petal tubes.

PETAL TUBES TAKE HONORS ON CAKES BOTH LARGE AND SMALL

Two beautiful examples of the wide range of flowers made possible by the versatile petal tubes. The heart-shaped cupcakes bloom with tiny carnations, pink wild flowers and forget-me-nots and the dramatic tier cake is ablaze with full-blown roses—yet the only difference in the tubes that produced them is size.

LITTLE HEARTS IN BLOOM

Pipe flowers first, using royal or boiled icing and tube 101s. Also make half-carnations. Dry.

Bake cakes in heart cupcake pans. Ice with white buttercream, then cover with pink poured fondant. To define the design, pipe stem arrangement first with tube 1, as shown in the cupcake on the plate. Position the tiny flowers on dots of icing, then trim with tube 65s leaves.

THE CAPTIVE HEART

The most romantic flower in all the world is the beautiful blushing rose. Here it is used in glowing colors for a cake lovely enough for a small wedding, ideal for an engagement party.

PIPE ROSES FIRST. Use royal icing and tube 104 to make full-blown roses. For the shaded color ef-fect in some of the roses, pipe center and first petals in deepest red, next row of petals in lighter red and final row in still lighter color. Make a single rose and bud with tube 126. Pipe many tube 67 leaves on wire stems. Mount large rose and bud on wires and tape to leaves.

PREPARE CAKE. Bake two-layer tiers—a 12" square and a 9" heart. Ice and assemble on cake board. Use Wilton Way III pattern for scalloped design on upper tier and mark. Mark a curving line around square tier as guide for vine border.

EDGE BASE OF BOTH TIERS with tube 7 balls. Edge top of base tier with tube 6 balls. Pipe curving vine with tube 3 and trim with tube 66 leaves.

Pipe freehand tube 3 stems on side of heart tier and add tube 66 leaves. Pipe a tube 5 top ball border. Do scalloped design with tube 2.

ARRANGE ROSES on icing mounds around base of heart tier. Add stemmed leaves in natural fashion. Set large rose and bud on cake top.

This masterpiece serves 48 guests at a party, 100 at a wedding reception.

ROSES HOLD CANDLES FOR A BIRTHDAY WISH

You just couldn't wish for a prettier cake! And roses turned into candle holders are a fresh, ingenious touch everyone will love. The petal tubes that shape the roses in a panoply of pinks also ruffle the rippling double borders. The very cake for that special young girl who's just turned sweet sixteen!

The long loaf cake is a very practical shape, too. It's neat and easy to serve, and the extended length gives the decorator a good opportunity for lavish trims.

STEP ONE. Make the rose candles. Attach wax paper square to a number 7 flower nail and pipe a tube 12 mound of royal icing in center. While icing is still wet push birthday candle into it. Then switch to tube 104 and pipe petals around the base of the candle, first making a row of three stand-up petals, then a row of five opening petals. Repeat for as many candles as you need in varied pink icing.

Make a number of regular tube 104 roses and buds in royal icing. Set all aside to dry. Pipe royal icing spikes on backs of six roses for cake sides. Allow to dry again.

STEP TWO. Prepare the cake. Bake a cake in a loaf pan, 4″ x 4″ x 16″ long. Ice smoothly with pale pink buttercream icing. Mark curves on sides and ends of cake to indicate position of ruffled borders.

Pipe a tube 8 ball border around base of cake. Pipe a tube 6 border around top edge of cake. Write birthday message on side of cake with tube 2. With tube 104 cover marks with a row of deep pink ruffles and pipe a row of pale pink ruffles above them. Trim ruffles with tube 3 beading.

STEP THREE. Position roses and rose candles on mounds of icing on cake top. Push spiked roses into cake sides. Trim with tube 66 leaves.

Light up the candles, turn down the lights and serve this blushing beauty of a cake to 16 very excited teenagers.

FOR SOMEONE SWEET . . . ONE PERFECT ROSE

Like an exquisite portrait, a single piped rose is mounted on a plaque and centered on a cake covered with smooth rolled fondant. Done in royal icing, the rose can become a keepsake for the person whose special day it honors. Such a dainty cake would suit so many occasions—a bridal shower, a Mother's Day tribute, even a shower cake for baby-to-be. Both rose and ripply ribbon borders are shaped, of course, with the standard petal tubes.

STEP ONE. Pipe the rose of royal icing with tube 124, forming the bud and first two rows of petals in yellow, the outer petals in white. Use the method described on page 13 for the classic rose, but make this rose with five rows of petals to give it the full rich look of a cabbage rose. Immediately after piping, dust fingers with cornstarch and furl edges of petals. When rose is dry, mount on wire stem. Pipe several tube 66 leaves on wires. Dry, then tape rose and leaves into a single spray with floral tape.

Make sky blue plaque with Color Flow technique. Draw 4½″ circle for pattern and tape to flat surface. Cover smoothly with waxed paper and outline with tube 2. Flow in thinned icing. Set aside to dry. (You may prefer to cut this plaque from rolled gum paste.)

STEP TWO. Bake a two-layer 10″ round fruit or pound cake 4″ high. Fill, then cover cake with rolled fondant. Place cake on serving tray.

STEP THREE. Add icing trims to cake. Pipe a row of tube 8 bulbs around base of cake, then trim bulbs with a row of tube 4 beads. Divide sides of cake into eighths, mark curves, then pipe zigzag ribbon scallops with tube 101, touching surface with wide end of tube and turning hand over so ribbon stands on edge. Trim points of scallops with tube 101s bows.

STEP FOUR. Position Color Flow plaque on cake top. Edge with tube 3 beads, then with double row of tube 101s stand-up ribbon scallops. Center rose on plaque. Serves 14 party guests.

Here are two lovely cakes that showcase the California poppy and the fluffy sweet pea.

POPPY SUNSHINE

PIPE FLOWERS FIRST. Make many royal icing California poppies with tube 103 petals, and 15 miniature poppies with tube 101s. Pipe tube 5 spikes on backs of about half the larger poppies.

BAKE, FILL AND ICE a 12" x 4" two-layer round cake. Divide cake side into fourths and mark about 1" down from top edge, leaving a 2" space between each division. Drop string guidelines for curves. Mark an 8" circle on cake top.

PIPE A TUBE 7 BALL BORDER at base of cake and a tube 6 border at top. Pipe double tube 104 curves, then tube 103 curves above them. Finish with tube 4 fleurs-de-lis. Fill in circle on cake top with tube 101s lattice. Ring lattice with poppies and push spiked flowers into cake side. Add more flowers at base. Secure tiny poppies to cherub figure. Serves 22.

SWEET PEA SERENADE

MAKE ROYAL ICING SWEET PEAS with tubes 101, 103 and 104. Make ornament by gluing four 2" bells to a petite ornament plate. Glue a kneeling cherub to top. Attach to 12" separator plate. Glue winged angels to four 5" Corinthian pillars.

BAKE, FILL AND ICE TWO-LAYER ROUND TIERS —16" x 4", 12" x 4" and 8" x 3". Use prepared 12" separator plate plus a second 12" plate and 5" Corinthian pillars between two lower tiers. Use 8" plates and angel-trimmed pillars above middle tier. Divide base tier in twelfths, mark at top edge and 1" up from bottom. Mark scallops on tier top. Divide side of middle tier by marking four 4" spaces on cake side directly below pillar openings. Divide remaining spaces in two. Divide side of top tier in eighths and mark 1½" up from base. Drop guidelines for all garlands. Pipe tube 8 base bulb borders on all tiers.

ON BASE TIER, pipe lower garland with tube 9 zigzags. Drop double tube 3 string. For upper garland, first pipe tube 103 ruffles, following guidelines, then top with tube 7 zigzags and tube 3 strings. Fill in scallops with tube 2 lattice. Frame with tube 4 beading and edge plate with tube 6.

ON MIDDLE TIER, pipe a tube 7 garland and trim with tube 3 strings and bows. Use tube 7 for reverse shell top border. Edge plate with tube 4.

ON TOP TIER, pipe a tube 7 garland and trim with tube 3 strings. Pipe a tube 6 top border.

FINISH WITH FLOWERS AS PICTURE SHOWS, attaching each with a dot of icing. Secure musical cherubs between pillars and set a cherub fountain on middle tier. Place cupid on top and surround with flowers. Pipe tube 65 leaves. Two lower tiers serve 186, top tier serves 30.

Garlands of wild roses circle a two-tier cake to announce an engagement . . . bow-tied arrangements of dainty daisies and forget-me-nots sweeten a bridal cake. Directions, page 30.

PETAL TUBES pipe the prettiest flowers to adorn sentimental cakes—and curving borders, too.

WILD ROSE GARLANDS *shown on page 28*

PIPE FLOWERS FIRST. Make many tube 103 wild roses and about 30 tube 102 wild roses in royal or boiled icing. Add tube 1 centers. Paint a plastic parasol with thinned royal icing. Dry, then add a tube 102 ruffle and topknot of small flowers.

BAKE, FILL AND ICE a two-layer square tier, 10" x 4" and a single-layer 6" round tier. Assemble on cake board. Pipe tube 16 shell borders around base and top of both tiers. Cover shells at base of 10" tier with a tube 124 ruffle. Edge with tube 3 beads. Write names on tier side with tube 2.

ATTACH FLOWERS. On 10" tier, drop tube 2 string guidelines for side garlands and cover with flowers. On 6" tier, circle base with more flowers. Mark a 4" circle on cake top and cover with a ring of flowers. Push parasol into center of circle. Trim all flowers with tube 66 leaves. Serve to 23.

DAISY BOUQUET, *shown on page 29*

MAKE TRIMS AHEAD. Pipe royal icing daisies with tubes 102 and 103 with tube 5 centers. Pipe smaller daisies with tubes 101 and 3, and forget-me-nots with tube 101s. Mount about a third of the flowers on wire stems.

Make lattice ornament. Use Wilton Way III pattern to pipe lattice in three sections on wax paper with tube 101s and royal icing. Edge with same tube. Cut a 4½" circle from rolled gum paste for base. Pipe a line of icing on base of center lattice piece, set on circle and pipe a line of icing on one side. Add second piece on an angle in same way, then third. Prop to dry. Edge with tube 2 beading and pipe a tube 101s bow.

To make little vase for bouquet, sugar-mold a shape in a 3" egg mold. Unmold and trim off two-thirds of large end with a taut thread. Trim off small end to flatten base. Hollow out remaining shape, dry thoroughly and trim with tube 2. Dry again, fill two-thirds full with royal icing and arrange stemmed flowers.

PREPARE CAKE. Bake two square two-layer tiers, 14" x 4" and 6" x 3", and one round tier, 10" x 3". Fill and ice all tiers with buttercream and assemble on cake board with 8" square separator plates and 5" Corinthian pillars.

ADD CAKE TRIMS. Edge base tier with tube 4B shells and trim with tube 103 ruffles. Edge tier top with tube 19 shells. Mark off a 6½" space for flower arrangements in center of each side and

pipe tube 103 bows.

On middle tier, pipe tube 16 shells around base and top with tube 104 ribbon swags. On top of base tier, pipe matching ribbon swag. Mark four scallop designs on side of tier and pipe tube 104 curves. Trim top edge of tier and separator plate with tube 16 reverse shells. Set bouquet within pillars.

On top tier, pipe a tube 16 base shell border, and a reverse shell border at top. Drop string guidelines for curves on cake sides and pipe with tube 103. Trim corners with tube 102 bows. Attach lattice ornament to cake top and position angel musician inside.

Arrange flowers on all tiers, attaching with dots of icing. Pipe tube 65 leaves. Two lower tiers of Daisy Bouquet serve 146, top tier 18.

VIOLET FANTASY *at right*

PIPE MANY VIOLETS in boiled or royal icing using tubes 101 and 101s.

MAKE HEART TRIMS. For stand-up heart on cake top, lay a 4" plastic heart on a flat surface and cover with a tube 124 ruffle. Pipe a tube 6 line of icing around inside edge of ruffles, and attach violets.

For curved hearts on upper tier, tape Wilton Way III pattern to 10" curved surface. Tape wax paper over it, then cover with tube 103 ruffles. Pipe a tube 4 line around inside edge of ruffle and attach violets. Make eight hearts and dry.

BAKE TIERS, using a pound cake or fruitcake recipe. Lower tier is two 14" round layers for a height of 3". For upper tier, bake a layer in a 10" round pan and one in a 10" top bevel pan. Fill tiers, cover with rolled fondant and assemble on cake board. Roll out untinted fondant and cut a 3½" circle for cake-top heart base.

Divide side of 14" tier in sixteenths and drop string guidelines. Divide upper tier in eighths and transfer arch and curve patterns.

DECORATE CAKE. Pipe tube 7 balls around base of bottom tier. Following guidelines, pipe tube 104 ruffles. Edge with tube 2 beads. Pipe tube 6 balls around base of upper tier. Following marked patterns, pipe tube 104 ruffled arches and curves. Edge with tube 2 beads.

TRIM WITH FLOWERS. Mound icing inside arches and attach violet cascades. Trim base tier with violets. Attach curved hearts to bevel surface with icing. Set fondant base on cake top and attach stand-up heart. Trim with violets. Serve to 50 party guests or 140 wedding guests.

PETAL TUBES FILL
A BASKET WITH BRIGHT PETUNIAS

The prettiest version of the basket cake you ever brought to your party table!

PIPE THE "LOLLIPOP" PETUNIAS in royal icing, almost like a morning glory. Fit a decorating cone with tube 104, stripe at wide end of tube with yellow icing and fill with white. Line a 1¼" lily nail with foil and pipe a circle of icing in well with wide end of tube down. With pink icing and same tube pipe five ruffled petals and brush together. Groove five lines to petal tips with pointed brush. Pipe center with tube 1. Let dry and remove from foil. For trumpet shape, pipe a spike of royal icing on back of blossom with tube 6. To make petunia buds, pipe base the same as flower then add pink ruffle, holding narrow end of tube straight up. When dry, mount on green calyx with wire stem and cover with tube 65s. Pipe several 67 leaves on wire stems.

PREPARE CAKE. Bake a two layer 8" x 4" loaf cake, 4" high. Fill and ice lightly with buttercream. Cover sides with green basketweave, using tube 4 for vertical lines and petal tube 102 for broad horizontal lines. Edge base and top of cake with tube 16 rope border. Arrange flowers, buds and stemmed leaves on mounds of icing and pipe more tube 67 leaves. Serve this showpiece to eight fascinated guests.

PETAL TUBES PLANT
A POT OF NASTURTIUMS

Another showpiece for summery party fun. All the flowers and leaves are shaped with petal tubes and the pot's a stack of little cakes. Start with the flowers and watch it grow!

FIRST MAKE FLOWERS. Pipe nasturtiums in brilliant sunny shades of orange, gold and red. Line a 1⅝" lily nail with foil, use royal icing and tube 103. Center flowers with tube 5 dots and artificial stamens. Make nasturtium leaves with tube 124 on number 7 flower nail. Pipe lines on leaves with tube 1. Mount flowers and leaves on wire.

PREPARE CAKE. Bake three 5" x 1½" round cake layers. Fill the cakes, chill and taper two lower layers with a sharp knife. Ice with buttercream, patting with a spatula for stucco effect. Set on serving tray.

ADD FLOWERS. Insert a Flower Spike in center of cake. Twist stems of flowers and leaves together and set bouquet in spike. So pretty, they won't want to eat it! Serve to six, making sure that everyone gets a nasturtium keepsake.

A WREATH OF RUFFLED PANSIES

Like butterflies in flight, these colorful flowers with lavishly ruffled petals brighten a dainty cake for a birthday or a bridal shower. Here gorgeous pansies are set on a shiny poured fondant cake to spotlight their delicate grace and brilliant color.

PIPE PANSIES with tube 103 and royal icing. Spatula-stripe decorating cone for vari-colored effect. Pipe a few pansy buds with tube 102, just as you would a rosebud, but make petals more ruffly. Mount buds on wire stems and pipe tube 2 sepals. Pipe a few tube 67 leaves on wires. Pipe spikes on the backs of about two dozen flowers for side trim.

BAKE A TWO-LAYER CAKE, 10″ square, each layer about 2″ high. Fill, ice with buttercream, then cover with poured fondant. Let icing set, then mark a 4½″ circle on cake top.

Edge base of cake with tube 7 balls and trim with tube 1 scallops. Pipe a tube 5 line around marked circle and fill with tinted fondant. Edge with tube 2 beading and tube 1 scallops. Write name with tube 1.

ADD FLOWER TRIM. Mark curves around corners of cake and attach pansies, using spiked flowers on side of cake. Attach more pansies in a wreath around circle. Trim all flowers with tube 67 leaves. Serve to 20 delighted party guests.

MORNING GLORY MAGIC

Inspired by an old-fashioned wallpaper print, morning glories twine around a cake with precisely-patterned borders. Make it for someone very special.

PIPE ROYAL ICING MORNING GLORIES just as described on page 13, but use just one tint of icing. For flowers on cake side, use tube 102 for base, tube 103 for outer edge. For flowers on cake top, use tube 103 for both base and outer edge. Finish with tube 1 lines and stamens. When dry, pipe tube 2 sepals on backs of all flowers and pipe royal icing spikes on backs of smaller flowers.

BAKE A 10″ ROUND TWO-LAYER CAKE using a pound cake or fruitcake recipe. Each layer should be about 2″ high. Cover with rolled fondant. Cut a

1″ strip of tinted fondant about 35″ long and wrap around base of cake, attaching with a little icing. Divide side of cake into sixteenths and mark a curving line for vine. Keep outer curves ½″ above strip and ½″ below top of cake.

TRIM CAKE with tube 1 scallops and dots. Pipe vine with tube 2 and add tube 66 leaves. Ice two marshmallows to top center of cake and attach larger flowers to them. Ring with more flowers and tube 67 leaves. Pipe icing on spikes of smaller flowers and push into cake side. Slice in 16 servings, using side flowers as guide.

MAKE HOLIDAYS HAPPIER WITH GLOWING CENTERPIECE CAKES

Use your petal tubes to pipe the trims for these beauties—pine cones, daffodils and violets.

A MERRY CHRISTMAS CAKE

PIPE ROYAL ICING TRIMS in advance. For pine cones, cover a plastic or paper cone with wax paper. Coat the tip with icing, about 1½″ down. Pipe the "petals" with tube 97, just as you would rose petals. Pipe an upstanding petal at top, then two more around it to form a bud shape. Moving down, circle the cone with five petals, then two rows of six petals. Finish with a final row of seven petals. As you pipe each row, turn narrow end of tube farther out, so final row is piped with tube held straight out from cone. Dry.

For pine needles, pipe a "V" shape, arms about 1¾″ long, with tube 2 on wax paper. Pipe two more narrower "V's" within it, points of all three touching. Pipe many of these sets and dry.

PREPARE AND DECORATE THE CAKE. Bake a two-layer 10″ round cake, fill and ice with buttercream. Lightly mark a 6″ circle on top and pipe tube 1 message with red piping gel within it. Pipe bottom rope border with tube 22, and a second tube 18 rope border on cake top, following marked circle. Do upright shell border around top edge with tube 18. Drop double tube 3 strings from tail of one shell to second one over. Continue dropping strings to form inter-laced effect. Add twirls at points of strings.

ARRANGE TRIMS. First secure pine cones to cake with mounds of icing. Surround cones with pine needle sets, piping a dot of icing on point of each "V" to secure. This cheery treat serves 14.

A GOLDEN CAKE FOR EASTER

PIPE SPRING FLOWERS FIRST in royal icing. Do violets with tube 101, add tube 1 dots. Pipe daffodil petals with tube 104, add a coiled cup with tube 3, ruffle it with tube 1 and pipe a tube 2 dot in center. Dry all flowers, then pipe royal icing spikes on backs of most daffodils.

PREPARE THE CAKE. Bake three layers—one in a 14″ base bevel pan, one in a 10″ round pan, and one in a 10″ top bevel pan. We recommend a firm pound cake recipe. Fill and ice the two 10″ layers with white buttercream, then set on rack and cover with yellow poured fondant. Ice 14″ base bevel layer with buttercream and cover with poured fondant. Assemble with 10″ layers and pipe a tube 6 bottom ball border. Pipe message with tube 101s as described on page 49.

FINISH WITH FLOWER TRIMS. Drop stems for daffodils on cake side with tube 3. Pull up long leaves with tube 70. Pipe a mound of icing on back of each spiked daffodil and push into cake side and top bevel. Secure a few more daffodils on cake top. Attach violets with dots of icing. Finish with violet leaves piped with tube 70. Base bevel layer serves eight, 10″ cake serves 14.

CHAPTER TWO

Pipe Striking Borders with Petal Tubes

WHILE THE PETAL TUBES are usually used to pipe beautiful flowers, don't overlook their ability to form striking borders. These tubes shape ruffles, swags and graceful curves to swing around a cake and give it a strong, rhythmic edging. Petal tube borders are so dominant and attractive that often they can be the only trim on a showpiece cake.

The petal tubes used most frequently for borders are the smaller ones—tubes 101s to 104, but any of the borders in this chapter may be enlarged by using larger petal tubes.

RUFFLES FRAME A SHOWER CAKE

PIPE THE FORGET-ME-NOTS in royal icing with tube 101s with tube 1 centers. These are made with the same method used for the wild rose on page 12. You will need about 450. Set aside to dry.

DECORATE THE PARASOL. Following the design on a small plastic parasol, pipe tube 101s ruffles in royal icing. Finish the trim by attaching forget-me-nots with dots of icing and tying a ribbon bow on the handle.

PREPARE THE CAKE. Bake two layers in 10″ round pans, each layer 2″ high. Fill, ice smoothly with buttercream and set on serving tray. Divide side of cake into tenths and mark about 1″ down from top edge. To the left of each of these marks, make a second mark, 1″ away. For scallop design on cake top, transfer Wilton Way III pattern, lining up points of scallops with marks on cake side.

PIPE THE CAKE TRIM. Edge base of cake with two lines of tube 4 bulbs. Drop double tube 2 guidelines from mark to mark on side of cake. With blue icing and tube 104, pipe a ruffle, following lower guideline as shown below. Lift off the upper section of guideline that crosses over. Add two more ruffles above first ruffle in white icing—pipe first with tube 103, second with tube 102. Edge top ruffle with tube 2 bulbs. Pipe a tube 2 top bulb border.

Following marked pattern, pipe a tube 102 ruffle on cake top and edge with tube 2 bulbs. Pipe a second bulb and fleur-de-lis design within scallops with tube 1. Now form ten cascades of forget-me-nots. Heap more flowers within curves of ruffles. Set parasol on top and serve to 14.

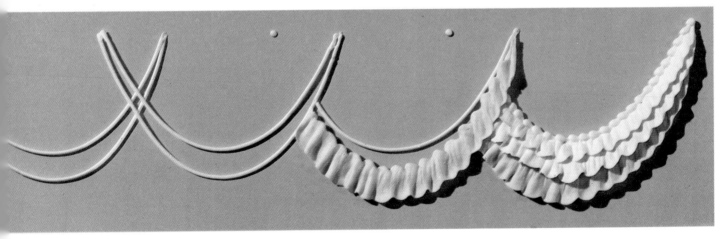

See how petal tubes can pipe showy borders to trim cakes very quickly. Each of the borders below is based on a petal tube curve or ruffle, then flowers or stringwork are added to finish the effect. Observe how contrasting tints show off the strong curves.

RHYTHM BORDER. Pipe a curve with tube 124, wide end of tube held against cake. As you reach the top of the curve, jiggle your hand twice, then continue in second curve. Trim the curves with trios of wild roses, petals piped with tube 101, centers with tube 1. A very effective border for base, side or top of cake.

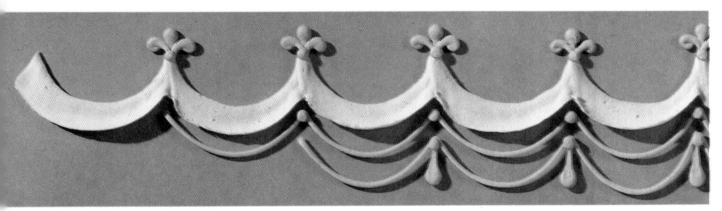

CRESTED BORDER. First pipe a series of even curves with tube 124, holding wide end of tube against cake, narrow end flaring slightly outward. Drop two tube 3 strings below curves. Finish with dots and bulbs on strings, fleurs-de-lis above curves, all piped with tube 3. A dramatic trim for top or side of cake.

DRAPED RUFFLE BORDER. First pipe evenly curved ruffles with tube 104. Above them drop tube 5 string. The string will support the tube 124 drapes piped above ruffles. Add little heart shapes piped with tube 5 at points of drapes. Use this border for the base of important cakes.

PETAL TUBE BORDERS MAKE IMPORTANT CAKE TRIMS

USE ONLY PETAL TUBES to create the borders shown on this page—then see page 43 for two beautiful cakes completely trimmed with them. The borders piped with petal tubes are so attractive that a cake needs little else for decoration.

SWEET PEA BORDERS

The same hand movements used for piping the sweet pea, page 12, create fluffy trims for the top and bottom edges of a cake.

TOP BORDER. With tube 104, pipe a sweet pea on the top of the cake. Pipe a second one, just below it, on the side of the cake. Continue piping sweet peas, first on top, then on side of cake. Result—a fluffy lei-like border, quickly done.

BASE BORDER. Use tube 104 again to pipe this pretty border. The technique is the same as piping a side petal of a sweet pea. First pipe a petal against side of cake, then a second one, just beyond it, against cake board or tray. Continue piping quick petals to form an easy, but intricate-looking border.

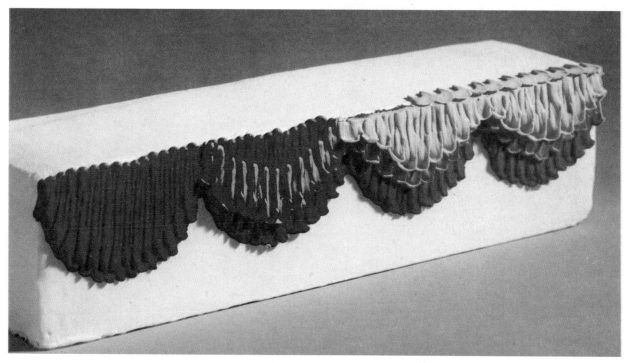

A TRIPLE TIER BORDER PIPED WITH PETAL TUBES

Divide and measure your cake before piping this ornate cake trim. The curves here are about 3″ wide and 2″ deep. Drop curved string guidelines, then pipe the border.

Hold tube 104 flat against surface, wide end up, and fill in the arc with tight zigzags. Within the piped curve, pipe a zigzag crescent in contrasting icing. Add a third layer of zigzags in a third color, top level with top of cake. Trim off excess icing on top edge of cake with a small spatula or knife.

Neaten the edge of the cake and complete the border by piping short curves with tube 102 on top of cake.

TRIM SHOW-OFF CAKES WITH PETAL TUBE BORDERS

A SQUARE CAKE GIVES GOOD LUCK WISHES. This little charmer can be done in a hurry! Bake and fill a two-layer square cake, each layer 2″ high. Ice in buttercream, and pipe tube 3 message.

Lightly mark the cake so borders will be even. Measure 1½″ in from two parallel sides and mark top of cake. Continue mark down both sides. Measure 3½″ in from sides and mark again. Divide these marked lines into halves on sides, fourths on top. Pipe a tube 6 base bulb border.

With tube 104, wide end held against cake, pipe curves from mark to mark, jiggling hand twice at points of curves. Pipe a second series of curves within first, using contrasting icing. Pipe tube 104 sweet peas down center of cake.

Cover bulbs at base of cake with a tube 104 "pleated" border, using same motion as used for piping shells. Serve to twelve.

A RUFFLY BON VOYAGE CAKE, *at right*. Nothing could be simpler, or more attractive, than this cake for a traveler. Just fill a two-layer, 10″ round cake and ice in warm yellow buttercream.

Tinted icing enhances the sweet pea borders, described on page 41. For base border fill a decorating cone fitted with tube 125 on one side with pink icing, the other side with orange icing. Pipe the bottom border. Letter message on top of cake with tube 101s (see page 49).

Fit a decorating cone with tube 104 and fill with pink icing on one side, yellow on the other. Pipe the top sweet pea border, following directions on page 41. Serve to 14.

TIER BORDERS TRIM A BIRTHDAY CAKE. Use the showy triple tier border shown on page 41.

Bake and fill a 12″ round, two-layer cake, each layer 2″ high. Fill and ice, then set on cake board. Divide cake side into tenths and mark on top and bottom edges. Make a second series of marks in center of cake side, each mark midway between marks at top and bottom of cake. Following these marks, lightly mark scallops on cake side. Mark ten scallops on cake top, each about 1½″ deep.

Now pipe triple tier borders on side of cake with tube 104. Do double tier border on top of cake with the same tube. Edge base of cake with a "pleated" shell motion border piped with tube 103. Pipe a matching border on top of cake with tube 103. Insert birthday tapers and serve to 22.

PETAL TUBES TRIM A LOVE CAKE IN A TRICE

Heart follows heart at top and around sides of this charming cake for a bridal shower or Valentine party. First pipe a dozen pink carnations, in boiled or buttercream icing and tube 103. If flowers are piped in buttercream, freeze.

BAKE A SQUARE TWO-LAYER CAKE, 8″ x 4″. Fill and ice with buttercream and use a 2″ heart cookie cutter to mark heart shapes on cake sides one inch below top edge, and on corners of cake top. Cover with tube 104 stand-out ribbon, starting at top of heart and bringing tube down to point in one motion.

PIPE BORDERS. Pipe a tube 6 line of icing around base of cake. Cover with tube 104 ribbon, using shell motion for pleated look. Pipe tube 104 curved ribbons below hearts on side. Start at corner, pipe four shell-motion pleats, then a curve. Continue around cake in a continuous motion, piping pleats between each heart. Edge cake top with tube 104 pleated ribbon. Pipe the same as base border, keeping wide end of tube on inner edge.

ADD BOUQUET. Mound a little icing at center of cake top and press in a cluster of carnations. Trim with tube 66 leaves piped with thinned icing. Serves twelve delighted guests.

PETAL TUBES RUFFLE A HEXAGON CAKE

Six sides make this cake six times as beautiful—each displays a flurry of ruffles and a cascade of sunny sweet peas. Sweet and special for the bride-to-be or any lady important to you. The shape of the cake makes measuring easy. Smooth poured fondant sets off the stand-out trims.

PIPE MANY SWEET PEAS with tube 104 petals and royal or boiled icing. Set aside to dry.

BAKE A TWO-LAYER CAKE in 12″ hexagon pans, each layer about 2″ high. Fill and ice with buttercream, then cover with poured fondant and set on foil-covered board cut to same shape. Mark center of each side 1″ above base and connect

with corners near top of cake.

DECORATE CAKE. Edge base with a tube 7 bulb border. Cover side marks with a row of tube 104 stand-out ruffles, going around all sides of cake in one continuous motion. Repeat with second row of ruffles above first, this time piped with tube 103. Edge with tube 3 beading.

TRIM WITH FLOWERS. Mound icing in center of cake top. Press in a marshmallow and attach sweet peas on dots of icing. Pipe diamond shapes with tube 7 zigzags, extending from top of cake to side. Attach flowers in six cascades. Trim all flowers with tube 66 leaves. Serve to 20 guests.

45

OUTSTANDING BORDERS FEATURING PETAL TUBES

Here is a group of big, exciting borders, each simply piped, each most attractive. Since they are large, careful measuring is needed to maintain a neat orderly effect. See how color adds to their charm. The scroll border at top is ideal for side trim, the other three borders are planned for the base of a cake or tier.

Try these borders on a practice board, then put one of them on a cake. You'll need very little other trim to make a masterpiece.

START WITH AN "S" SCROLL piped with tube 102. Add tube 2 flowers, tube 65s leaves.

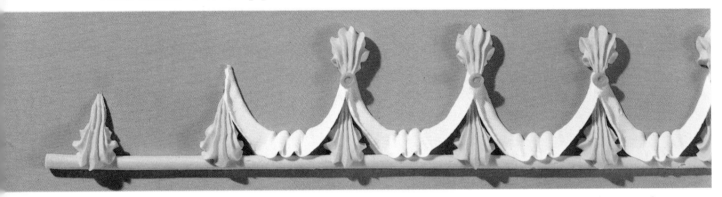

START WITH A TUBE 9 LINE. Pipe tube 18 shells, drape with tube 103, finish with tube 3 curls.

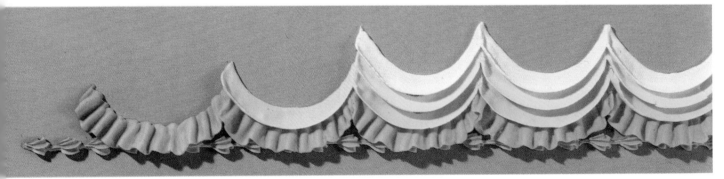

START WITH TUBE 13 SHELLS, add a ruffle and triple drapes with tube 103.

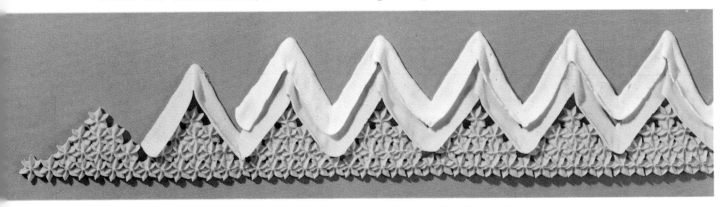

START WITH STARS piped with tube 17. Outline twice with tube 103.

46

PETITE FLOWERY BORDERS FEATURING PETAL TUBES

Petal tubes can pipe sweet dainty borders, too, that look even prettier when accented with flowers. Each of these except for the bow border, starts with a curved string guideline to keep an even, uniform look. All are shown in actual size.

Practice these borders—then pipe one or more of them on any cake you'd like to look delicate and dainty. You're sure to dream up some original border designs of your own.

PIPE TUBE 101s SCALLOPS, trim with tube 1 dots, tube 24 flowers, tube 65s leaves.

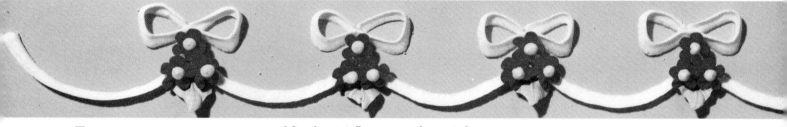

TUBE 101s PIPES BOWS AND CURVES. Add tube 24 flowers, tube 65s leaves.

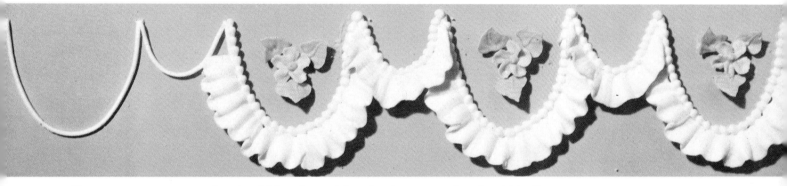

Do DOUBLE RUFFLES with tube 101, edge with tube 1, trim with tube 101s forget-me-nots.

START WITH TUBE 5 BULBS, do ruffles with tube 102, bows with tube 1, roses with tube 59.

PETAL TUBES TRIM A CAKE TO ANNOUNCE AN ENGAGEMENT

Here's a bright new way to add a personal touch to a cake—trim it with a decorative monogram.

MAKE ROSEBUDS in advance in royal icing and tube 104. You'll need about 40.

PREPARE THE CAKE. Bake a two-layer cake in 10″ square pans, each layer 2″ high. Fill, then ice with buttercream and set on cake board. Lightly mark a 5″ square on top center of cake. Make your own pattern for initials of the couple and transfer to center of square. Ours are about 1¾″ high. Divide each side into fifths and mark on edge. Use Wilton Way III pattern to mark line on sides.

PIPE BASE BORDER with tube 22 shells. Frame each shell with tube 104. Pipe curving line on cake side with tube 3, then pull out stems. Attach rosebuds on dots of icing and add tube 65 leaves. Pipe a tube 14 shell border on top edge of cake, then pipe a tube 104 "frame" over it. Draw tube along, almost flat, and move your hand quickly up and down at marks to give fluted effect.

Pipe initials with tube 101s as described on facing page. Outline center square with tube 101s scallops, leaving about 1½″ at top left corner free. Pipe a spray of tube 3 stems, attach several rosebuds and finish with tube 65 leaves. Add rosebuds to other three corners. Serves 20.

PIPE DECORATIVE INITIALS WITH PETAL TUBES

Lettering is one of the abilities of this tube family. See the cakes on pages 21 and 37 for examples. Large letters may be combined to form attractive monograms that give a unique touch to cakes. Use tube 101s for this work, unless you want really large initials. The ones shown below are actual size.

To pipe a monogram, first sketch the letters on graph paper. This gives you an opportunity to use your creativeness in combining the letters and adding curved flourishes to complete the design. Transfer your pattern to the iced cake.

Hold tube 101s as flat as possible, full width of the tube just touching surface. For vertical strokes, pull straight down. For curves, the wide end of tube should be on the inner edge of the curve as you begin. For horizontal strokes, pull straight across, producing a narrow line. Extra decorative flourishes, like those shown below, are added after the main letter is piped. You may decide to trim your initials with tiny flowers and leaves after they are piped.

Lettering done with a petal tube has the character and charm of that done with an old-fashioned quill pen. Practice and experiment with this technique. You'll add a new dimension to your decorating skill.

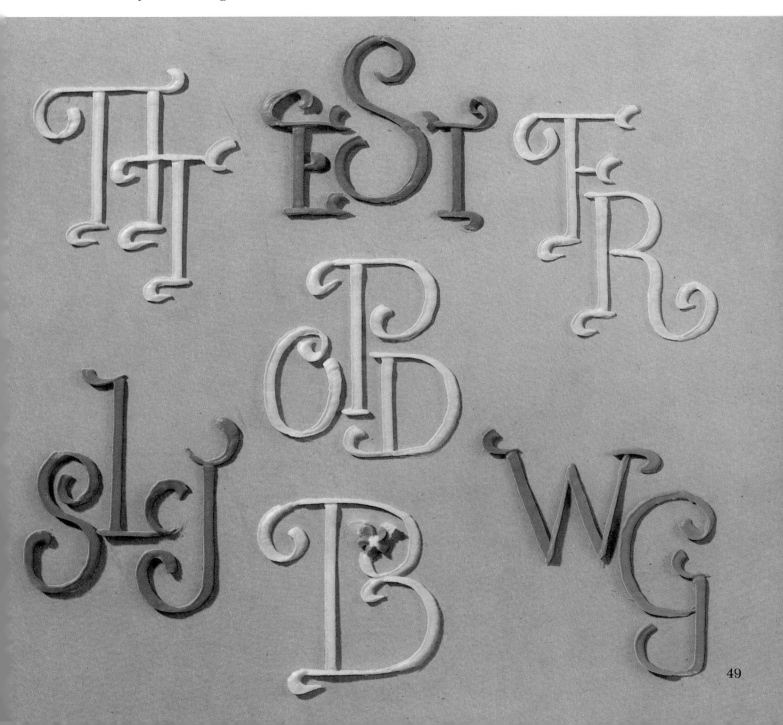

49

CHAPTER THREE

Lace, Lattice and Stringwork Piped with Plain Round Tubes

Explore the myriad uses of these simplest of tubes! With openings ranging from pinhole-tiny to ½″ in diameter, they pipe the most ethereal lace pieces, dainty to bold borders and even substantial three-dimensional figures. Browse through the next five chapters to see a summary of the near-miracles the round tubes can produce. All the standard round tubes and samples of what they do are shown on pages 52 and 53.

IN THIS CHAPTER, we show some of the uses of the smallest of the round tubes—tubes 000, ls, 1 and 2. See how they can pipe airy stand-up wings, veil-like embroidery, and curved forms as delicate as snowflakes. The use of these little tools demands a steady hand and careful, even pressure—the results are beautiful!

THE PRETTIEST PRESENT

A ribbon edged in dainty lace ties up this elegant little cake. Shiny poured fondant sets off the polka dots and cluster of roses. Make it as a beautiful gift for a birthday, anniversary or any important occasion.

STEP ONE. Use tube 1 and Wilton Way III pattern to pipe the lace pieces. Egg white royal icing is strongest for lace piping. Tape patterns to stiff surface and cover smoothly with wax paper. You'll need about 90 pieces.

Pipe the roses with tube 104 and three tints of icing, deepest in center, palest at outer petals. Let roses and lace dry.

STEP TWO. Cover a two-layer, 8″ square cake with buttercream, then poured fondant. Mark the exact center of the top surface of the cake, then the center of each side at top and bottom edges. Pipe a tube 48 ribbon from top center to base of cake, following marks, then pipe a second ribbon beside it, sides touching. Edge the ribbon with tube 1 beading, then trim it with tube 1 dots. Use tube 2 to pipe polka dots all over cake, then add a tube 6 bottom ball border.

STEP THREE. Arrange the roses in the center of the cake, securing on mounds of icing. Pipe tube 66 leaves. Now attach the lace pieces, one by one. Pipe a tiny line of icing at base of each piece, then set in position, holding an instant until set. Be sure to keep all pieces at a uniform 45° angle. This little masterpiece serves twelve.

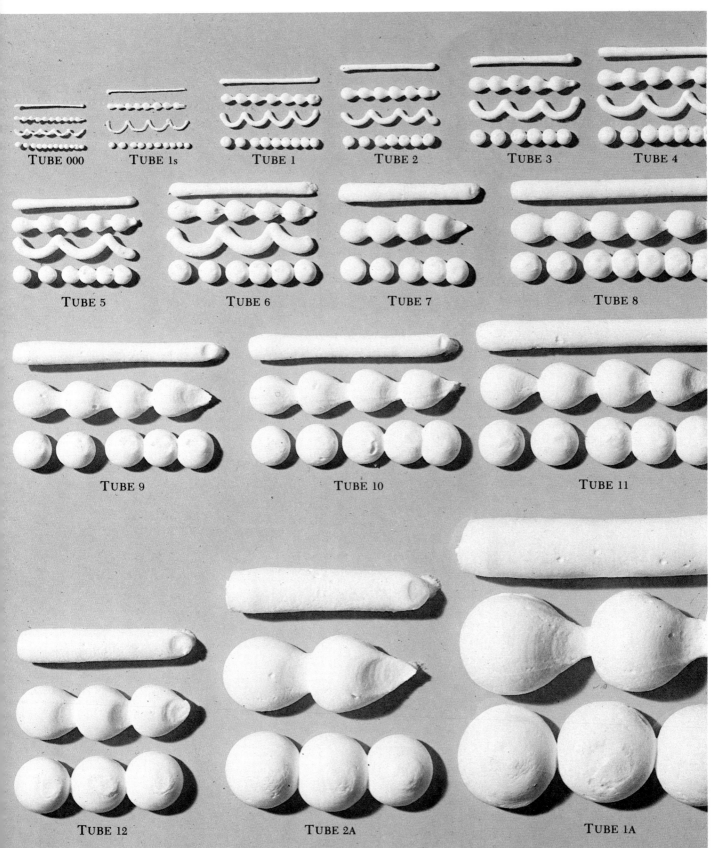

TUBE 000   TUBE 1s   TUBE 1   TUBE 2   TUBE 3   TUBE 4

TUBE 5   TUBE 6   TUBE 7   TUBE 8

TUBE 9   TUBE 10   TUBE 11

TUBE 12   TUBE 2A   TUBE 1A

THE WONDER-WORKING ROUND TUBES

Just a glance at the page at left will show you the enormous range of sizes of the standard round tubes. Tube 000 pipes a line as fine as a hair—tube 1A pipes one a full ½" across and a ball 1" in diameter. All of the examples are actual size.

THE SMALLEST ROUND TUBES, 000, 1s, 1, 2 and 3 pipe delicate lace, fragile constructions done on net, airy lattice and the neat beading that often edges a design. They also pipe the curving stringwork so traditional and lovely a part of decorating, some of it seemingly suspended in air. Small round tubes make lacy wings, shaped three-dimensional lattice and lace piped on Australian nails, dainty "printed" designs, cornelli, embroidery, and the most refined fine line borders and motifs. And, of course, the small round tubes are indispensable for piping decorative script and initials and block letters to personalize a cake. For an interesting sub-group, see the "L" series of small tubes on page 68.

THE INTERMEDIATE SIZES of round tubes, 4 through 9, do stronger line-work, have an important role in over-piping and pipe many attractive garland and ball borders. These tubes also play a part in figure piping and form the foundation of some of the prettiest icing flowers.

THE LARGEST OF ROUND TUBES, tubes 10 through 2A and 1A, are really fun to use. They allow a decorator to turn sculptor and pipe the most dramatic high relief and upright figures. Skillful use of these tubes can launch swans across icing ponds, cause turkeys to strut and teddy bears to wish "happy birthday" to an enchanted child. Use them to make bunnies and baby chicks scamper on Easter cakes and pretty dolls pose below a Christmas tree. They'll even set a bird singing on an icing branch! Chapters Six and Seven show a sampling of these near-miracles of the decorator's art. Turn to these big tubes, too, for quick showy borders on out-size tier and large display cakes.

THE STANDARD ROUND TUBES offer great rewards to the decorator, but they give a challenge, too. Since the forms they create are so clear and simple, a sure hand and careful pressure control is demanded. The results are worth the effort. Without the round tubes, many of the most beautiful effects of decorating would not exist.

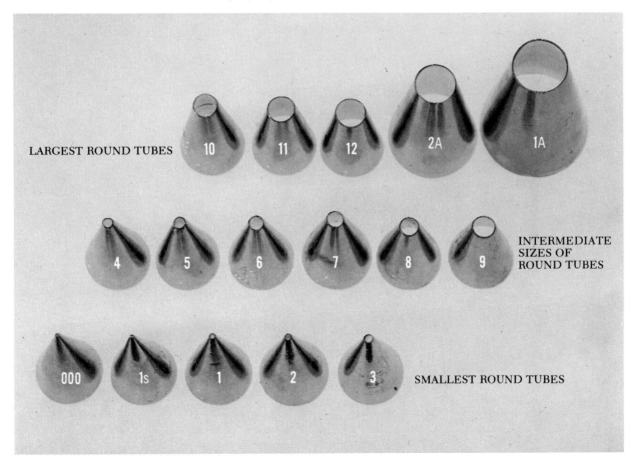

LARGEST ROUND TUBES   10   11   12   2A   1A

4   5   6   7   8   9   INTERMEDIATE SIZES OF ROUND TUBES

000   1s   1   2   3   SMALLEST ROUND TUBES

CIRCLES OF DELICATE LACE RING A RADIANT CAKE

All the fairytale decorations on this lovely cake—the fragile lace pieces, the tiny fantasy flowers, the beaded borders—are made with just three round tubes. All patterns are in Wilton Way III Pattern Book.

PIPE LACE PIECES. Tape pattern to stiff surface and cover smoothly with wax paper. Use egg white royal icing and tube 1. You'll need about 300.

BAKE AND FILL a 12″ round two-layer cake, each layer 2″ high. Use a fruitcake or pound cake recipe. Cover with rolled fondant and place on a 16″ foil-covered cake board.

Divide cake sides into sixths, then transfer circle-and-curves pattern. Mark circle on cake top with a 4″ cookie cutter.

PIPE FREEHAND FLOWERS within all circles, using tube 2 for larger flowers, tube 1 for smaller flowers and leaves. Pipe a tube 6 base bulb border. Cover lower side curves and side circles with tube 1 beading. Pipe curves below circles with graduated tube 2 dots and do fleurs-de-lis with same tube. Pipe circle on cake top with graduated tube 2 dots and trim with fleurs-de-lis.

ATTACH LACE PIECES. Pipe a dot of royal icing on base of a lace piece, then hold in position an instant until set. First do circles, then curves below them. Be sure to keep all pieces on a uniform 45° angle. This radiant showpiece serves 22 party guests, or 68 at a wedding reception.

ADD PIPING TO NET FOR A FROTHY CAKE TRIM
Please turn the page for description of this dainty Valentine cake.

55

This delightful technique creates the frothiest of all cake trims. Here, just two of many ways to "embroider" net with icing. In one, the net is simply gathered and covered with icing dots. In the other, a pattern and stiffened net are used to shape fantastic butterflies.

VALENTINE RUFFLES *shown on page 55*

PREPARE TRIMS FIRST. Cut a strip of nylon net 1½" wide by about 40" and gather near one edge for top heart ornament. Cut a second strip 2¾" by three yards long, gather and attach to a 14" foil-covered cake board with royal icing.

The rosy stand-up hearts are made of gum paste. Roll out thinly, cut one large heart and ten small hearts using Wilton Way III patterns or 3"

and 1" heart cutters. Dry flat. Attach net ruffle to large heart with royal icing. Paint a popsicle stick with thinned icing, dry and attach to back of heart with a tiny piece of gum paste moistened with egg white. Cut a second large heart, paint back of first heart with egg white, and lay second heart (still wet) on it, sandwich fashion. Dry. Cut ten 5" lengths of cloth-covered florists' wire. Lay on backs of dried small hearts, attaching with royal icing. Paint back of each heart with egg white and immediately lay a second gum paste heart, still wet, on it. Dry all hearts, then trim front of large heart with tube 1 and bead edges of small hearts with the same tube.

BAKE, FILL AND ICE two-layer tiers—10" round, each layer 2" high and 6" heart, each layer 1½" high. Assemble on prepared cake board and divide lower tier side into tenths. Drop string guidelines for curves and transfer heart patterns.

DECORATING IS FAST AND EASY! Pipe a tube 8 bottom ball border at base of larger tier. Outline hearts with tube 2, fill with tube 1 dots. Pipe curves

with graduated tube 2 beading and trim with tiny hearts. Edge top with tube 7 balls and add tube 2 scallops. Pipe a tube 7 ball border at base of heart tier, a tube 6 border at top. Do hearts and scallops with tube 2.

Twist stems of small hearts together to form two bouquets, wrap with white floral tape and tie with bows. Push into 10" tier. Push stick on large heart into cake top. Thin royal icing enough so it will form a bead and scatter tube 2 dots over net ruffles on heart and cake board. Serve to 20.

BUTTERFLIES A-FLUTTER *at right*

A breathtaking illusion! At first glance these butterflies in brilliant colors seem almost real—and in motion! Use Wilton Way III patterns.

MAKE BUTTERFLY ORNAMENT. For a shaped construction like this, first stiffen the nylon net. Stretch it over an open box, and spray several times with clear acrylic spray, drying between each spraying. Tape butterfly patterns to stiff surface, tape wax paper, then stiffened net over them and pipe with tube 2 and royal icing. Tape petal patterns to outside of a small Flower Former, cover with wax paper, then stiffened net and pipe with tube 2. Do leaves the same way, but tape patterns to inside of former. Spray all pieces again and dry. Cut out shapes with a sharp knife.

On wax paper, prop two wings together in "V" shape on styrofoam blocks. Pipe a line of royal icing in center and paint with egg white. Dry, then lay an 8" length of fine uncovered wire on icing line and pipe a tube 6 body. Insert artificial stamens for antennae.

Cut a 3½" circle from thinly rolled gum paste and cut a hole near the edge with tube 9. When dry, pipe a tube 9 mound of royal icing in center, insert leaves and petals. Add tube 1 stamens.

BAKE, FILL AND ICE THE TIERS—a two-layer 10" square, each layer 2" high, and a single-layer 6" round tier. Assemble on cake board and transfer butterfly pattern to base tier. Pipe tube 6 ball borders and pipe butterflies with tube 1. Drop double strings below them with tube 2. Pipe borders on top tier with tube 5, drop strings with tube 2 and fill in dotted design with tube 1. Secure gum paste circle, with flower, to cake top. Twist wires on butterflies together, wrap with white floral tape, and insert in hole in circle. Serve cake to 23 party guests or serve lower tier to 50 wedding guests. Top tier is the bride's to freeze for the first anniversary.

SYMPHONY ... A GLORIOUS BRIDAL CAKE CROWNED BY A NET ORNAMENT

This stately formal cake, fit for a princess, is decorated by using only round tubes. Delicate lace pieces soften the angles and a see-through ornament piped on net crowns the top tier. Tier sides are trimmed with stylized sprays of wheat. All patterns for this elegant cake are in Wilton Way III Pattern Book.

PIPE LACE IN ADVANCE

Tape patterns to a stiff surface, tape wax paper over, then pipe in royal icing and tube 1. You will need about 300 pieces. Set aside to dry.

CONSTRUCT THE ORNAMENT

USE GUM PASTE FOR THE BASE. Roll out the gum paste to a thickness of ½″ and cut smaller hexagon for lower base. Roll out thinly and cut larger hexagon for upper base. Dry thoroughly.

PIPE SIDE AND TOP SECTIONS. First stiffen nylon net by stretching over an open box and spraying several times with clear acrylic spray. Dry between each spraying. Tape patterns to a rigid surface, tape wax paper over, then tape stiffened net over the wax paper. Pipe all designs with tube 1s. When thoroughly dry, trim out pieces with a sharp X-acto knife.

ASSEMBLE ORNAMENT with royal icing. Attach upper hexagon to lower hexagon base. Start with the net side panel for the back. Pipe a line of icing on edge of base, set net section on it. Pipe an adjacent line on base and a line on side of net piece and attach second net panel. Hold until set. Continue until all five side panels are in position. Pipe double beading with tube 1 at base and all joining angles at sides. Dry.

Assemble roof sections on sides the same way. Finish all seams with tube 1 beading. Add a little finial with tubes 4 and 1.

DECORATE THE CAKE

BAKE TWO-LAYER HEXAGON TIERS, 15″, 9″ and 6″. Finished height of two larger tiers should be about 4″, that of 6″ tier, 3″. Ice smoothly in buttercream and assemble with 5″ Corinthian pillars and 9″ hexagon separator plates.

Mark curves on base and top tiers as shown. Transfer wheat patterns to all three tiers.

DECORATE THE TIERS. Pipe wheat designs on all tiers with tube 2. Pipe bottom ball border on all tiers with tube 4, top border with tube 2. Edge lower separator plate with tube 6 scallops.

Pipe curve on sides of base tier with tube 1 beading. Extend beading on top of tier to outer corner of separator plate.

Pipe tube 1 beading on corners of middle tier and extend on top of tier to lower corners of top tier. Outline curves on sides of top tier with tube 1 beading.

ADD LACE PIECES, starting at top of cake. Secure ornament to cake top, then trim with lace. Attach each lace piece separately, piping a tiny line of icing at base of piece then holding in position an instant until set. Be sure to keep a uniform angle on all pieces. Work your way down the cake, adding lace as pictured. On tops of base and middle tiers, add a second row of tube 1 beading after lace is attached, so lace pieces are framed in beading. Set cupids within pillars, and another within top ornament.

Top tier of this regal centerpiece serves six, two lower tiers serve 88.

PIPED NET MAKES THE SWEETEST BABY CARRIAGE

This lacy, see-through carriage is the cutest trim you could put on a cake for a shower for a new baby. It's a lovely keepsake for Mother, too—the carriage is set on a gum paste plaque to lift off the cake before serving, and treasure for many years as a reminder of the happy event. The carriage is piped in net sections, then assembled—the dainty cake is covered with embroidery done with a round tube.

MAKE THE CARRIAGE FIRST

After this dainty little ornament is finished, the cake can be decorated in a hurry. Patterns are in Wilton Way III Pattern Book.

FIRST CUT THE CARRIAGE BOTTOM and handle supports from thinly rolled gum paste. Roll a cylinder of gum paste for handle. Cut a 5½″ circle for base of ornament. Stiffen net as described on

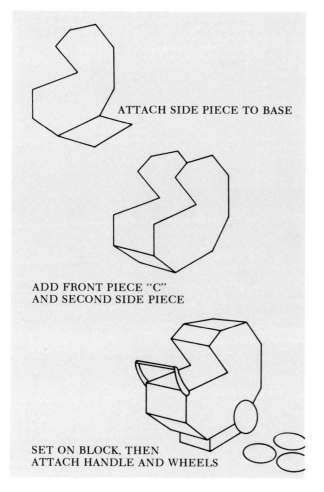

ATTACH SIDE PIECE TO BASE

ADD FRONT PIECE "C"
AND SECOND SIDE PIECE

SET ON BLOCK, THEN
ATTACH HANDLE AND WHEELS

page 59, tape patterns to a stiff surface and tape net over them. Do all piping and assembly with royal icing and tube 1. After net pieces have dried, spray again and dry. Cut out along outlines with a sharp knife.

ASSEMBLE AS DIAGRAM SHOWS. Pipe a line of icing on one edge of gum paste bottom and set side piece on it. Pipe a line of icing on line "C" of side piece, and a line on front edge of bottom. Add piece "C", then attach second side piece. Hold each section a moment to set. Finish assembling front of carriage, then do back and top. Dry thoroughly, then pipe a double line of beading on all seams for extra strength.

WHEN DRY, SET CARRIAGE on a small box or block of styrofoam ¾″ high. Attach wheels, handle supports and handle. After final drying, carriage will stand by itself and may be attached to gum paste base with dots of cing. Edge base with tube 5 beading. Notch the ends of a 7″ length of 1″ satin ribbon and print message with tube 1.

DECORATE THE CAKE

PIPE MANY DROP FLOWERS with tube 225 and royal or boiled icing. Add tube 2 centers and dry.

BAKE A 10′ ROUND two-layer cake, each layer 2″ high. Fill and ice with buttercream, then cover with poured fondant. Set on serving tray and pipe bulb-and-dot "embroidered" flowers with tube 1. An easy way to insure the even effect of the embroidery is to cut a 4″ strip of squared graph paper long enough to wrap around the cake. Mark the squares at 1″ intervals, pin to cake side and prick through marks with a pin. This will guide placement of flowers.

PIPE A TUBE 5 LINE of icing around base of cake, then attach drop flowers with dots of icing. Set ornament on top and add a ribbon bow to handle. Place message ribbon on cake top. Serve to 14 admiring guests after presenting the baby carriage to the new mother.

LATTICE GIVES A SUMMERY, OPEN TOUCH

LATTICE, DONE WITH SMALL ROUND TUBES, is a traditional and always-lovely technique for cake trim. In piping lattice, first drop a string guideline or mark the cake for the lattice area. For most precise results use egg white royal icing, thinned to flow easily from the tube. Be sure there are no lumps in the icing. Always start near the center of the design, fill in to one edge, then fill in to other edge. Add cross strokes in the same manner. Touch tube to attach, lift tube slightly and let string *drop*, then touch to attach again.

This winsome cake uses lattice in a new way—dropped from a built-up curved edge to frame a little bouquet. Use patterns in Wilton Way III Pattern Book.

DECORATE THE CAKE

FIRST PIPE THE FLOWERS in boiled or royal icing. Roses, wild roses and buds are done with tube 102—forget-me-nots and violets with tube 101s, tube 1 for centers. Allow to dry.

BAKE A TWO-LAYER, 8″ SQUARE CAKE. Finished height should be about 4″. Cover with rolled fondant and set on a 12″ square cake board. Following patterns, mark lattice designs with a toothpick on top and sides.

FILL IN SQUARE in center of cake top by dropping touching parallel lines with tube 1. This gives an interesting textured surface. Pipe marked lattice pattern, first with tube 6, then over-pipe with tubes 5 and 4. Pipe and over-pipe tapering wedge at corners (see picture at left). Fill in each side separately with tube 2 lattice. Bead all edges with tube 2.

PIPE A LINE ON CAKE BOARD, ½″ away from bottom of cake with tube 5. This will support lattice. Pipe a tube 7 upright bulb on each corner of cake for attaching flowers. Fill in lattice and bead edges with tube 2. Secure flowers to corners with dots of icing. Arrange flowers in a cluster on cake top, then trim all flowers with tube 65 leaves. This airy little masterpiece will serve twelve.

SUMMER PALACE . . . A LATTICED DREAM CAKE FOR THE BRIDE

Patterns are in Wilton Way III Pattern Book.

PIPE DAISIES IN A NEW WAY from royal or boiled icing. Each flower is made in two steps with tube 2. First pipe a six-petaled flower by starting near edge of nail and piping three touching strokes to center for each petal. Dry within curved form. Pipe a second daisy with shorter petals and dry in curved form. Secure smaller daisy to larger one with a dot of icing and pipe a tube 5 center. Touch with yellow-tinted sugar.

PIPE DELICATE LATTICE WINGS with tube 1 and egg white royal icing. Tape patterns to glass or stiff cardboard and tape wax paper over them. Outline designs and fill in with lattice. When dry, over-pipe all curved lines and center lines of top ornament. Dry, turn over and over-pipe again.

Cut a 5″ circle from rolled gum paste to serve as base for top ornament. Cut a second 4″ circle for heart-box ornament base. Dry.

MAKE THE LATTICED BOX by using a heart cupcake pan as a mold. Lightly grease two heart shapes of the pan with white vegetable shortening. Outline with tube 1 and royal icing about ¼″ up from base of heart, then fill in with lattice. Add tube 1 beading to edges. Set pan in warm oven for one or two minutes to melt shortening and gently remove lattice hearts. Secure one heart to 4″ base with icing. Pipe icing on rear curves and set second heart on it in open position, propping with cotton balls to dry. Mound icing within box, attach flowers and edge base with tube 5.

FIGURE PIPE BIRD in royal icing exactly the same as the bird on page 147. Use tube 1 for wings, tube 3 for body. Insert a wire in lower part of body.

ASSEMBLE TOP ORNAMENT on gum paste circle. Attach complete lattice wing to circle with dots of royal icing. Pipe a line of icing down center of wing and set a half-wing against it. Place wire on bird against icing line. Add second half-wing to other side. Pipe tube 2 beading where wings join. Prop with cotton balls to dry. Trim with flowers and edge base with tube 5 beading.

BAKE AND FILL THE TIERS, each two layers. Base tier is 16″ round, middle tier 12″ round. Layers for each should be 2″ high. Top tier is 8″ round, each layer 1½″ high. Ice and assemble with clear dividers and 12″ and 8″ separator plates.

Divide sides of base and middle tiers into eighths and mark at top and bottom edges. Transfer lattice pattern to top of base tier, scroll patterns to sides of all tiers. Pipe tube 6 bottom ball borders on all three tiers.

ON BASE TIER, do scrolls with tube 5, over-pipe with tube 4, then with tube 3. Finish with three rows of tube 2. Drop string guidelines for lattice curves on side, matching at top edge with marked top lattice pattern. Following guidelines, pipe zigzag garlands with tube 8, then over-pipe twice with tube 6. Fill in lattice with tube 1, then edge lattice curves on side with tube 3 beading and pipe top border with same tube. Edge lattice design on top of tier with tube 2. Mound icing in center of tier and arrange daisies. Attach daisies below garlands with icing.

ON MIDDLE TIER, pipe side scrolls with tube 5 and over-pipe with tube 4, then with two rows of tube 2. Drop string guidelines for lattice on side of tier and mark scallops on tier top. Leave ¼″ free space between scallops for wings. Pipe garlands, fill in lattice, add beading as for base tier. Add heart box and attach daisies on side.

ON TOP TIER, pipe heart-and-scroll designs just as for scrolls on middle tier. Starting about 1″ from top, attach daisies in garlands. Pipe tube 5 ball border at top edge.

WHEN CAKE IS IN PLACE on the reception table, attach the fragile lattice wings with dots of icing. Secure ornament to top tier with icing and trim with daisies. The two lower tiers serve 186, top tier serves 30 guests.

LAVISH LACE PIECES ADORN A REGAL CAKE

Large lace pieces in an intricate design are piped separately, then attached, to create a cake of refined loveliness. A lace tiara is the crowning touch. Decorate this beauty as the centerpiece of an important party, or for a wedding reception.

PIPE ROSES AND BUDS in boiled or royal icing with tube 104. Use a deeper-tinted icing for the centers of the flowers. When dry, mount on wire stems. Pipe tube 66 leaves on wire and dry. Form roses and leaves into a curving spray.

PIPE LACE PIECES in egg white royal icing with tube 1. Tape Wilton Way III patterns for side pieces to glass or a stiff board and tape wax paper smoothly over them. Over-pipe main curving lines for strength. Dry flat. Tape patterns for tiara

to a 6″ curved form, pipe, then over-pipe main curves and dry on form.

PREPARE THE CAKE. Bake and fill a two-layer cake in 12″ hexagon pans. Finished height should be 4″. Use a firm pound cake or fruitcake recipe. Cover with rolled fondant and set on cake board. Cut a 4½″ circle from a 1″ slice of cake, or styrofoam, and ice with royal icing to support tiara. Secure to cake top.

ATTACH LACE PIECES with dots of royal icing. First form tiara, then secure side pieces to corners of cake and add side-center motifs. Set the rose spray on the cake and serve to 20 party guests. Or, at a wedding reception, cut in 50 pieces.

66

TRIM A CAKE WITH APPLIED LACE IN A RICH FLOWER DESIGN

Exquisite lace, piped right on the surface, trims a regal cake, elegant enough for the most important party, lovely enough for a bride's intimate reception. The lace is piped in a pale ecru against lustrous white fondant—roses in delicate peach complete the subtle color scheme.

PIPE ROSES AND BUDS IN TWO TONES in royal or boiled icing. Pipe tube 66 leaves on wire.

PREPARE CAKE. Use a pound cake recipe to bake a layer in a 14″ base bevel pan, one in a 10″ round pan, 2″ high, and one in a 10″ top bevel pan. Fill the two 10″ layers, ice in buttercream and cover with poured fondant. Ice base bevel layer in buttercream, cover with poured fondant and assemble on cake board with 10″ cake. Divide top and bottom bevel surfaces in tenths and mark.

DECORATE WITH ROYAL ICING and round tubes. Transfer Wilton Way III patterns to cake, following marks. Outline flower and bow designs with tube 1, then pipe a second outline within shapes. Let outlines crust, then thin icing to a more flowing consistency and fill in between outlines. Use a cone with tiny cut opening. Add sprays of dots.

  Pipe a tube 5 bulb border at edge of base bevel, and a tube 1 border where base bevel meets 10″ cake. Add a row of scallops above it. Arrange flowers and leaves on cake top. Serve to 21 party guests, or to 72 at a bridal reception.

67

THE DAINTIEST OF ALL CAKES . . . PIPED WITH THE TINIEST OF TUBES

Cobwebby lattice, fine enough to hang by a thread, sets off lace piped directly on the cake.

Decorators who like the challenge of precise, delicate work will enjoy using the "L" series of tubes. These tubes are similar to the standard round tubes. Tube 00L produces a line as fine as that piped by tube 000—tube 0L corresponds to tube 1s. Tube 1L is a little finer than tube 1 and tube 2L is about the same as tube 1. The cone-shapes of the "L" tubes are more slender than those of standard round tubes and are useful for piping in hard-to-reach areas.

DECORATE THE CAKE

PIPE ROYAL ICING TRIMS IN ADVANCE. Pipe the delicate bluebells in peach icing with tube 65 as shown in Chapter Fourteen. You will need 48. Mount a dozen flowers on wire stems and pipe tube 65s leaves on wire. Pipe twelve ovals on wax paper with tube 4, following Wilton Way III patterns. When dry, add tube 2L beading.

PREPARE CAKE. This cake is a fruitcake covered with marzipan, then royal icing in the English manner. This keeps the cake in perfect condition for many days, allowing you to work unhurriedly. Bake a layer in a 14″ base bevel pan. Bake two or three layers in 10″ round pans so that the round layers will have a final height of 4″. Assemble all layers with apricot preserves as a filling. Insert a Flower Spike in center of cake.

MARK PATTERNS. Mark the circle on top center of cake following pattern. Outline with royal icing

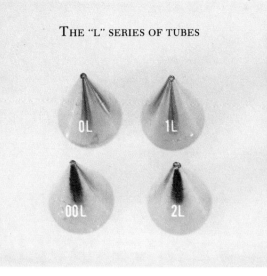

THE "L" SERIES OF TUBES

and tube 6, then overpipe with tube 6, two lines of tube 4 and a final tube 2 line. Dry thoroughly.

Carefully cut out the center circle of the pattern and mark the scalloped edge of the lattice on cake top. Mark end points of radiating lines accurately on top of piped circle and scalloped edge. Mark twelve flowers on cake top, corresponding to curves of scallops. To do this, mark just the centers of flowers and dots for loops of petals. Mark smaller flowers extending from top to side of cake, and large flower-and-leaf patterns on cake side. Mark position of tops of twelve ovals on side of 10″ cake, about 1″ up from bevel.

PIPE LACE MOTIFS. *Use egg white royal icing for all*

trim. Starting on cake top, pipe the flowers with tube 00L and finish with tube 0L beading and accents. Keep the pattern in view as you pipe, and let petal curves extend to marked dots. Continue piping motifs on cake side in the same way.

PIPE SCALLOPED LATTICE PATTERN on cake top with tube 0L. The picture shows finished lattice in actual size. Refer to pattern as you pipe. First connect marked points from circle to scallop edge in diagonal direction. Go back and pipe a second series of strings in the same direction between each piped string. Dry, then pipe strings in opposing direction. When lattice has dried, scatter with tube 00L dots. Bead circle and scalloped edges with tube 2L.

ATTACH OVALS on dots of icing at marks on side of cake and on bevel surface. Attach flowers within ovals and trim with tube 65s leaves. Drop tube 2L strings from top of one oval to the next. Drop strings from slightly above bases of ovals. Strings will touch cake at centers of curves only.

Pipe tube 0L lattice to connect ovals, suspending from strings and oval sides as shown. Scatter tube 00L dots on lattice.

FINISH THE TRIM by dropping curved tube 2L strings on bevel. Add curves of tube 0L dots. Border the cake with tube 4 bulbs and trim with tube 2L dots. Set bouquet in flower spike. Serve wedding cake-sized pieces to 72 guests.

JOY ... A SOARING BRIDAL
CAKE TRIMMED WITH LACY WINGS

Joy is truly a bride's delight—rosy tiers are sweetened with daisy garlands, given a lift with lace wings and crowned with a hand-fashioned ornament that's a froth of flowery lace. The lace pattern repeats the forms of the flowers in a free, curving design.

Joy is a decorator's delight too—this impressive, pretty cake is very quick and easy to put together—even if you're not experienced in tube work. The perky lace wings are done with tube 2, so the piping is quickly done, no over-piping is needed and the wings are much less fragile than most. Borders are simple but effective. Round tubes do all the decorating.

DO TRIMS IN ADVANCE

PIPE LACE PIECES. Use egg white royal icing and tube 2. Fill in centers of daisies, then cover with dots. Cut a 4″ circle from rolled gum paste as base for ornament—or, if you prefer, make base with Color Flow method on wax paper. Outline a 4″ circle with tube 2 and fill in with thinned icing.

ASSEMBLE ORNAMENT. Divide edge of circular base in sixths and mark. Pipe dots of icing on bottom of complete lace piece and set on base, outer edges on opposite marks of base. Pipe a line of icing down center of complete lace piece, pipe dots on bottom of a half-piece and set half-piece in position, edge on one of marks on base. Add other three half-pieces the same way. Prop with cotton balls to dry.

PIPE DAISIES in royal icing. These are seven-petaled flowers, each petal formed with three strokes of tube 3. Pipe a tube 5 yellow center, then sprinkle with a mixture of edible glitter and yellow-tinted sugar for sparkle. Dry within curved form. Mount about two dozen flowers on cloth-covered florists' wire stems. Twist stems together to form a bouquet to set within pillars.

PREPARE AND DECORATE CAKE

BAKE TWO-LAYER TIERS—14″ round, each layer about 2″ high, and 8″ round, each layer about 1½″ high. Fill and ice smoothly. Prepare two 9″ separator plates for six pillars by gluing six stud plates to *plain side* of each plate. Assemble the tiers with these plates, pushing sides with four projections into surface of cake. Use six 5″ Corinthian pillars. Divide each tier into sixths

and mark on top edge. Mark curves for daisy garlands on side of lower tier.

ON LOWER TIER, pipe a tube 11 line around base. Pipe tube 7 balls above and below line, then a third series of balls on top of line. Pipe top ball border with tube 6 and edge separator plate with same tube. Attach daisies to tier side with dots of icing, then pipe little bows above them with tube 3. Set daisy bouquet within pillars and add a few more flowers on separator plate.

ON UPPER TIER, pipe a line around base with tube 6. Complete triple ball border with the same tube, just as you did bottom border on lower tier. Pipe top ball border with tube 5. Attach daisy clusters to tier side with dots of icing. Secure ornament to top and trim with flowers.

ADD LACE WINGS to both tiers. Pipe dots of icing on inner edges of each lace piece and set in position on marks. Hold a moment to set.

Lower tier of Joy serves 92 guests, upper tier serves 30.

71

STRINGWORK FINISHES THE BORDERS
ON A BEAUTIFUL, TRADITIONAL BRIDAL CAKE

ROUND TUBES DO ALL THE DECORATING on Rose Ballet, a lovely formal cake. Classic bulbs and garlands circle the tiers, then are trimmed and enhanced with stringwork. Roses in varied tints of pink add the finishing touch.

Review the rules for piping stringwork in beautiful, even curves. First of all, keep your work at eye level, as you would in piping any side trim. Raise the cake on a stool, box or any sturdy support—or stand on a stepstool to bring yourself to the height of an upper tier. Use icing thinned with corn syrup or piping gel so it is of the proper consistency to flow evenly from the tube. Too thin, the curves will droop, too thick the string will break—so practice a few drapes before piping them on a cake.

When you are ready to pipe stringwork, hold the tube straight out, perpendicular to the cake. Touch to attach, then move *straight out* as the string drops, maintaining light, even pressure. Touch to attach again. *Never* follow the string down with your tube. Most important, keep moving in an even relaxed rhythm. Follow these simple rules and your stringwork will always be even and graceful—and there is no lovelier trim for a cake than delicate stringwork.

DECORATE ROSE BALLET

STEP ONE. Pipe roses in several sizes and tints. Use boiled or royal icing and tubes 104, 103 and 101. Set aside to dry.

Glue an Angelino figure to each of four 5″ Grecian pillars. This gives the pillars a whole new decorative effect.

STEP TWO. Prepare the tiers. Bake two-layer bottom tier in 16″ round pans, each layer 2″ high. Middle tier consists of two layers, each 2″ high, baked in 12″ round pans. Two 8″ layers, each 1½″ high, make up top tier. Fill each tier, cover with marzipan, then with tinted rolled fondant to give a perfectly smooth background for decorating. Assemble on foil-covered cake board with 8″ separator plates and prepared pillars.

Divide base tier into twelfths and mark on top edge. Divide middle tier into twelfths, using base tier as guide, and mark 2″ up from bottom. Make a second series of marks on top edge of tier, midway between marks below. Divide top tier into twelfths and mark 1″ up from bottom and on top edge. Drop string guidelines for all garlands.

STEP THREE. Decorate base tier. Pipe bottom bulb border with tube 2A, then drape with tube 3 strings. Pipe garlands from mark to mark on top edge of tier with tube 12. Use a counterclockwise circular motion, starting with light pressure, increasing pressure and lifting tube to let the icing build up in the center of the curve, then decreasing pressure as you move to end of each garland. Drape lower edges of garlands with tube 3 and drop a second series of tube 2 strings on upper edges of garlands.

Connect points of garlands with scallops on top of tier. Use tube 4 in a tight circular motion.

STEP FOUR. Decorate middle tier. Pipe bulb border at base with tube 2A and light pressure. Drape with tube 3 strings. Follow guidelines to pipe lower garlands with tube 5, starting with light pressure, increasing pressure and lifting tube in center, then decreasing pressure as you near end of garland. Drape a tube 3 string over garlands, then drop a second series of tube 2 strings above them. Pipe tube 2 bows and streamers. Pipe upper garlands with tube 5 and drape with strings just as you did lower garlands. Pipe a little zigzag with tube 2 between each garland. Pipe scallops on top of tier with tube 3 and circular motion, increasing pressure in centers of scallops. Pipe fleurs-de-lis in shell motion with tube 2. Edge separator plate with tube 2 garlands, following scallops on edge of plate, and finish with tube 2 strings.

STEP FIVE. Decorate top tier. Pipe tube 4 garlands around base of tier and drape with tube 3 strings. Make two little twirls at points of strings with tube 3, using heavy, then light pressure. Pipe tube 4 garlands from mark to mark on upper edge of tier. Drop tube 3 strings below and on each garland, tube 2 strings above them. Do scallops on top of tier with tube 3 and zigzag motion.

STEP SIX. Add trims to all tiers. Attach roses with mounds of icing, decreasing in size as you move up tiers. Form cascades on bottom tier. Attach four little cupid figures between pillars and set trios of roses at their bases. Secure a small rose between each garland at bottom of top tier. Set a love bird ornament on top of cake and wreath with flowers. Trim ornament with more flowers. Finish by piping white leaves with tube 66 on bottom tier, tube 65 on two upper tiers.

Serve two lower tiers of Rose Ballet to 186 guests, top tier to 30.

STRINGWORK ADDS GRACE TO SHOWY TOP BORDERS

Pipe basic icing forms—shells, garlands, curves, flowers and fleurs-de-lis. Then embellish them with the graceful curves of dropped stringwork and watch a beautiful border take shape!

You need not limit yourself to just round tubes for the underlying structures and accents. Experiment with star tubes, specialty tubes or tubes in almost any family. You'll be amazed at the interesting borders you'll produce. Drop the string rhythmically to achieve graceful, even curves. For large borders it is best to measure and mark the cake top. *All stringwork for the borders on these pages was piped with tube 2.*

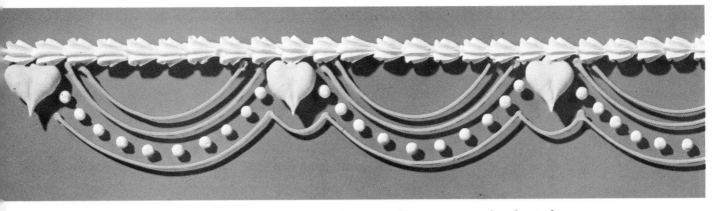

LOVE BORDER adds tube 353 hearts to tube 16 shells. Accent with tube 4 dots.

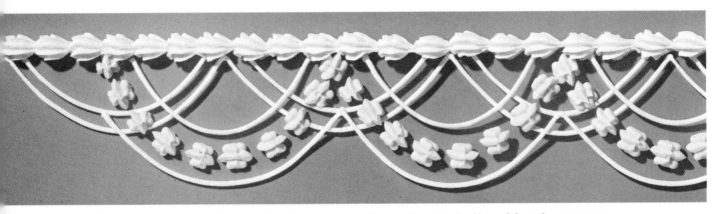

GEOMETRIC BORDER drops string in a pattern from tube 16 shells, adds tube 340 trim.

BOW-TIED BORDER drapes triple strings and bows over a tube 5 garland. Pipe flowers with tube 3.

FLOWERY BORDER begins with tube 5 garlands, adds tube 224 flowers, tube 65 leaves.

FRENCH BORDER combines tube 8 bulbs and tube 6 fleurs-de-lis. Strings are interlaced.

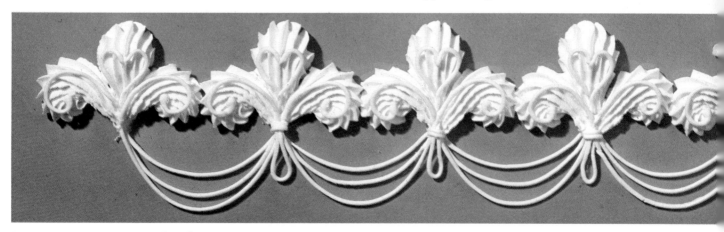

BAROQUE BORDER trims tube 199 curved shells with tube 3 and dropped strings.

CLASSIC FLEURS-DE-LIS with tube 506 are overpiped with tube 2, loops and string added.

Stringwork adds a dressed-up look to any cake and is really easy to do. After you've done a few of these variations, try some new string border designs of your own.

Just keep a few rules in your mind as you pipe and your stringwork will always drop in beautiful even curves. First thin the icing so it flows easily through the tube. *Keep your work at eye level,* raising the cake if necessary on a box or pile of books. Touch the tube to the surface to attach, *pull it straight out,* keeping a light even pressure. Let the string drop by itself, then come back and touch again. Keep moving quickly and rhythmically as you pipe.

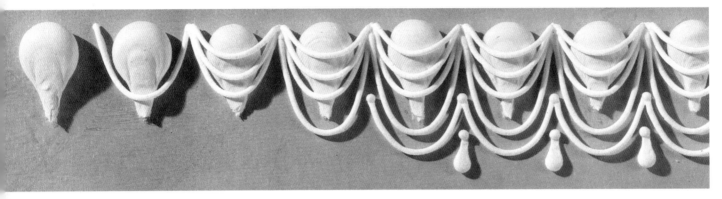

DRAPED BULB BORDER, ideal for the top edge of a cake. First pipe a series of tube 12 bulbs, just as you would an upright shell. Over them pipe triple strings with tube 2. Drop a fourth series of strings that fall just below the tails of the bulbs and add parallel strings below. Finish with small tube 2 bulbs and dots.

DRESSMAKER BORDER gives a sweet touch to cake side. Do it all with tube 2. Pipe a row of even string drapes and frame them with scallops. Add dots and bulb-petal flowers and leaves.

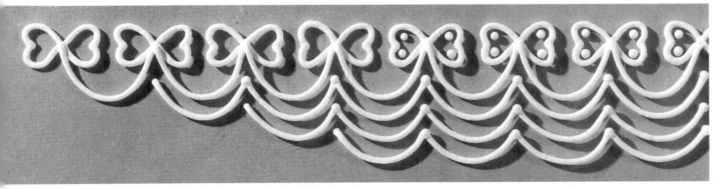

BUTTERFLY BORDER for cake side is sweet as a song. Pipe a row of figure eight bows with tube 2, then connect them with strings. Add parallel triple strings below them and pipe dots in wings.

INTERLACED BORDER makes a handsome, elaborate trim for cake side or top. Use tube 2 to drop triple strings. Starting at mid-point of the curve, drop a second set of triple strings. Continue dropping sets of strings to form the interlaced border. Use tube 2 again to pipe fleurs-de-lis at the points of the strings for a finished look.

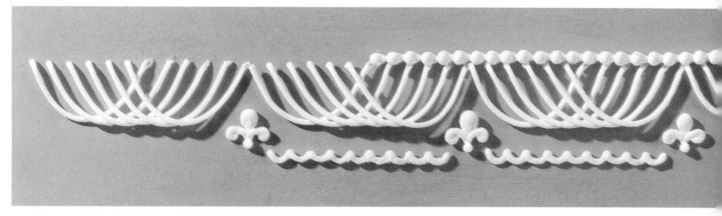

TAILORED BORDER is effective for the top edge of a cake. Drop a tube 2 string drape. Move about ¼" away from its beginning and drop a second string. Continue until you have dropped six string drapes. Circle the cake with these sets of strings. Below each set pipe a row of tiny scallops, and pipe fleurs-de-lis between them. Finish at top with shell-motion tube 2 bulbs.

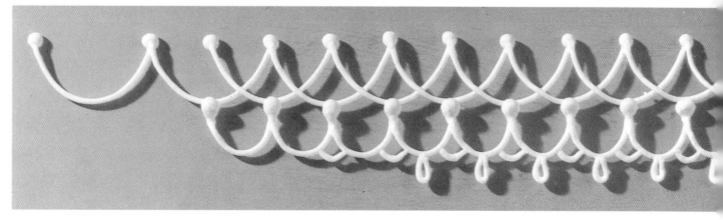

LOOP BORDER gives a lacy look to top edge or side of a cake, or may be "floated" from an upper tier. Drop a string curve, then starting at mid-point drop a second curve. Apply a slight extra pressure as you attach string to form the decorative bulb effect. When you have completed this series of drapes, add a second series of strings, attaching each to center of curve above. Connect them with short string curves, then add loops to finish the border.

77

DELICATE STRINGWORK CIRCLES A LATTICED CAKE

Small round tubes pipe the ethereal trim on this cake—formal enough for a small bridal reception, pretty enough for an engagement announcement or a christening party.

STEP ONE. Pipe petunias in royal or boiled icing, using tube 104 for petals. Dry, then brush centers with thinned yellow icing, pipe tube 16 stars and push in a few artificial stamens. Dry.

Bake a 10″ round two-layer cake, each layer about 2″ high. Fill, ice smoothly with buttercream and set on serving tray. Divide side in twelfths and mark about 1½″ up from base for garlands. Use Wilton Way III pattern for design on cake top, lining up with marks on side.

STEP TWO. Pipe a tube 7 bottom bulb border and trim with tube 2 dots. Drop tube 2 string guidelines from mark to mark on cake side, then pipe zigzag garlands with tube 7, lifting tube in center of each garland to build up. Over-pipe garland with same tube for extra depth. Drop tube 2 guidelines above garlands to define upper curves of lattice. Pipe lattice with tube 1, then frame with tube 1 beading. Use tube 1 to pipe four parallel rows of string, starting with row just above lattice. Finish with dots and fleurs-de-lis.

Cake-top trim is done with tube 1. Fill in scallop design with lattice and edge with beading. Drop string curves just beyond beading, then pipe series of graduated dots extending to edge of cake. Pipe a tube 4 top bulb border.

Ice a marshmallow to center of cake and attach a petunia to it with a mound of icing. Circle with more petunias and trim with tube 65 leaves. Serves 14 at a party, 48 at a wedding reception.

TARANTELLA
Decorating directions, page 80

SUSPENDED STRING LOOPS MAKE THE AIRIEST TRIM

BEAUTIFUL AIRBORNE STRINGWORK is done the same as regular stringwork described on page 76. After the first string loops are dropped, others are dropped from them. Just keep a light touch as you attach string to string, and make sure your icing is thinned to the correct consistency. Use egg white royal icing. Let a row of loops dry before attaching the next.

TARANTELLA *shown on page 79*

PIPE MANY DROP FLOWERS in royal icing with tubes 26 and 35 and add tube 1 centers. Dry. Glue six 2″ plastic bells to a petite ornament plate, trim with flowers, tube 65 leaves and a bow. Attach to a 9″ hexagon separator plate. Trim cherub with flowers, attaching with dots of icing.

BAKE, FILL AND ICE TWO-LAYER HEXAGON TIERS, 12″ x 4″ and 9″ x 3″. Assemble with prepared separator plate, second 9″ plate and six 5″ pillars.

Pipe a tube 7 bulb border at base of lower tier and trim with tube 1 scallops. Pipe a tube 5 top bulb border and use the same tube to outline separator plate. Add tube 1 scallops and dots.

On upper tier pipe a tube 5 bottom bulb border and a tube 3 border at top. Pipe a double scallop and loop design on top of tier.

DO ALL STRINGWORK WITH TUBE 1. The scalloped edge of the separator plate is a spacing guide. On top tier drop a row of strings just below top border. Add more rows to form points in center of sides. Drop a row of strings from separator plate, attaching to indentations in edge. Drop strings from first row to form points at pillars.

On base tier, drop strings from just below top border. Add succeeding rows of string to form points over corners of tier. Attach flowers, trim with tube 65 leaves and set cupid on cake top. Lower tier serves 50, upper tier serves 22 guests.

MINUET *shown at right*

PREPARE TRIMS. Pipe flowers in royal or boiled icing. Use tube 101 for roses and buds, tube 101s for forget-me-nots. Paint two 9″ and two 6″ heart separator plates with thinned royal icing to match icing used on cake. Also paint a standing cherub, a fountain cherub, three 5″ and three 3″ pillars. Circle fountain cherub with flowers and secure to 9″ plate. Add tube 65s leaves. Attach flowers to 6″ plate.

Make top ornament base. Cut a 3″ circle from thinly rolled gum paste and a 2¾″ circle from gum paste rolled to ¼″ thickness. Dry and attach smaller circle to top of larger with royal icing. Set upside down on a small weighted glass and drop curve-upon-curve of string from smaller circle. When dry, turn over, secure standing cherub and trim with flowers and leaves.

BAKE TWO-LAYER TIERS—14″ x 4″ round, 9″ x 4″ and 6″ x 3″ heart. Fill, ice and assemble with prepared pillars and plates. Divide base tier in thirteenths and mark midway on side. Mark again just below top edge, and add second series of marks between each for a total of 26. Divide each curve of middle tier in tenths, leaving a small space at point of tier and mark just below top edge. Divide top tier in fourteenths and mark below top edge. Scallops on plates will guide.

PIPE BORDERS. On bottom tier, use tube 6 for base, tube 5 for top. On middle tier pipe tube 5 base border, tube 4 top border. Pipe a tube 4 border at base of top tier, tube 3 at top. Edge separator plates with tube 4 scallops and dots.

PIPE ALL STRINGWORK WITH TUBE 1. Study the picture for the patterns we used. Pipe the tiny loops on a knife blade and transfer to string curves with a damp brush. Attach a rose to each mark on side of base tier and surround with forget-me-nots. Trim stringwork on side of middle tier with rosebuds. Set ornament on top of cake and complete flower trim. Serve two lower tiers to 120, top tier to twelve wedding guests.

80

ROUND TUBES PIPE LACE AND LATTICE IN THREE-DIMENSIONAL FORMS

There just couldn't be a sweeter trim for a cake than see-through lacy forms of lattice piped on Australian nails. These metal shapes on stems make it possible to pipe crescent curves, arches, baskets and vases in delicate, open line work.

The technique is simple. Lightly but thoroughly grease the nail with solid white vegetable shortening. Pipe the design on the nail, being careful to stop your piping just above the open edge. Dry, then set in a warm oven for just a minute or two to melt the shortening. Gently slide the completed icing form off the nail. Use *egg white royal icing* and a small round tube for this work. Once you've piped a few of these pretty trims, you'll dream up dozens of ways to use them on cakes. Begin with this flowery treat—it's a lovely centerpiece for a special party, or will serve beautifully for a wedding or anniversary celebration.

PIPE TRIMS IN ADVANCE

MAKE MANY DROP FLOWERS in royal icing with tubes 35, 26 and 131. Add tube 2 centers and dry. Mount most of the flowers on cloth-covered florists' wire stems and twist stems together to form into five bouquets. Tape stems with floral tape, push into a block of styrofoam and pipe tube 65 leaves directly on the flower stems.

PIPE LATTICE FORMS in egg white royal icing and

tube 1. You will need twelve crescent designs, but make extras. Study the Wilton Way III patterns but pipe the designs freehand. First pipe the daisy shapes in center of curving sides of the nail, then fill in with lattice. Pipe a row of dots on upper edge of form.

Pipe a complete basket for center of cake on the stovepipe nail. Pipe four baskets with open spaces for corners of upper tier. First pipe the daisy edges, then complete with lattice. Cut a 3" circle from thinly rolled gum paste and cut an opening in the center with base of any standard tube. When dry, pipe a line of icing around bottom of complete basket and set on circle.

BAKE AND DECORATE THE CAKE

BAKE AND FILL two-layer square tiers. Lower tier is 12" x 4", upper tier 8" x 3". Ice smoothly in *boiled icing* and assemble on cake board. On lower tier, mark each side in exact center about 1" up from base. On upper tier, make marks at top edge 1" in from each corner. Divide these spaces in thirds and mark on sides 1" below top edge.

ON UPPER TIER pipe a tube 8 bottom ball border and a tube 3 top border. Drop triple tube 2 strings on side of tier from marks. Set basket on base on top of tier, edge with tube 2 beading and double row of scallops. Finish with bulbs and dots.

ON LOWER TIER, pipe a tube 10 ball border at base, trim with tube 2 strings and dots. Pipe a tube 4 border at top.

ADD TRIMS. Push bouquets into cake at corners of upper tier. Pipe a line of icing around base and sides of a partial basket and gently fit around corner of tier and bouquet. Do the same with the other three partial baskets. Pipe a row of tube 2 scallops around baskets and base of tier. Push stem of bouquet into center of basket on cake top, through hole in base.

On lower tier, use marks on cake side to position crescent lattice. Pipe a line of icing around open edge of a crescent and hold to center side for a moment to set. Add a crescent design on either side. Do the same on the other three sides of the tier, then drop triple tube 2 strings from corners of tier to ends of crescents. Attach flowers to tier sides as picture shows and trim with tube 65 leaves.

This sunshiny treat serves 48 guests at a party, 104 at a wedding reception.

LACY, DIMENSIONAL CURVES GLORIFY A MASTERPIECE CAKE

Airy forms piped on Australian nails give this masterpiece a breathtaking beauty. Decorate it as an exquisite wedding cake, or for the most formal party.

PIPE LATTICE SHAPES with egg white royal icing and tube 1. You will need a flower center piped on the number 3 domed nail, six petals piped on the arch nail, using Wilton Way III pattern, twelve large border shapes and 24 crescents.

Thoroughly grease all nails with white vegetable shortening before beginning. The picture above shows design of lattice. When piping crescents, be sure to keep the piped lines ¼" above open edge of nail.

Pipe tube 1 beading on upper curves of crescents and borders and at edges of petals and dome. When dry, place in a warm oven for a few minutes, then gently slide shapes off nails.

Pipe tube 225 drop flowers in royal icing with tube 1 centers. Dry.

BAKE A FRUITCAKE in a 16" base bevel pan and sufficient layers in 12" round pans to achieve a finished height of 4". Assemble and cover with marzipan, then royal icing in the English manner. Measure side of cake and divide in twelfths, then twenty-fourths, and cut pattern for 24 inverted arches. Arches should be 1½" high. Mark on side of cake about ½" up from bevel.

DECORATE WITH ROYAL ICING. Pipe a tube 4 bulb border at base of bevel, a tube 2 bulb border at upper edge of bevel. Form twelve tiny clusters of flowers on top edge of cake, lining up with arch pattern. Pipe tube 65s leaves. Pipe arches with tube 4, then over-pipe with tubes 3 and 2. Pipe a tube 1 line on both sides of arches and add tube 3 balls and fleurs-de-lis.

FINISH WITH LATTICE SHAPES, attaching with dots of icing. Place dome in center of cake top and secure petals around it. Trim with flowers. Using flower clusters and arches as guide, secure borders to cake top at edge, one at a time. Add tube 1 beading. Using arches as guide, circle bevel with crescents. Trim borders and crescents with flowers and tube 65s leaves. This elegant creation will serve 28 as a party dessert, 85 at a wedding reception.

CHAPTER FOUR

Round Tubes Pipe Dots, Lines and Built-up Over-piping

Leaf through this chapter to see the amazing variety of effects produced by dots and lines piped with plain round tubes. See how these simple forms can "print" a cake like a calico pattern, veil it with lace-like cornelli and create borders from dainty to dramatically bold. Basic round tube dots and lines can also "embroider" a design and make lifelike flowers. The tiniest round tubes produce the delicate borders and motifs of the fine line technique. Line piped upon line results in the strong light-and-shadow effects of over-piping.

DOTS AND LINES
TRIM HOLIDAY COOKIES

Cookies in a variety of shapes, your own imagination, and simple dots and lines piped with small tubes add up to a jar full of the most attractive confections ever created for the holidays! Start with the recipe below, or use your own favorite firm cookie recipe.

ROLL-OUT COOKIES

1¼ cups butter
2 cups sugar
2 eggs
5 cups flour
2 teaspoons baking powder
1 teaspoon salt
½ cup milk
¼ teaspoon grated orange peel

Cream butter and sugar together, then add eggs and beat until fluffy. Sift dry ingredients to-

gether and add alternately to creamed mixture with milk. If mixture is too sticky, add a little more flour so that it is easy to handle and roll out.

Divide dough in thirds. Tint one portion green by kneading in liquid food color. Tint second portion pink and leave the third untinted. Keep dough you are not working with well wrapped in plastic. Roll out to ⅛" thickness, cut out shapes and bake in a 375°F oven about eight minutes, or until done. This recipe yields about four dozen large cookies.

FOR COOKIES IN THE JAR, use royal icing thinned with gel or corn syrup and tinted in cheerful colors. Tube 2 pipes all the freehand designs in combinations of dots and lines. Here is a good chance to use your imagination in dreaming up pretty patterns. Pipe a snowflake on a round cookie, mass dots for a Christmas wreath or make a smiling face. Decorate a tree-shaped cookie, trim hearts with flowers or repeated lines, harness a reindeer or just outline a star or an angel figure and add dot flowers.

FOR BOY AND GIRL COOKIES, first mark outline for colored areas lightly with a pin. Fill in areas with closely set parallel lines piped with tube 1. Pipe curves and dots for features and details after colored areas have set a bit. This line technique gives an interesting texture to the finished cookie. Hang the decorated cookies on the tree, use them as place cards, or arrange a bright assortment on a tray to pass to guests.

ROUND TUBES PATTERN PARTY CAKES WITH DOTS AND LINES

It's amazing how the simplest of forms piped with small round tubes can trim a cake beautifully—and give it a distinct personality. Here are two easy-to-pipe charmers, one calico-printed, the other sweetened with lacy cornelli. Do it all with icing lines and dots.

A PERKY BIRTHDAY CAKE

Gay dot flowers in a bright calico pattern and a curving message make a tribute that's cheerful and sophisticated.

BAKE, FILL AND ICE a two-layer 10″ round cake, each layer 2″ high. Set on serving tray or foil-covered cake board. Divide side into eighths and transfer Wilton Way III pattern. Mark a 4½″ circle on cake top and make pattern for greeting on an 8″ paper circle. Print letters ⅝″ high and make sure all verticals point toward center of circle. Transfer to cake top.

DO ALL LINES AND DOTS with tube 2. First do the side flower-and-stem-design, then edge with beading and scallops. Pipe scallops and dots on circle on cake top, then do lettering. Finish with a tube 8 bulb border at base, tube 6 at top. Push in

birthday candles, light them and serve with a flourish to 14!

A LACY SHOWER CAKE

Bells ring out the happy news on a cake with tailored charm—its angles softened with the curving lines of cornelli. Patterns are in Wilton Way III Pattern Book.

MAKE BELLS IN THE COLOR FLOW TECHNIQUE. You will need ten. Outline patterns with tube 1 and flow in thinned icing. When dry, pipe designs with tube 1. Dry again.

BAKE, FILL AND ICE a two-layer 10″ square cake, each layer about 2″ high. Transfer patterns to top and side. Fill in areas with tube 1 cornelli, piping continuous curving lines, never touching. Keep the curves tight and as close as possible. Do the lettering and the curving blue ribbon with tube 4. Pipe the two little rings with the same tube. Attach the bells on mounds of icing. Finish by piping a tube 8 ball border at base and trimming with tube 4. Serve at an engagement party to 20 admiring guests.

STRING OF PEARLS. Very easy to achieve, very pretty on cake side or top edge. Start with tube 2 and drop double string guidelines. At their points, pipe little hearts and bows. String slightly separated dots along guidelines, then add tube 4 fleur-de-lis and flower trim.

TWIN HEARTS is patterned with a 1⅜" heart cutter, or trace Wilton Way III pattern. Mark pairs of facing hearts, leaving about ½" between each pair. Make flowers and tiny leaves with tube 2, then pipe the hearts with tube 6, adding a curved "V" to each.

ROCOCO BORDER looks lavish on side or top of a cake but can be done very quickly. Cut your own shield-shape pattern, 3⅝" wide, 3" high, from folded paper, or use Wilton Way III pattern. Pipe all the curved "C's" with tube 5, then trim with tube 2 flowers. Color contrast adds to the charm.

POPCORN BORDER is cute and colorful and just the thing for a Christmas cake. Do it all with tube 2. Drop curved guidelines, then fill in with triple white dots for "popcorn". Add red dots for "cranberries" and tie it up with perky bows.

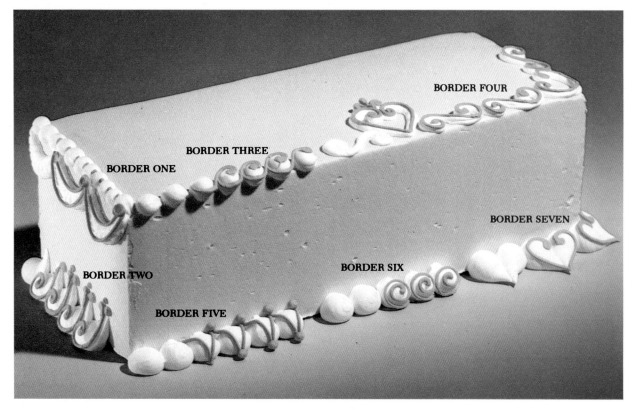

EMBELLISH BASIC ICING FORMS . . . CREATE INTERESTING NEW BORDERS

BORDER ONE starts with a classic tube 4 zigzag garland draped over a guideline. Add tube 2 strings and twirls, then above it pipe tube 4 bulbs and trim with tube 2 dots.

FOR BORDER TWO, pipe a row of tube 5 curved shells, then add contrasting tube 2 trim.

BORDERS THREE, FIVE AND SIX all begin with a row of tube 4 balls. Trim them with contrasting "C's," "V's" or spirals, piped with tube 2 and watch attractive borders take form. Dots complete the tailored look on Border Five.

BORDER FOUR adds a heart shape to a row of "S" curves and turns the corner with a "C". Do it all with tube 4, then go back and over-pipe with tube 2. This pretty border makes the trim on the cake on the next page.

BORDER SEVEN begins with a puffy heart. Form the hearts with touching shells piped with tube 5. Accent them with contrasting tube 2 hearts.

CURVING LINES, PIPED WITH ROUND TUBES
BORDER A PRETTY SHEET CAKE

Yes, a sheet cake can look very festive, even when it's decorated in just a short time, and without the glamor of piped flowers. This practical cake shape, so easy to cut and serve, is often the most difficult one to decorate with originality. Here, simple curves piped with round tubes and a skillful use of color give the sheet cake real distinction. The top expanse is trimmed with a baroque panel to enclose a name or message.

BAKE A TWO-LAYER SHEET CAKE, 9″ x 13″. Put the layers together with your favorite filling and ice smoothly in buttercream. Make the quick design for the top panel by imprinting twice with a Pattern Press. On top edge, mark the exact center of each side of the cake. Do the same at the base.

DO ALL THE DECORATING IN BUTTERCREAM with round tubes. Start with white icing and tube 5.

Pipe a ball on base of cake at each corner and at centers of sides. Above the balls pipe inverted hearts ending in curves. Fill in spaces between them with reverse shells.

Continuing with white icing, pipe heart shapes on cake top at each marked point. Add curved "C's" on each corner, then complete top border with "S" shapes. Pipe the marked center design, adding curves and flourishes.

CHANGE TO PINK ICING and tube 3, and over-pipe the base border, following curves of shells and hearts. Do the same on the top border. Now pipe the name with tube 2 and use the same tube to trim the panel with bulb-petal flowers and leaves. This simple but very pretty cake serves 24 party guests.

92

SHORT LINES OF ICING
EMBROIDER A CAKE WITH ROSES

Short strokes of icing done with tube 1 give an amazingly realistic effect of crewel embroidery. Use Wilton Way III patterns for this cake, or experiment with some of your own favorite needlework designs.

This cake was made for a small Valentine celebration, but if you need to serve a large gathering, put the same designs on a sheet cake.

BAKE A TWO-LAYER 9″ HEART CAKE, each layer 2″ high. Fill, then ice smoothly with buttercream and set on cake board cut the same shape. Transfer crewel pattern to top and sides.

DO ALL TRIM WITH ROUND TUBES and buttercream icing. Use tube 1 for embroidery. Cover petals with short strokes, starting at outside of petal and working in. Go back and over-pipe the main petal shapes for rounded appearance. Fill in cen-

ters with yellow dot stamens. Pipe two-tone green leaves with lines of icing and bead the center vein. The script message is also piped with short lines of icing.

PIPE A BALL BORDER at base of cake with tube 7 and add tube 2 string scallops above it. Pipe a tube 6 ball border at top, then add tube 2 scallops on cake side below it, and on cake top.

Center your party table with this pretty "embroidered" creation, and serve to twelve.

93

ROUND TUBES PIPE REALISTIC ICING FLOWERS

The same tubes that turn simple lines and dots into fanciful trims, "embroidery" and a multitude of borders, can also form two of the prettiest flowers. These easy-to-pipe blossoms make very unusual cake trims.

SUMMER CLOVER

The sweetest of all meadow flowers starts with a ball, then is covered with fine lines for the string-like petals.

To pipe right on the cake, first pipe a ball with tube 12 with buttercream or boiled icing. Cover it with tiny tube 1 lines, starting at the top, and the flower's in bloom.

To make a clover bouquet, pipe a tube 8 calyx and add a florists' wire stem. Now pipe a tube 12 ball on the calyx, brush smooth and add tube 1 petals. Pipe tube 2 green sepals below the flower. The clover leaf is piped on a number 7 nail with tube 102. Pipe three heart shapes, points touching, then brush together. For the characteristic two-tone look, brush with thinned paste color. When dry, attach to a wire stem with icing and bind to flowers with floral tape. Only royal icing can be used for stemmed flowers.

LILIES OF THE VALLEY
BLOOM ON A BRIDAL CAKE

These dainty signs of spring are truly the bride's

own flower. Pipe them on a serenely lovely cake, trimmed with classic curves. You may do all decorating in buttercream, or use boiled icing for the leaves and flowers.

PREPARE THE TIERS. Bake a two-layer 15" petal tier and a two-layer 10" round tier, each layer 2" high. For the top tier, bake two 1½" high layers in 6" round pans, and a cake in a blossom pan. Fill the layers, ice with buttercream and assemble on an 18" cake board. Use 12" round separator plates and 5" Corinthian pillars.

Using base tier as guide, divide middle tier in eighths and mark halfway up the side. Drop string guidelines for garlands. Mark a vine on upper side of tier, curves corresponding to guidelines below. Divide top tier in sixths and drop guidelines for garlands.

ON BASE TIER, drop guidelines for garlands. Pipe long leaves with tube 114 and pipe stems with tube 2. Edge base and top with tube 6 bulbs. Pipe zigzag garlands with tube 9, then drop tube 3 strings and loops. Edge separator plate with tube 5, then pipe tube 70 leaves within petal curves on tier top. Add tube 2 stems.

ON MIDDLE TIER, pipe base bulb border with tube 6, top border with tube 5. Do zigzag garlands with tube 8 and drape with tube 3 string. Pipe the vine and stems with tube 3, then add tube 70 long, curving leaves.

PIPE BOTTOM AND TOP BORDERS on top tier with tube 4. Pipe zigzag garlands with tube 6 and add tube 3 strings and bows. Pipe tube 4 bulbs at the base of the blossom tier and do garlands with tube 6. Add stringwork and beading with tube 3.

NOW PIPE ALL THE FLOWERS. This is a short-cut version of the lily of the valley that produces a very pretty bell-like blossom. Simply pipe a dot just below a stem with tube 2, then pull out four tiny points with the same tube. Set a tiny white bird on top of the cake and gather a strip of tulle to surround a plate from a petite ornament base. Glue petite couple to plate and place ornament within pillars.

Lily of the Valley—spring's loveliest bridal cake—is ready for the reception table. Serve two lower tiers to 110 wedding guests, top tier serves 20.

Any discussion of the uses of round tubes for line effects would not be complete without an exploration of the *fine line technique.*

In this technique, only the smallest of the round tubes are used—000, 1s or tubes in the "L" family shown on page 68—00L and 0L. Using lines formed with these tiny tubes, the most delicate curved borders and decorative motifs are piped. Since the borders are so small, two or more different designs are often set close together on a cake. The cakes, too, are of modest dimensions, but so unique and dainty they achieve an important effect. Motifs often use a series of repeated parallel lines to increase a color effect.

This fine line technique, as is true of many others, originated in Europe. The Wilton-American method has adapted it, and given it a new freedom in color and design. This meticulous technique is best displayed on cakes covered with poured or rolled fondant.

ROYAL ICING is best for fine line piping. Thin it with about one teaspoon of piping gel to a fourth-cup of icing. Experiment with the icing—you may wish to add more gel for effortless, even lines.

USE A SMALL CONE, made of a parchment paper triangle, half the size of the usual cone.

THREE METHODS OF PIPING

THE DROP METHOD FOR CAKE TOP. Hold your cone straight up, about ⅜" above the surface, and let the icing drop to form the design. Keep a very light, even pressure so lines have exactly the same thickness. Go as far as you can with the piping, stop pressure and lift away—then start your work again.

THE GLIDING METHOD FOR CAKE TOP. Hold your cone rather flat as if writing, at about a 30° angle to the surface. Just glide it over the surface, varying your speed and pressure to produce a varied line, from fine to a little thicker.

THE DRAWN METHOD FOR CAKE SIDE. Hold cone straight out, tube touching cake, and draw the design. You may start or stop at any time and the break will not be visible. As with all work on cake side, *be sure to have your work at eye level.*

PRACTICE IS NEEDED so that your work becomes easy and automatic. Start by tracing patterns with a wax paper overlay. Then go on to create beautiful little designs of your own. You'll really enjoy decorating cakes in this technique.

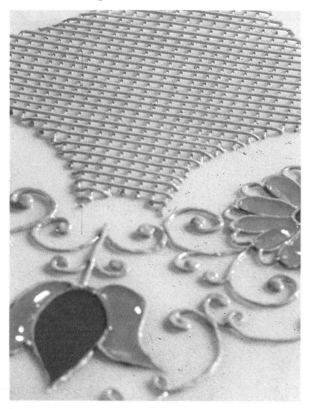

A CAKE PATTERNED WITH FINE LINE FLOWERS

Glittering piping gel fills in the flower petals on this petite cake done in the fine line technique. The picture above shows an enlarged detail.

PREPARE THE CAKE. Bake and fill an 8" x 3" square cake. Use a firm pound cake or fruit cake recipe. Cover with marzipan, then rolled fondant. If you are not experienced in fine line work, first tape cake-top pattern (in Wilton Way III Pattern Book) to a stiff board or glass and tape wax paper over it. Thin royal icing with piping gel to the consistency that is easiest for you to work with. Practice-pipe the design with tube 1s. After you are familiar with it, you may need only to transfer the shape of the lattice center and the flower shapes to the cake top. Transfer "E" shapes to cake sides.

PIPE THE TOP DESIGN with tube 1s. All work is done in the drop method. Pipe a tube 6 bottom ball border, then pipe the "E's" on cake side with tube 1s and the drawn method. Fill in between them with "c" shapes.

Thin piping gel with water to an easy-flowing consistency. Use a cone with a tiny cut opening to fill in the petal areas. Display this glittering little masterpiece with pride! Serves twelve.

THE FINE LINE TECHNIQUE CREATES IMAGINATIVE BORDERS

These tiny borders in the fine line technique give just a hint of the versatility this method can achieve. All are shown actual size.

Fit a small parchment cone with a tiny round tube. Fill the cone with royal icing mixed with piping gel. A proportion of one part gel to four parts icing was used here. Or use piping gel alone for a sparkling effect.

Now tape Wilton Way III pattern to a stiff surface, tape wax paper smoothly over it and practice the borders. Follow the method noted below each border. (Methods are described on page 97.) For Border One, pipe the sweeping upward curve, then, without stopping, the short "E" curve below it. For Border Two, pipe all diagonal lines in same direction first, then go back and pipe diagonals in the opposite direction. Borders Three, Four and Five are done in a continuous movement. For Border Six, pipe a series of "C" shapes, pausing just long enough to build up thickness, then go back and drop curves below all "C's".

In Border Seven, a continuous curving line is dropped, then a second curving line is piped over it to form medallions. Each motif in Border Eight is formed of two "V's".

Now pipe some original border designs of your own. As a guide to spacing, pipe on wax paper taped over squared graph paper. Soon, evenly spaced piping will become automatic.

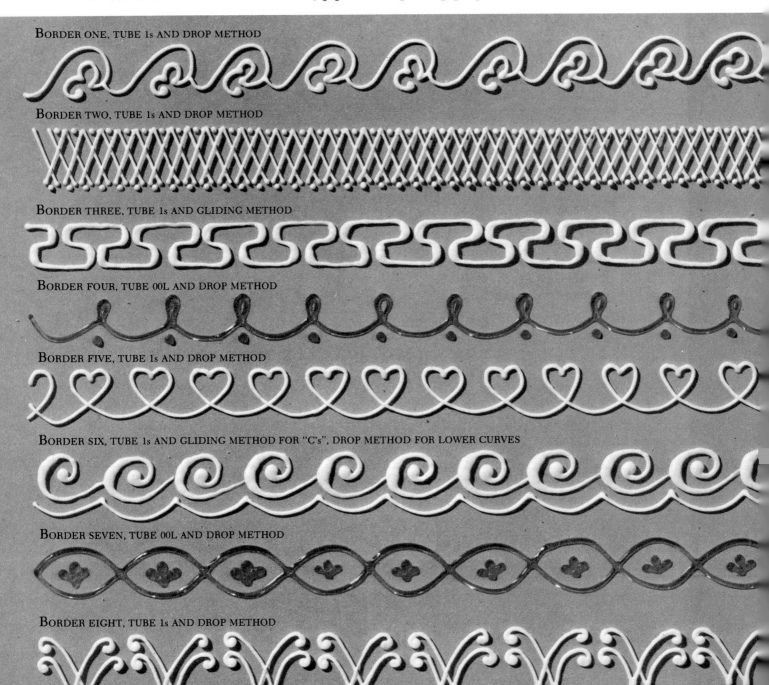

BORDER ONE, TUBE 1s AND DROP METHOD

BORDER TWO, TUBE 1s AND DROP METHOD

BORDER THREE, TUBE 1s AND GLIDING METHOD

BORDER FOUR, TUBE 00L AND DROP METHOD

BORDER FIVE, TUBE 1s AND DROP METHOD

BORDER SIX, TUBE 1s AND GLIDING METHOD FOR "C's", DROP METHOD FOR LOWER CURVES

BORDER SEVEN, TUBE 00L AND DROP METHOD

BORDER EIGHT, TUBE 1s AND DROP METHOD

A GROUP OF DECORATIVE FINE LINE MOTIFS

Pretty, curving designs are fun to pipe in the fine line technique. Space a number of them on a cake top and add borders to complete the decoration. Use them as the only trim on petits fours, or choose just one to center a petite cake, then ring it with fine line borders.

First practice these motifs by tracing Wilton Way III patterns covered with wax paper. All are piped with tube 000, all are shown here in actual size. Use royal icing thinned with piping gel, the methods indicated below and described on page 97, and add shining accents of gel.

Motifs, as well as borders, in the fine line technique often make use of a continuous line. Start piping at a certain point and pipe the curves without stopping until the design is complete. In the picture below, the Scale, Fern, Flower, Diamond Curve, Tree and Fan designs were all done in a continuous line. Begin at the point marked on the pattern with an arrow—then pipe all the curves without stopping.

This continuous line gives a special grace and fluidity to the trim.

Design and pipe fine line motifs of your own. An easy way to start is to trace a small cookie cutter in round, diamond, star or heart shape. Loop in and out of the outline in graceful curves. When you have piped a design you especially like, put it on a cake. Lightly press the cutter to the cake surface to serve as a guide.

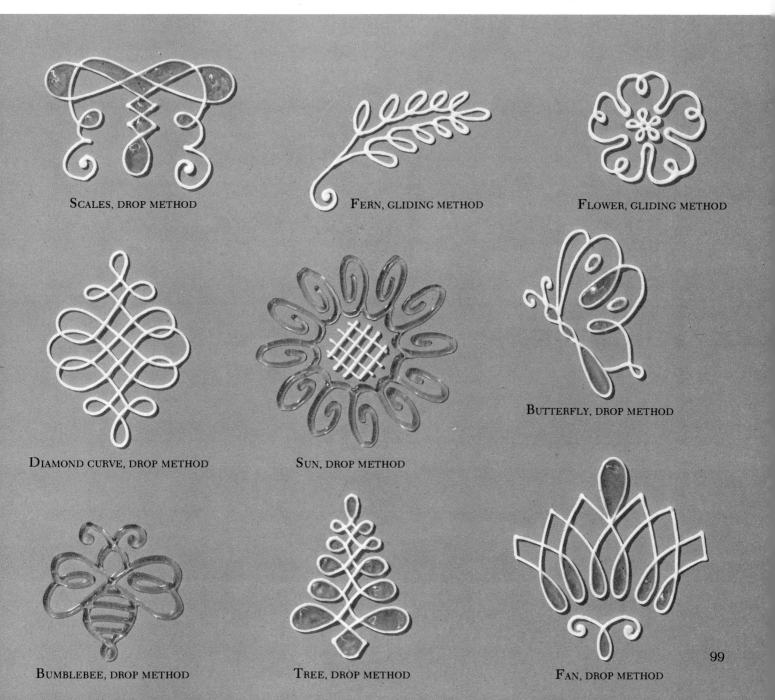

SCALES, DROP METHOD

FERN, GLIDING METHOD

FLOWER, GLIDING METHOD

DIAMOND CURVE, DROP METHOD

SUN, DROP METHOD

BUTTERFLY, DROP METHOD

BUMBLEBEE, DROP METHOD

TREE, DROP METHOD

FAN, DROP METHOD

ELEGANT SWEETS TRIMMED WITH FINE LINE PIPING

Simple designs, meticulously executed with a tiny round tube, and daintily tinted icing produce stylish cakes with continental flair.

A TRAY OF PETITS FOURS

To really impress your guests, bring out a tray of these tiny cakes after an elegant luncheon, or let them star on the sweet table at a reception.

Start by baking a butter or sponge cake in an 11" x 17" cookie sheet. Height should be no more than ¾". Cut in half, stack and fill with jam. Chill, then trim off crisp edges. For squares, cut in 1¾" strips, then slice in 1¾" pieces. For circles use a 1¾" biscuit cutter. Brush the cakes with hot apricot glaze to seal crumbs, ice with buttercream and cover with poured fondant.

You'll enjoy using your originality to pipe the dainty trims. First use tube 000 or 00L and Wilton Way III patterns to pipe the designs on wax paper. Use tinted or chocolate fondant, thinned with a few drops of water for piping. Then pipe the designs freehand on the cakes. Soon you'll be creating your own pretty designs. Even a simple spiral makes a graceful trim when centered with a tiny drop flower.

A SPRAY OF TULIPS *at right*

The most delicate line work creates a springtime pattern on a sunny cake. Repeated lines and borders emphasize the color and form.

BAKE AND FILL a 10" x 3" round cake. Ice with buttercream, then cover with poured fondant. Transfer Wilton Way III pattern to cake top. You need only transfer the main lines of the design.

PIPE THE FLOWER SPRAY with tube 000 and royal icing thinned with piping gel. Use the drop method, explained on page 97. After forms of flowers are piped, repeat the shapes with curved parallel lines. Pipe the outer edges and center lines of the leaves, then fill in with diagonal lines.

PIPE THE BORDERS with tube 000, first practicing on wax paper. For green border on top edge of cake, pipe scallops and loops, then add "C" curves with the drop method. Pipe the inner pink border in the gliding method for a thick-and-thin effect. Circle the base of the cake with a tube 6 ball border, then add scalloped border above it in the drawn method. Serve this dainty creation to 14.

A DAINTY MASTERPIECE, DRAWN WITH THE FINEST TUBE

THE FINE LINE TECHNIQUE, done with the smallest of round tubes, is used for this outstanding example of the decorator's art. Delicately tinted icing sets off the design of flowers in a cornucopia and adds variety to the graceful borders.

Before starting to decorate, we suggest you practice the designs first. Tape the Wilton Way III pattern for the top design to a stiff surface and tape wax paper over it. Fit a tiny decorating cone with tube 000 or tube 00L and fill with royal icing thinned with piping gel. Holding your tube straight up about ⅜" above the surface, trace the design. After your eye and hand are accustomed to the tiny forms, you will need to transfer only the main shapes of the flowers and cornucopia, giving you freedom in filling in details.

Practice the borders, too, in the same manner. After you have done this, you will only need to trasnsfer the dots on the pattern to the cake. To design an original border, just cover a piece of graph paper marked in ¼" squares with wax paper. All the borders on this cake were done in ¾" modules. Pipe curves, loops and angles and repeat them each ¾", confining the design to three squares, then repeating it. You'll be surprised at the pretty patterns you'll invent.

PREPARE THE CAKE. Bake a two-layer cake in 9" oval pans. Use a fruitcake or pound cake recipe. Cover with rolled fondant and place on serving tray. Transfer patterns by pricking through with a pin, using minimal marking. Prick only through marked dots on border patterns, or just mark ¾" spaces to fill in your own design.

USE TUBE 000 OR 00L for all decorating. Fill your cone with thinned royal icing and use the drop method for top motif. For the yellow border on top edge of cake, use the gliding method. Pipe a tube 3 bulb border around base of cake, then use the drawn method for the two borders on upper and lower side. (See methods, page 97.) For side borders, be sure to raise the cake to eye level.

Display this lovely little centerpiece at any important occasion—or present it to someone very special. Serves twelve.

LINE-UPON-LINE GIVES DIMENSION TO OVER-PIPING

ONLY OVER-PIPING will give this rich three-dimensional quality to a cake. In this technique, line is piped upon line for a built-up effect that emphasizes rich curving designs, and gives a fascinating play of light and shadow to the cake surface. Sometimes line work with a round tube is built on a star tube foundation, as shown on page 178, but the use of only round tubes for the succeeding lines gives a special crispness and clarity to the sculptured effect.

Over-piping is not difficult to do—all it needs is a steady hand and a careful eye. Allow the piped line to dry a few minutes before adding another on it. In this cheery holiday cake, green and scar-

let stylized flowers set off the simple built-up curves. If you haven't experienced the fun of this technique, this cake gives a wonderful opportunity to begin. Only round tubes are used. For the over-piping, buttercream icing is acceptable.

A HAPPY HOLIDAY CAKE

PREPARE THE CAKE. Bake a two-layer cake in 10″ round pans, making sure each layer is about 2″ high. Fill, then ice very smoothly in buttercream to provide a ridge-free surface for the handsome over-piping.

Transfer Wilton Way III pattern to top of cake. Following marked scallops on cake top, divide side into twelfths and mark on side of cake 1″ up from base. This will be guide for side scallops. Transfer flower pattern to cake side.

DECORATE THE CAKE TOP. Do message, sprays of stems and bows with tube 2. Pipe petals with tube 4, squeezing heavily at base, then relaxing pressure as you move out to a point. Center flowers with tube 2 dots. Pipe leaves the same as petals, again using tube 4.

Pipe long scrolls and inner scallops with tube 5, following pattern accurately. Wait a short time for these lines to dry before adding second lines with tube 4. Let them drop on the first curves, holding tube slightly above surface. Now over-pipe again with tube 3. Border the inner curves of the scallops with tube 3 dots. Do outer scallops with tube 4, dry, then over-pipe with tube 3. Add little tube 3 dots to points of all scallops. Pipe a ball border on edge of cake with tube 5 and trim with tube 2 dots.

DECORATE THE CAKE SIDE. Pipe a tube 5 ball border at base and trim with tube 3 dots. Drop a tube 5 string from mark to mark for scallops, keeping curves even in depth. Dry and over-pipe by dropping a second string with tube 4. Dry again, then add a third string with tube 3. Pipe stems with tube 2 and add leaves and flowers with tube 4, just as for top of cake. Edge inner curves of scallops with tube 2 dots, then add dots piped with tubes 4 and 2 to points of scallops. This stand-out Christmas cake serves 14.

LAVISH OVER-PIPED CURVES CIRCLE A ROSY HEART

Just the most striking and beautiful love cake you could decorate—and all the extravagant curves are deeply over-piped with round tubes. Make it to announce an engagement, celebrate Valentine's day in a never-before way, or even for a small wedding reception.

PREPARE THE GUM PASTE TRIMS. Cut many forget-me-nots from thinly rolled gum paste and pipe tube 2 centers. Mold an angelica and dry.

BAKE THE CAKE in 9″ heart pans—two layers, each 2″ high. Fill and ice smoothly. Buttercream may be used for this cake, but it is easier to cover the cake with marzipan, then royal icing in the English manner. Then do piping in royal icing. Also bake a half-egg in an egg cupcake pan, ice with buttercream and cover with poured fondant. When icing sets, pipe ornamented initials on egg with tube 1. Transfer Wilton Way III patterns to cake top and sides.

Do OVER-PIPING ON CAKE TOP, starting with outer edge of design. Remember to wait a short time for a line to dry before piping another one on it. Design consists of five rows. Pipe outer row with tube 1 and edge with tube 1 dots. Second row is piped with tube 2, over-piped with tube 1. Pipe third row with tube 3 and overpipe twice, with tubes 2 and 1. Fourth row is piped with tube 3, then over-piped three times with tubes 3, 2 and 1. Final innermost row is piped with tube 5 and over-piped with tubes 5, 4, 3, and 2.

OVER-PIPE SIDE OF CAKE, starting with top row. First pipe a tube 5 bulb border at base. Top row is a tube 1 line edged with tube 1 dots. Next row is piped with tube 2, over-piped with tube 1. Third row is piped with tubes 3, 2 and 1. Pipe fourth row with tubes 3, 3, 2 and 1. Final, lowest row is piped with tubes 5, 5, 4, 3 and 2.

PUT EVERYTHING TOGETHER. Cover cake with tube 1 cornelli between over-piping on top and side. Set egg cake in position and attach angelica on a mound of icing. Cover mound with flowers, attaching each on a dot of icing. Scatter flowers around angelica and egg and mass more flowers at points of cake.

Serve this extravanganza to twelve guests at a party or to 28 at a wedding reception.

CHAPTER FIVE

Script and Printing with Round Tubes

A MESSAGE OR A NAME piped on a cake always makes it more memorable to the person for whom it was decorated. But script and printing can do much more than that.

The beautiful curving lines of script can pattern a whole cake top with a swirling design. Monograms can give distinction and style to even the simplest cake. Pipe block printing in interesting arrangements and trim it with lines, dots and drop flowers. Fill-in letters can make a cake come alive with color and excitement. All too often a message is simply piped on a cake almost as an afterthought. The beautiful cakes in this chapter will inspire you to make script and printing a strong central design element on a skillfully decorated cake.

The technique of writing or printing on a cake top is easily learned. Thin the icing so it flows easily from the tube, using corn syrup or piping gel. Use tube 1, 2 or 3. Hold the cone as flat as possible and just glide over the surface, tube barely touching. Don't dig into the surface or hold the cone above it. If you are inexperienced in this technique, practice for a few minutes a day on the back of a cookie sheet. Soon your work will gain a real character. Then go on to some of the highly styled letters shown in this chapter.

Even if your handwriting is less than perfect, you can achieve a beautiful script style. That's because you are using your whole arm to write—not just your fingers.

EASTER JOY

A simple sheet cake becomes a work of art when adorned with these beautiful letters in the medieval style. Read page 117 for a description of the fill-in technique, then decorate the cake.

BAKE A 9″ x 13″ SHEET CAKE in two layers. Fill, ice with buttercream, then cover with poured fondant to give a perfectly smooth and shining background for the message.

TRANSFER PATTERN from The Wilton Way III Pattern Book to the cake top. Outline all the letters with tube 1 and royal icing, let crust, then fill in with thinned icing and a cone with a tiny opening cut from the tip. Dry.

Trim the letters with sparkling piping gel. First pipe the exuberant curves, then add dots with tube 000 or 00L. Pipe a plume border at base of cake with tube 7 curved shells and boiled icing, then outline and add dots with tube 000 and piping gel. This springtime masterpiece serves 24 party guests.

A SCRIPT MESSAGE GLORIFIES A VALENTINE CAKE

See how script, dressed up with swirling initials, can make a sweet Valentine even sweeter. Plan your script before you put it on a cake, adding curves to complement the space.

PIPE THE FURLED ROSES in advance in royal or boiled icing and tube 59. Dry. Bake, fill and ice a two-layer 9″ heart cake. Set on doily-trimmed cake board. Divide each curved side of cake into sixths and mark about 1″ up from base. Drop string guidelines for ruffles. Mark a heart shape 1″ in from edge on top of cake.

EDGE BASE OF CAKE with a tube 16 shell border. Pipe the ruffles, following guidelines, with tube 102. Finish with tube 1 beading. Above ruffles, drop double tube 1 strings and a row of tiny loops piped with same tube.

PIPE MESSAGE ON CAKE TOP with thinned icing and tube 1, adding curves and flourishes to conform to heart shape. Outline marked heart with a double tube 1 string, then add a row of tiny loops. Pipe a tube 14 shell border and cover it with a tube 102 ruffle. Edge ruffle with tube 1 beading. Finish this pretty tribute by attaching the roses with icing and trimming with tube 65 leaves. Serve to twelve at a Valentine party.

A SCRIPT ALPHABET

Practice this alphabet with Wilton Way III patterns. The gel letters were piped with tube 1s, the yellow letters with tube 1 and thinned icing.

For the decorative build-up on the down strokes of the initials, hesitate an instant as you pipe, giving a short back and forth movement.

SCRIPT GREETINGS FOR CELEBRATION CAKES

These often-used greetings show how the initial letters set the style for script. Although every decorator develops her own characteristic writing style, it's wise to practice script designs occasionally to give greater variety to your decorating. "Good Luck" and "Bon Voyage" are piped in a breezy casual style, well suited for a cake for an informal party, while "Shalom" is done in a dignified, traditional design.

Note how important it is that the small letters follow the same slant as the beginning initial.

All these greetings were piped in a mixture of half piping gel, half royal icing. Shown in reduced size here, they are large enough to be the main decoration on a cake top. "Good Luck" is 5″ wide, "Happy Birthday" is 6½″ wide. Practice them, using Wilton Way III patterns to extend your script-writing technique.

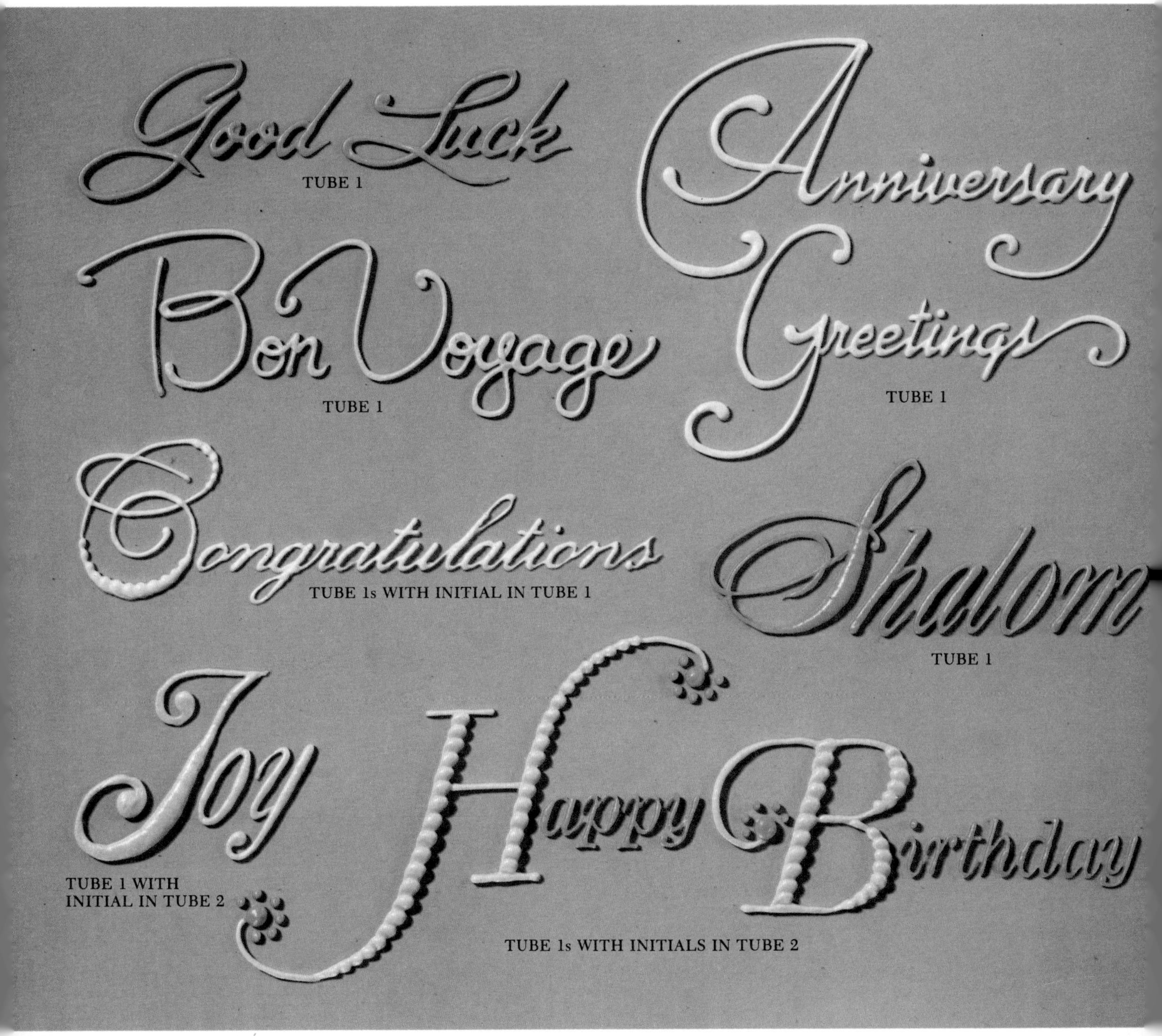

Good Luck
TUBE 1

Anniversary

Bon Voyage
TUBE 1

Greetings
TUBE 1

Congratulations
TUBE 1s WITH INITIAL IN TUBE 1

Shalom
TUBE 1

Joy
TUBE 1 WITH
INITIAL IN TUBE 2

Happy Birthday
TUBE 1s WITH INITIALS IN TUBE 2

Add a beautiful personal touch to cakes for almost any occasion with a script monogram. Even a wedding cake gains personality when adorned with a graceful monogram.

Make your own monogram designs by combining Wilton Way III patterns for script initials. Plan the design on parchment paper first, then transfer to the cake. If you are adding a sparkling trim of piping gel, pipe the gel loops and curves first, then pipe the letters in royal icing mixed with an equal amount of gel. Achieve the thick and thin look of the letters by varying the speed and pressure of your piping.

One lovely way to use a monogram on a cake top is to frame it with one or several fine line borders. These designs, shown here in reduced size, are quite large—"DKN" is 4½" in height.

TUBE 1

TUBE 1s

TUBE 1

TUBE 1s FOR GEL,
TUBE 1 FOR ICING

TUBE 1

TUBE 1s FOR GEL,
TUBE 1 FOR ICING

TUBE 1

CCGGOOQQSS
EEFHHIILTT*LOVE
AAKKMNNNWXYZ
DPR*GREETINGS

abcdeegoopqss
ffiijllt*father's day
kkvvvwwwxxxyyzzz
hmnru*new year

ROUND TUBES PIPE TRIM BLOCK LETTERS

TAILORED BLOCK LETTERS are ideal for messages on many cakes—most especially, birthday cakes. In piping them, use the same hand position, as close to horizontal as possible, as you would use for script. Thin the icing, too, with piping gel or corn syrup, so it flows effortlessly out of the tube. Glide your tube over the surface, barely touch-ing it, never digging in or lifting above surface as you form the stroke.

Since the forms of block letters are so simple and clear, piping them calls for even greater con-trol than that needed for script. Any flaw is immediately apparent. Learn to keep a light, completely even pressure. Stop pressure entirely before lifting away as you complete a stroke—then the lines are cut off cleanly. They will not extend too long or end in a lump.

All block letters are formed of curves, verticals, horizontals or diagonals, so practice these lines repeatedly on the back of a cookie sheet to gain control. Then use Wilton Way III patterns to practice individual letters. Each is a combination of curved lines or of straight lines piped in various directions.

Put the letters together into words. Be careful of the spacing between the letters—too much

and the word falls apart—too little and the word looks cramped and hard to read. Soon printing in icing will become easy and automatic, and you'll enjoy the crisp forms of the letters and the exciting color effects you can achieve with icing in contrasting tints.

USE THE ROUND TUBE that best suits the size of the letter. Patterns for the letters at left, shown here in reduced size, are ¾″ high. All the pink letters were piped with tube 1, the yellow letters were piped with tube 3 for a stronger impression.

WELCOME HOME!

Pipe a bold message on a sheet cake and surprise someone dear who's coming home! Though the trims are flowery, this easy-to-serve cake has a tailored look that makes it just as appropriate for a man as for a woman.

STEP ONE. Bake a two-layer sheet cake in 9″ x 13″ pans. Fill, then ice smoothly in buttercream and place on cake board. Transfer Wilton Way III message and heart patterns to top and sides.

Make drop flowers in boiled icing with tubes 225 and 26. Add tube 2 centers and dry.

STEP TWO. Pipe a tube 32 shell border at base of cake and trim it with tube 14 curves. Do top border with tube 16 shells. Now pipe the message and straight lines of the frame with tube 5.

STEP THREE. Finish the cake with flowers, attaching each on a dot of icing. First dress up the letters and outline marked curves of the frame with flowers. Outline the heart shapes with more flowers and complete the trim with tube 65s leaves. Serve to 24.

DRESS UP BLOCK LETTERS FOR LIVELY CAKE TRIMS

Plain block letters will gain a lot of personality when you add some creative touches of your own. Take a few minutes to plan and practice your message before you pipe it on a cake. You'll be delighted when you see how color, extra-fancy initials or just simple design can give your lettering more interest and make the cake much more appealing.

All the messages on this page were piped with tube 3 and thinned royal icing. Buttercream or boiled icing works well too. Use Wilton Way III patterns to practice them, then use your own ideas to personalize your cakes with glorified block letters.

"Happy Anniversary" adds twirls to initials and some of the smaller letters to give a perky touch. "Hello!" puts the letters on a slant, then gets a trim of tube 1 dots in piping gel to make a much greater impact. "Hi, baby!" is piped in simple style, sweetened with little flowers.

"Good Luck" is piped in two colors with added curves and "Happy Halloween" becomes more decorative by an interesting placement of the letters. Pipe a posy instead of an "O" to make "mom" as pretty as she is. Put a little more love into the message at the bottom by repeating the lines in related colors.

116

THE FILL-IN LETTERING TECHNIQUE GIVES LOTS OF ROOM FOR CREATIVITY

Here's a technique that's really fun to do and gives a spectacular effect on any cake! It calls for the same careful pressure control as script or block lettering but adds a whole new dimension by borrowing from the Color Flow method. In the fill-in style, the work is done on the cake.

Start by using a letter style broad enough to show off the color areas. The Wilton Way III Pattern Book contains several suitable styles. Plan the message or monogram on paper—then transfer it to the cake. Outline the letters accurately with tube 1 and royal icing. Since the outlining is usually done in a contrasting color, use light even pressure for a uniform line. Let the outlines crust, then fill in the areas with royal icing thinned enough to flow easily from a cone with a tiny cut tip. After the letters have dried, you might wish to add contrasting icing or gel trim.

"Peace" is elaborated with curves of shining gel piped with tube 1s after the letters have dried. For "Aloha," fill in the lower part of a letter with pink icing, then immediately fill in the upper part with yellow thinned icing. Outline "Hooray!" with tube 1s lines of blue gel and add decorative red gel dots to "Bravo!" This page gives just a hint of all the exciting possibilities of the fill-in technique.

117

...-IN LETTERS TURN A CAKE
...EAUTIFUL CHRISTMAS CARD

There's ... ...as greeting than ... ...istening fill-in mess ... ...reen of holly. The ... ...rs are piped on a g... ...off before serving. The gu... ...easure it. Gum paste makes the ... ...nolly, too.

Only the fill-in ... ...ique will pipe a letter style like this—with extreme contrast of thick and thin strokes.

MAKE PLAQUE AND HOLLY. Roll gum paste ⅛″ thick and cut out center plaque using Wilton Way III pattern. Roll green-tinted paste as thin as possible and cut out leaves with the holly cutter. Dry on and within curved surface. Roll small pieces of gum paste between your fingers for berries. Dry all thoroughly.

PIPE LETTERING. Transfer pattern to plaque. (You may do this with tracing paper, if you like, since the plaque is not intended to be edible.) Outline letters with tube 1s and royal icing thinned with gel or corn syrup. Use the same tube for holly trim. Dry, then thin piping gel with water, one part water to four parts gel. Fill in letter areas with this mixture and a cone with cut tip. Pipe a tube 2 royal icing outline around plaque and top with tube 1s gel dots.

BAKE AND FILL a two-layer 12″ square cake, each layer 2″ high. Ice with buttercream. Transfer pattern to sides of cake. Pipe a tube 7 bulb border at base of cake, a tube 5 border at top. Pipe the side pattern with tube 4, then over-pipe with tube 2 and add tube 1s gel dots. Place plaque on cake top on mounds of icing, then add holly clusters by attaching with dots of icing. Serve this cheery treat to 36 at a memorable Christmas party.

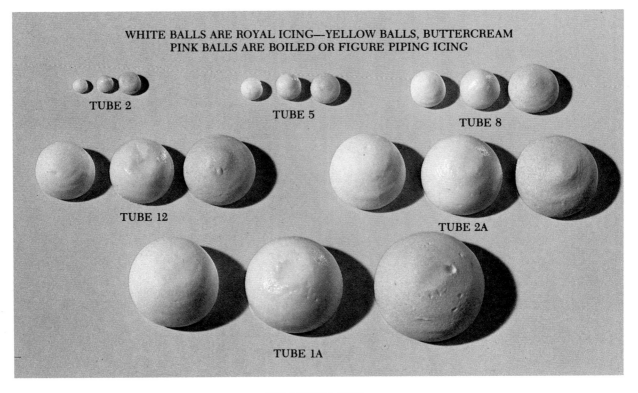

WHITE BALLS ARE ROYAL ICING—YELLOW BALLS, BUTTERCREAM
PINK BALLS ARE BOILED OR FIGURE PIPING ICING

TUBE 2

TUBE 5

TUBE 8

TUBE 12

TUBE 2A

TUBE 1A

CHAPTER SIX

High Relief Figure Piping

ROUND TUBES, which pipe the most delicate lace, lattice, script and fine line work, also excel at creating the boldest and most dramatic of icing forms—those produced by figure piping.

In this technique, rounded, dimensional figures are formed by the larger round tubes. The technique is basically the same as piping a ball. Lightly touch tube to surface, exert pressure as you lift the tube to let the form build up and stop pressure completely before lifting away. Important: *always keep the tip of the tube buried in the icing* as you pipe.

THERE ARE TWO BROAD TYPES of figure piping—*upright* or completely three-dimensional, discussed in Chapter Seven, and *high relief* in which the base of the sculptural figure rests on the cake. This chapter shows you some of the magical results of high relief figure piping.

ICINGS TO USE. Choose the icing that best suits your purpose. *Royal icing* is best for figures in multiple parts to be assembled, and for figures to save for souvenirs. *Boiled* or *figure piping icing* is easy to handle and used for most figures. Don't use it for figures you wish to pipe days in ad-

vance. *Buttercream*, stiffened with additional confectioners' sugar, is fine for edible figures piped right on the cake. Study the picture above to see how different icings produce various sizes of forms when piped with the same tube.

A GLOWING HARVEST CAKE

Here, two icings were used to pipe the colorful fruits. The realistic basket on cake top is a lasting keepsake and holds a royal icing harvest. The fruit wreaths on cake side were piped in buttercream, directly on the cake. All the fruits are just rounded ball shapes.

PIPE THE ROYAL ICING BASKET. Use an Australian nail in stovepipe shape and pipe the basket on it with tube 2. See page 83 for technique. Use a single string for the vertical weaving, a double string for horizontals. Using Wilton Way III pattern, pipe the handle on wax paper, then overpipe twice, using tube 2 again. Paint a 5½" separator plate with thinned royal icing, dry, then trim with tube 3 strings and balls. Pipe a tube 3 bow on wax paper.

Secure basket to plate and fill with royal icing. Pipe tube 5 balls for fruit, then attach handle with icing. Add tube 3 grapes, starting at tip of cluster, and pipe a few more tube 5 balls on plate. Drape handle with tube 3 and attach bow.

PREPARE THE CAKE. Bake, fill and ice a two-layer 12″ round cake, each layer 2″ high. Set on serving tray, and divide side into eighths. Use Wilton Way III pattern to mark wreaths, or use a 2½″ cookie cutter. Pipe a tube 9 ball border and trim with tube 5 string.

PIPE THE FRUIT WREATHS IN BUTTERCREAM. First pipe the larger fruits with tube 4, then fill in with smaller tube 3 fruits and grapes. Add tube 2 bows and ribbons.

Pipe a tube 5 line around top edge of cake. Pipe a tube 5 ball border on it, and one on either side for triple border. Set plate with basket on cake top and edge with tube 5 bulbs and balls. Lift off plate and basket before serving to 22.

HIGH RELIEF FIGURE PIPING PAINTS A NURSERY RHYME ON A CAKE

Thrill a little girl with this charming cake! Mary stands in her flower garden while a row of tiny girls dance around the cake. Mary is done with the easiest method of high relief figure piping—mark a stick figure on the cake, then pipe over it with large tubes. Use Wilton Way III pattern to start—but soon this method will allow you to pipe a figure in almost any position—just by following your own stick figure sketch.

Figure piping or boiled icing is best for piping the figures on this cake, but buttercream may also be used. Stiffen it to hold the rounded forms.

PREPARE THE CAKE. Bake a two-layer cake in 8" square pans, each layer 2" high. Fill, then ice with buttercream, top yellow, sides a grassy green. Apply a 2" strip of green icing on top of cake and roughen with a spatula. Mark pattern for figure on top of cake. Divide each side of cake into sixths and mark 1" up from base of cake.

FIGURE PIPE MARY. Follow the picture below for the easy steps. First pipe message with tube 2. Pipe a base to build up full skirt with tube 12. Start at hem with heavy pressure and pull up to waist as you decrease pressure sharply. Pipe two tube 12 bulbs for pantaloons, pausing briefly to let icing build up.

Over-pipe the skirt with tube 12 in six "folds", letting icing build up at hem. Pipe bodice in a large bulb shape, and use lighter pressure for two balls for puffed sleeves, using tube 12 again. Pipe a short line for neck with tube 4, then pipe a large tube 12 ball for head.

Finish the figure by piping tube 10 bulbs for feet and tube 4 for arms. Add balls for hands. Pipe features and hair with tube 2, add hair bows, and trim on dress and pantaloons with tube 1. Fill in folds at hem with tube 1 dots.

PIPE THE TINY GIRLS on cake side in a similar manner. At each mark, pull up skirt with five strokes of tube 5, pipe sleeves and bodice with tube 4, head and arms with tube 3. Pipe a tube 3 ball where arms join. Hair is done with two tube 2 curves, then features piped with tube 000.

DECORATE THE CAKE. Pipe a tube 7 ball border at base, a tube 6 border at top edge. Pipe a spray of tube 1 stems in each of Mary's hands, then pipe curling tube 1 fingers. Pipe each bell flower with three strokes of tube 3, drawing to a point.

Plant the garden. Pipe curving tube 1 stems, then add bell flowers. Fill in with tube 1 grass. Serve this enchanting treat to twelve little girls.

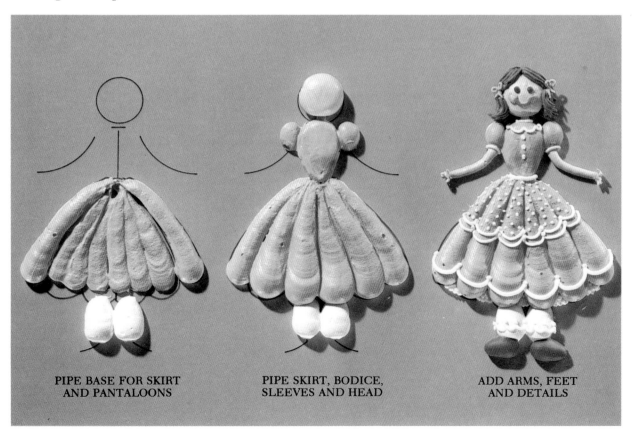

PIPE BASE FOR SKIRT AND PANTALOONS

PIPE SKIRT, BODICE, SLEEVES AND HEAD

ADD ARMS, FEET AND DETAILS

SWAN MEDALLION FEATURES HIGH RELIEF
FIGURE PIPING

This fairytale bridal cake is highlighted by the graceful curving forms of swans, figure piped on pale blue medallions. A beautiful monogram showing the couple's initials adorns the base tier, and water lilies are the appropriate flower trim. Any bride will feel like a princess when she sees this cake at her wedding celebration.

FIGURE PIPE THE SWANS

Pipe these designs in advance on gum paste plaques—then they are easily placed on the cake when time to decorate.

Roll out tinted gum paste thinly and cut the plaques using a 2″ cookie cutter or Wilton Way III pattern. Cut four circles and dry on a 14″ curved form for base tier. Also cut two ovals for monogram and dry on a 14″ form. Cut six circles for middle tier and dry on a 10″ curved form.

The swans are quickly piped by following an outline in a variation of the stick figure method. Transfer pattern to circles by pricking through with a pin. Use royal icing for piping. First pipe the neck with tube 5, exerting a little extra pressure to form head, then relaxing pressure and continuing in a smooth curve. Tuck tube 2 into front of the head and pull out to form curved beak. Use tube 11 for the body. Pipe a curved shell shape, letting body build up at front and relaxing pressure as you move back to a pointed tail. Tuck tube 5 into the body and pipe another curved shell for wing, ending in a point. Indent eye with a toothpick. Pipe an equal number of swans facing left and right for base and middle tiers. Edge circles with tube 2 beading.

MAKE A SCRIPT PATTERN for couple's initials and transfer to gum paste ovals. Pipe with tube 2. (Page 113 gives directions.)

PIPE WATER LILIES with tube 80 in royal icing mixed with a small amount of piping gel. Follow the directions in Chapter Sixteen. Dry all trims.

PREPARE AND DECORATE THE BRIDAL CAKE

BAKE AND FILL THE TIERS. For base tier bake two 2″ high layers in 14″ round pans. Middle tier is two 10″ round layers, each 2″ high. Top tier is two 1½″ high layers baked in 6″ pans. Bake a cake in the blossom pan for the little dome. Ice tiers in buttercream and assemble with 11″ separator plates and 5″ Corinthian pillars.

Transfer Wilton Way III side trim designs to base and middle tiers—or mark your own patterns, allowing space for ovals and swan medallions. Divide side of top tier in twelfths and mark 1″ down from top edge.

DECORATE BASE TIER. Pipe base border with tube 17—double curved shells followed by single shells. Attach ovals and medallions to front and back of cake on mounds of icing, then pipe side designs with tube 14. Pipe a tube 17 top border, similar to base border. Edge separator plate with tube 17 curved shells. Secure a cherub fountain figure to center of plate.

ON MIDDLE TIER, pipe a base border of curved tube 17 shells, then edge with tube 16 shells. Attach medallions with icing and pipe side design with tube 14. Finish top edge with a tube 16 reverse shell border.

DECORATE TOP TIER. Use tube 16 for all trim. Pipe a curved shell border, then edge with shells. At marked points on tier side, pipe upright shells and connect with "C" scrolls. Trim with stars at touching points. Pipe a second series of upright shells and join at top edge with curved shells. Pipe scrolls and upright shells on blossom cake, following petal curves.

TRIM WITH FLOWERS. Use royal icing to secure flowers around cupid figure and to attach flowers to base and top of pillars. Form four clusters on top of middle tier and trim blossom cake with a wreath and cluster of flowers.

Serve two lower tiers of Swan Medallion to 140 guests, top tier to 20.

A STORK FLIES TO A BABY SHOWER

Traditional baby pink and blue flowers frame a sunny scene on this most delightful of all shower cakes. In the sky, a stork bears the precious bundle. High relief figure piping with round tubes pipes the snowy stork with his outspread wings. The new mother will be especially pleased because the plaque can be lifted off the cake and saved as a souvenir of a happy occasion.

PREPARE THE PLAQUE

Work back and forth, creating parts of the scene and figure piping the stork, allowing an area to set a few minutes as you go on to another. Use royal icing for all decorating.

STEP ONE. Roll out gum paste to ⅛″ thickness and use Wilton Way III pattern to cut out plaque. Dry, then transfer stork and house patterns to plaque. For clouds and landscape, use pattern to cut stencils from light cardboard.

STEP TWO. Hold cloud stencil against plaque and apply icing with a small spatula, moving edge of blade smoothly across surface. Let icing dry, then use background stencil with pale green icing. Dry, then hold foreground stencil against plaque and apply deeper green icing.

STEP THREE. Pipe areas of house with close-set tube 1 lines, then flatten with a small knife. Do trunks of trees with repeated lines of tube 1, and fill in foliage with a multitude of tube 1 bulbs. Add tube 1s flowers and grass.

FIGURE PIPE THE STORK

STEP ONE. Use pattern as guide and royal icing. Pipe the head with tube 8 and heavy pressure, then relax pressure and move back smoothly to form neck. Pipe a large shell shape for the diaper with tube 8. Do the back wing with feathered strokes of tube 101. Use tube 8 and heavy pressure to pipe the rounded body, relaxing pressure at points of legs. Now build up the front wing with lines of tube 8. Over-pipe for wing feathers with tube 101, first doing outer row of feathers, then inner row.

STEP TWO. Pipe long pointed beak with tube 4. Do upper legs with tube 6 lines, adding a knob at joints, then pipe lower legs with tube 4. Pipe the baby's head and little legs with tube 2. The tails of the diaper are done with tube 101. Use tube 1s for baby's hair and nose and add feathery texture to stork's body with the same tube. Finish by edging the entire plaque with tube 1 beading.

DECORATE THE CAKE

STEP ONE. Pipe wild roses in boiled or royal icing with tube 103. Add tube 1 centers and dry within curved form.

STEP TWO. Bake a two-layer 9″ x 13″ sheet cake. Fill and ice smoothly with buttercream. Pipe a tube 8 ball border at bottom and trim with tube 4 string. Pipe message on cake side with tube 3, then pipe a tube 5 top ball border.

Set flat sugar cubes on cake top to support plaque and pipe a dot of royal icing on each. Set plaque carefully in position. Mound icing on corners of cake and attach flowers, each with a dot of icing. Trim flowers with tube 66 leaves and you've finished the prettiest centerpiece ever to grace a shower table! Lift off the plaque and serve the cake to 24.

SCENE IS DONE WITH STENCILS

PIPE LINES TO BUILD UP FRONT WING

A WICKED WITCH RIDES ACROSS THE HALLOWEEN SKY!
(SHE'S REALLY SWEET... DONE WITH HIGH RELIEF FIGURE PIPING)

Royal or boiled icing, a few round tubes and a gum paste sky make the eery scene. Set it on a chocolate cake, garnish with a few plump pumpkins and you'll have a creation the trick-or-treaters will rush home for! The high relief figure piping technique makes piping the witch a quick task.

FIGURE PIPE THE WITCH

STEP ONE. First make the plaque using Wilton Way III patterns. Roll out blue-tinted gum paste ⅛" thick and cut out circle for sky. Roll out yellow gum paste 1/16" thick, cut out moon and stars, and while still wet, brush backs with egg white. Gently press to circle as pattern indicates and allow to dry thoroughly.

STEP TWO. Transfer witch pattern to plaque. Either boiled, figure piping or royal icing may be used, but piping with royal icing makes the plaque a lasting keepsake. Use tube 3 for the face. First pipe an oval, then tuck tube in, squeeze and relax pressure to pull out a long beaked nose. Curve a shell shape to make cheek and chin, then add a ball for neck. Pipe the right arm (in the background) with tube 6, using even pressure. Do shoes with a curve of tube 5, relaxing pressure to pull to a point. Add another squeeze for heels.

Pipe long oval body with heavy pressure and tube 8. Tuck the same tube into lower part of body and pipe long curves for skirt, relaxing pressure to end in points. Pipe broomstick with tube 2. Pipe triangular hat and add brim with lines of tube 5. Brush to smooth. Pipe scarf with same tube. Pipe long curves with tube 2 for hair.

STEP THREE. Pipe left, forward arm with tube 6, using heavy pressure at shoulder. Pipe tube 2 lines for cuffs. Pipe a tube 2 ball for left hand, then pipe fingers for both hands with the same tube, curving them around broomstick. Do straw for broom with lines of tube 2. Finally, add a tube 1 dot for eye.

BAKE AND DECORATE THE HALLOWEEN CAKE

STEP ONE. Bake a two-layer 10" round cake. Fill and ice the cake with chocolate buttercream and use buttercream for all decorating. Set cake on serving tray. To pipe pumpkins, first pipe a tube 8 ball at base of cake. Cover with lines piped with same tube, increasing pressure at center for plump effect. Finish with a tube 2 spiral for stem.

STEP TWO. Pipe tube 233 brown "grass" around base of cake. On top edge, pipe graduated "C" curves with tube 7, then pipe inner curved outline with tube 5. Set five or six flat sugar cubes on cake top and place plaque on them. Turn the lights low and call the children! Serve to 14.

START WITH HEAD, ARM AND SHOES   **ADD BODY, SKIRT AND HAT**   **COMPLETE THE FIGURE**

SERENE SWANS FLOAT ON A WEDDING TIER

This petite wedding cake is trimmed with bouquets and sprays of airy daisies piped in the Philippine manner, but its highlight is a quartet of poetic swans that drift across the lower tier. While fully three-dimensional, they are piped in the high relief technique.

PIPE THE SWANS

These are made in royal icing in sections, then put together to create upright forms.

STEP ONE. Tape Wilton Way III patterns to a stiff surface and cover smoothly with wax paper. With tube 8, use heavy pressure to form head, then relax pressure, move down in a curve for neck. Use light pressure and tuck tube into head to pipe beak. Add a short stroke for raised area above beak. Now pull out a heavy curving form for body, using maximum pressure, then relaxing as you near pointed tail. Pipe two facing sides of the body.

For wings, use Color Flow technique. Outline with tube 2 and flow in heavily with thinned icing. Pipe a tube 1 bow on wax paper.

STEP TWO. Assemble the swan with royal icing. Secure the two halves of the body together, pipe a line of icing to fill seam and brush smooth. Attach wings to sides of body and prop to dry. Pipe short tube 1 lines for feathers. Attach bow to neck and add tube 1 streamers. Paint crown and beak with thinned food color and paint dots for the eyes.

BAKE AND DECORATE THE CAKE

STEP ONE. Pipe daisies on wires in the Philippine manner, as described in Chapter Sixteen. When dry, twist stems together to form eight sprays for base tier. Form a wreath to place between tiers and a bouquet for top tier.

Glue a 2″ plastic bell to plate of a petite ornament base. Line with clear plastic, fill with royal icing and insert bouquet.

STEP TWO. Bake and fill two-layer tiers—a 12″ square, 4″ high and a 8″ round, 3″ high. Ice sides in white buttercream, tops in pale green boiled icing. Assemble with 9″ round separator plates and 5″ Corinthian pillars. Transfer Wilton Way III patterns to tier sides.

STEP THREE. On base tier, pipe side design with tube 6 and over-pipe with tube 4. Pipe triple bulb border at bottom with tube 7, at top with tube 6. Edge separator plate with tube 6.

On top tier, pipe side designs with tube 6 and over-pipe with tube 4. Pipe base triple bulb border with tube 6, top border with tube 5. Pipe scallops and dots on top of tier with tube 2.

STEP FOUR. Set daisy wreath within pillars and attach sprays to base tier. Secure bouquet to top of cake, then set swans in place. Before cutting the cake, present the flower sprays and swans to members of the wedding party. Base tier serves 72, top tier 30 guests.

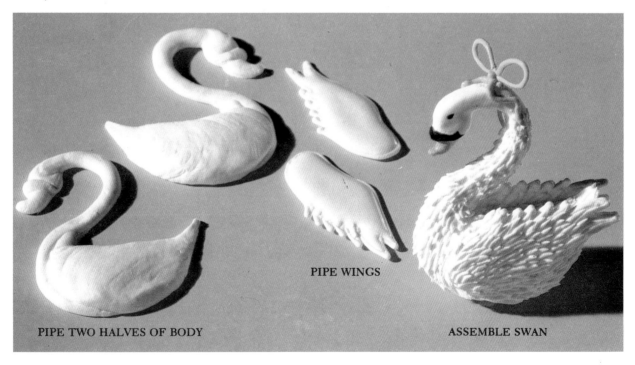

PIPE WINGS

PIPE TWO HALVES OF BODY

ASSEMBLE SWAN

CHAPTER SEVEN

Upright Figure Piping
with Round Tubes

UPRIGHT FIGURE PIPING is done with the same technique and careful pressure control as high relief figure piping described in Chapter Six, but the results are even more dramatic. The figures produced are fully upright and three-dimensional and almost seem to have a life of their own! The only limit to the types of figures and their poses is your own imagination.

A cake trimmed with upright figures is always the center of attention at a party, but for the most enthusiastic appreciation, bake a cake for a child. Top it with clowns, animal pets or toys, and watch his eyes light up!

Review page 120 for appropriate icings and technique, then pipe some upright figures on a cake and win some applause of your own!

A TURKEY TROT CAKE

Decorate this spectacular cake as the finale for Thanksgiving dinner, or serve it at any fall gathering. It's sure to be talked about long after the party's over. Boiled icing covers the cake, boiled or figure piping icing is used for the turkeys, pumpkins and corn.

PIPE PUMPKINS on a marshmallow base. Insert a toothpick in the bottom of a marshmallow to twirl it as you pipe. Use tube 11 to start at the base and move up. Increase pressure and lift tube slightly to plump out sides, then decrease pressure as you move to top center of marshmallow. Repeat until marshmallow is completely covered, then pipe a tube 11 stem and dry on wax paper.

PIPE CORN ON WAX PAPER. Pipe a tube 5 line about 2" long. Cover it with rows of tube 4 kernels, done

the same as a bulb border. Pipe tube 65 long leaves for husks and dry.

BAKE A TWO-LAYER CAKE in 10" round pans, making sure each layer is about 2" high. Assemble with your favorite filling, ice sides orange and top beige and set on a 14" or larger serving tray. Pipe a tube 5 bulb border at bottom, a tube 7 border at top. Divide side into eighths and mark about 1" up from bottom of cake.

PIPE THE TURKEYS. The magnificent tail of each turkey is formed with a fan of shells. Use Wilton Way III pattern to define the shape, or mark the fan shape freehand, 3½" high, 3¾" wide, the center at marked point. Pipe long radiating shells with tube 11, starting first at top center and drawing to center mark. Pipe tube 7 scallops on edges of shells, then a second row of scallops within first row.

The body is formed with a large inverted shell piped with tube 1A and brown icing. Hold tube straight up and exert heavy pressure at base—decrease pressure as you finish off a little above center of fan. Change to orange icing, tuck tube 11 into tail of shell, pull straight up to form neck, then exert more pressure to form ball for head. On either side of body, pipe a curved shell with tube 11 for wings.

Pull out yellow beak with tube 2 and pipe feet with three short lines with same tube. Add a curve with tube 1 and red icing. Pipe tube 1 dots for eyes. The proud turkey is complete! Pipe seven more to circle the cake.

Arrange pumpkins and corn on cake top and display your creation. Serve to 14.

Did you know that teddy bears are the all-time favorite playthings for babies and toddlers? Here these loveable little pets cluster on a tier cake, complete with tiny gifts. Two hold paper parasols to show that the party is a shower for the new arrival. The entire cake is decorated with round tubes in a rather sophisticated color scheme to please the new mother.

Teddy bears are easy and fun to figure pipe. Once you've mastered the technique of piping them, you're well on your way to becoming an expert figure piper. Many other people and animal figures start in the identical way, with only the details varied. These figures show, too, how just a turn of the head can give personality and add interest to a figure.

To support upright figures like these, a toothpick is often inserted in the body. Remember to dampen the pick before inserting it—otherwise the icing may collapse as the pick is inserted.

FIGURE PIPE THE BEARS

Boiled or figure piping icing is easiest to use. You may pipe the bears right on the cake, but it is easier to pipe them on wax paper and dry them before placing on the cake.

STEP ONE. Pipe an upright cone-shape body with tube 1A held straight up. Use heavy pressure, gradually relaxing as you move up. Stop pressure completely and move away. Immediately insert a dampened toothpick in body. Tuck tube 2A into the body and pull out the four legs, using even pressure. Curve front legs as preparation for holding parasols or present. Pipe a round ball for head with tube 12.

STEP TWO. Insert tube 4 into front of head and pull out the nose. Add ears with two quick curves of tube 2. Add white dots for eyes with tube 2, then pipe second dots on top of these with piping gel and tube 1. Pipe a heart shape at front of nose with tube 1 and gel. Insert handles of paper parasols into arms of two of the bears. Dry the finished bears thoroughly.

Dip sugar cubes in thinned royal icing and dry. Pipe ribbons with tube 1.

DECORATE THE CAKE

STEP ONE. Bake a two-layer tier in 10" round pans, fill and ice. Bake a single layer in a 6" round pan, ice and assemble tiers on serving tray. Divide lower tier into sixteenths and mark about 1" up from base as guides for dropped strings. Using these marks as guides, divide tier into eighths and mark about 1" from top edge of tier.

STEP TWO. Pipe a tube 10 line around base of lower tier. Do lettering with tube 3 in space within two marks on upper side of tier. Drape tube 8 scallops from mark to mark near base of tier, leaving spaces below greeting empty. Add balls with same tube. Drape tube 9 scallops from mark to mark on upper part of tier, leaving space holding greeting empty. Pipe a tube 8 ball border around top edge of tier.

On upper tier, run a tube 9 line around base. Pipe a tube 6 ball border on top edge of tier.

Arrange bears and sugar cube presents on cake, attaching with dots of icing. Serve to 17 guests—upper tier serves three, lower tier 14.

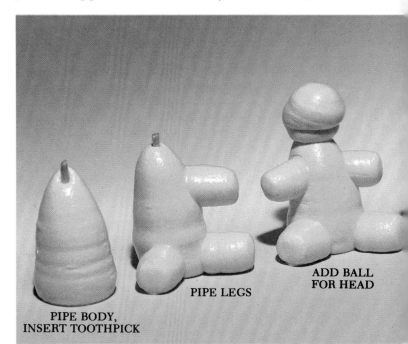

PIPE BODY,
INSERT TOOTHPICK

PIPE LEGS

ADD BALL
FOR HEAD

LARGE ROUND TUBES TURN CAKES INTO
EASTER SURPRISES

There couldn't be a more charming centerpiece for your Easter table than one of these cakes trimmed with figure piped bunnies or chicks!

A BASKET OF BUNNIES

PIPE THIS CUTE LITTLE FAMILY with figure piping icing on wax paper. For upright bunnies use tube 2A and heavy pressure to pipe a teardrop shape. Decrease pressure gradually as you move up, keeping tube buried in icing, stopping pressure, then moving away. Immediately insert a dampened toothpick into body for support. Tuck tube 11 into body and squeeze heavily to pull out rear legs, decreasing pressure as you move to paws. Pipe the front legs the same way, using even pressure. Pipe a tube 11 ball for tail.

Set tube 2A over toothpick in body and pipe pear-shaped head. Tuck tube 11 into lower part of head and pull out round cheeks with light pressure. Insert dampened toothpicks in head to support ears. Let head set a few minutes, then pipe ears on toothpicks with tube 5, first on one

side, then the other. Finish the bunny with features and ear accents piped with pink gel and tube 000.

Pipe crouching bunnies in a similar way, following the diagram. Pipe oval eggs with tinted icing and tube 11. Dry bunnies and eggs.

BAKE A TWO-LAYER 9″ OVAL CAKE. Fill, then chill the cake and taper to 7½″ x 5½″ at base with a sharp knife. Ice side yellow, top green. Do basket weaving with tube 46 vertical lines, tube 48 horizontals. Pipe top and bottom rope borders and handles with tube 16.

Set bunnies and eggs on cake top and fill in with tube 233 grass. Add a ribbon bow. Serve the Easter basket to twelve.

YELLOW CHICKS
SCAMPER AROUND A TIER

PREPARE THE CAKE. Pipe drop flowers in royal icing and spring pastels with tubes 224 and 106. Add tube 2 centers and dry.

Bake and fill a two-layer 10″ round tier and a single-layer 6″ round tier. Ice with buttercream and assemble.

Pipe a tube 6 bulb border at base of 10″ tier, a tube 5 border at top. Do random stems on side of tier with tube 2. Pipe top and bottom bulb borders on 6″ tier with tube 5.

PIPE THE CHICKS right on the cake with stiffened buttercream or figure piping icing. The little parade on the side of 6″ tier is done in the high relief method described on page 120. Pipe a ball for head with tube 4. Use heavy pressure to form body, decreasing pressure as you move back to pointed tail. Tuck tube into body and exert light pressure to pull out a pointed wing. Finish the chick with tube 2 legs and eyes and a tube 65s pointed beak.

Mark a 2″ circle on top of cake and pipe a ring of icing with tube 6 for nest. Cover with tube 233. Pipe chicks, one in nest, one out, in the upright method, using the same tubes as were used for chicks on side of tier. First pipe body and wings, then head, eyes and beak.

Finish the cake by attaching drop flowers with dots of icing. Serve lower tier to 14, the top tier to four delighted children.

Would you like to make extra surprises for the children? Bake cupcakes, ice and top each with a chick in a nest. Set one at each place.

CROUCHING BUNNY   UPRIGHT BUNNY

FIGURE PIPING CREATES A JOLLY CAKE

Bake a layer cake and a cake in a ball pan. Ice, put together and decorate in sunny colors. Figure pipe cheerful little clowns in relaxed positions and pose them on the cake. You've created a happy masterpiece that will make any child laugh—and most grown-ups chuckle too!

DECORATE THE CAKE

A cake with such an unusual construction needs just the simplest decorating to make it an outstanding background for the figure piped clowns. Just three tubes do it all.

STEP ONE. Bake a two-layer cake in 10″ round pans and a 6″ ball cake. Fill and ice the layer cake a sunny yellow with buttercream. Divide cake in tenths and mark midway on side.

STEP TWO. Fill the ball cake and slice off the base to give it stability. Set on a 3″ corrugated cardboard circle and ice thinly with yellow buttercream. Hold a taut string around widest part of ball to mark its circumference. Divide in fourths and mark. Hold a taut string from top center of ball to marks and down to base to divide in four segments. Insert four dowels in center of layer cake and clip off level with top. This will give support to the ball cake. Set on serving tray and assemble with ball cake.

STEP THREE. Drop string guidelines for scallops from mark to mark on layer cake. Fill in area from scallops to base of cake with tube 16 stars. Pipe a tube 17 star border on top edge of cake.

STEP FOUR. Outline segments of ball cake with tube 3 string, and fill in areas with tube 16 stars in contrasting buttercream. Let icing set a little before you pipe clowns.

FIGURE PIPE THE CLOWNS

Pipe the clowns right on the cake in figure piping icing. Review page 135 for basic method and have fun creating these lovable little people. Do clowns seated on layer cake first.

STEP ONE. Hold tube 1A straight up, just touching surface of cake, and exert steady pressure to pipe body, lifting tube as icing builds up. Stop pressure, move away and insert a damp toothpick for support. Insert tube 2A into body and pull out legs, using even pressure. Curve them for relaxed poses. Pipe arms with tube 12.

STEP TWO. Change to red icing and pipe zigzag cuffs on legs and arms with tube 13. Pipe a collar around top of body with same tube. Now hold tube 2A straight up and pipe a ball for head, covering tip of toothpick. Pipe shell shapes for feet with tube 12. Pipe balls for hands with tube 3, then add thumbs and ears with same tube and very light pressure. Finish by piping features and hair with tube 1. Serve to 26. Layer cake slices into 14 pieces, ball cake into twelve.

SEVEN CLOWNS ON A CAKE MAKE A CHILD'S BIRTHDAY VERY HAPPY

MAKE THE COOKIES, using your favorite recipe or the one on page 86. Use Wilton Way III patterns to cut out the letters and number of the birthday year. Lay them on dampened popsicle sticks extending from their bases, then bake. These will be inserted in the cake. Outline the cookies with tube 2 and thinned icing.

BAKE A 16″ x 4″ LOAF CAKE. Swirl with boiled icing and set on an 18″ x 8″ cake board. (Extra space in front of the cake is needed for clowns.) Pipe a ball border at base with tube 8. Insert cookie

letters in cake and attach number with icing.

PIPE THE CLOWNS right on the cake and board as described on page 139. Use figure piping icing, tube 1A for bodies, 2A for legs and arms, tube 5 for collars and cuffs, tube 8 for heads and shoes, tube 2A for pointed hats. Pipe features, buttons, hair and hands with tube 2. For crouching clown, see directions for squirrel, page 144. Serve to 16 party guests.

THE DOLLS' CHRISTMAS TREE . . . A CAKE ENHANCED WITH FIGURE PIPING

MAKE THE COOKIE TREE. Use patterns to cut out dough made from recipe on page 86. Bake and outline each section with tube 1 and royal icing. Thin the icing and flow in areas. Dry, assemble with royal icing and pipe tube 4 balls.

BAKE, FILL AND ICE two-layer 10″ and single layer 6″ tiers. Assemble tiers. Divide lower tier in eighths, mark midway on side, drop guidelines. Pipe a tube 8 ball border at base of lower tier. Following guidelines, pipe tube 104 ruffles and top with tube 3 beading. Add bright dots with

tube 4. Pipe a tube 6 ball border on top of tier. Do ball borders on upper tier with tube 6.

TO FIGURE PIPE THE DOLLS, review page 135 and pipe right on the cake in figure piping icing. Dolls on lower tier require no toothpick for support. Pipe tube 2A body and tube 11 legs. Dry, then pipe ruffles for skirt with tube 102. For green doll, use tube 104 ruffle. Pipe tube 7 arms, tube 101 collar and cuffs, tube 7 head and shoes, add tube 4 hands. Pipe all details with tube 1. Serves 17.

FIGURE PIPING CREATES AN ADORABLE ORNAMENT
FOR A CHRISTENING CAKE

Bake and decorate a ruffly square layer cake for the christening celebration—then top it with this sweet ornament! The proud new parents will treasure it for years.

MAKE THE ORNAMENT FIRST

We chose to figure pipe the baby in royal icing for its long lasting qualities. The dainty pillow on which baby sits is formed of styrofoam. If you prefer, carve a slice of firm pound cake into a pillow shape, and use boiled or figure piping icing—however the ornament will then have a much briefer life.

CARVE A PILLOW SHAPE from a 4″ x 4″ piece of styrofoam, 1″ thick. Cover with royal icing, dry, then brush a coat of thinned icing over the pillow for a smooth surface. Pipe tiny dot flowers with tube 1. Pipe a tube 1 hair bow on wax paper. Dry both pillow and bow thoroughly.

PIPE THE FIGURE RIGHT ON THE PILLOW. This cunning figure is done in a similar method to the teddy bear, so review page 135 for directions. First pipe a tube 1A body and insert a damp toothpick for support.

INSERT TUBE 11 INTO BODY and pull out legs, piping them in natural curved positions. Turn tube sharply to form feet. Set the same tube over protruding toothpick and pipe an elongated ball for baby's head.

FORM ROUND CHEEKS by tucking tube 2 into head. Use the same tube for button nose, two curves for ears and tiny toes. Pipe a tube 101 ruffle around base of body for skirt. Pipe arms with tube 11.

FINISH THE FIGURE by piping a tube 101 ruffle for collar and adding tube 2 fingers. Pipe curling hair, eyes and mouth with tube 1. Attach dried hair bow. Add a tube 101 ruffle around pillow and edge with tube 2 beading. Set aside to dry.

DECORATE THE CAKE

BAKE, FILL AND ICE an 8″ square two-layer cake. Divide each side in fourths and mark 1″ up from base. Drop string guidelines for ruffles.

PIPE MESSAGE with tube 2. Do ball border at base and top of cake with tube 4. Following guidelines, pipe tube 104 ruffles and edge with tube 3 beading and fleurs-de-lis. Add ruffles and beading around top edge with same tubes. Sprinkle tube 1 dot flowers on top of cake. Place a 3″ square of plastic wrap on top center of cake and set ornament in position. Lift off before serving this dainty creation to twelve guests.

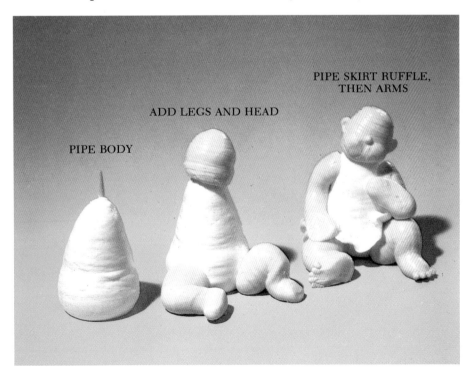

PIPE BODY

ADD LEGS AND HEAD

PIPE SKIRT RUFFLE, THEN ARMS

ROUND TUBES BRING FRIENDLY ANIMALS TO LIFE

PIPE THE LIONS in stiffened buttercream, boiled or figure piping icing. Mrs. Lion and Mr. Lion are identical except for the mane. Use tube 1A to pipe the body, starting with heavy pressure at rear. Move to front, then pull tube straight up to full height of head. Insert a dampened toothpick at an angle where the ear will be piped for support. Tuck tube 8 into body to pipe legs. Pipe chin and cheeks with tube 8 balls, then add a stroke with the same tube for nose. Do ears with two quick curves of tube 5.

Pipe toes with tube 5. Use piping gel and tube 1 to pipe a little heart on nose and two bright eyes. Pipe mane and tuft on tail with tube 1. Dry.

PIPE THE SQUIRRELS in royal icing. For upright squirrel, pipe pear-shaped head with tube 12 and dry. Pipe body with tube 1A, using heavy pressure at base and relaxing as you move up. Insert a dampened toothpick for support and dry.

Clip off toothpick and secure head to body with icing. Pipe a curving tube 12 tail and support with a damp toothpick. Pipe legs with tube 7. To finish, do perky ears with tube 80, cover tail with tube 1s fur and pipe eyes and mouth with piping gel and tube 1. Attach a marzipan acorn to paws with icing.

The crouching squirrel is done in almost the same way and with the same tubes. Follow the steps below to pipe the figure.

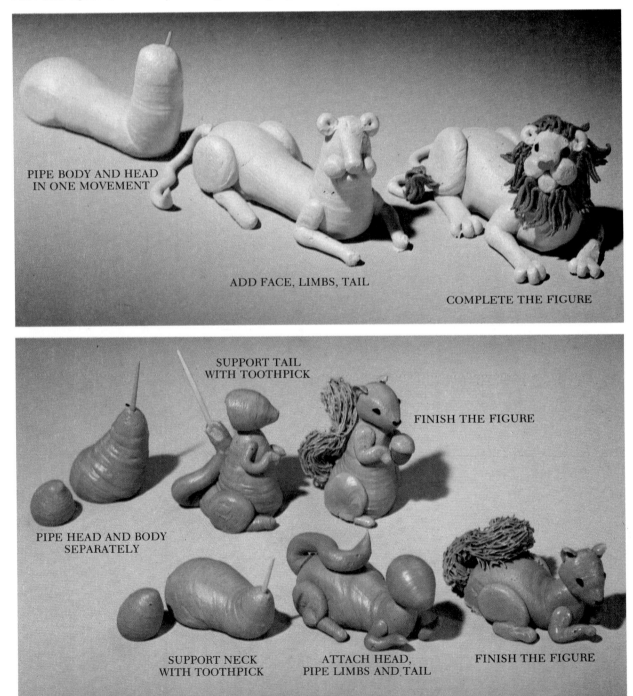

PIPE BODY AND HEAD IN ONE MOVEMENT

ADD FACE, LIMBS, TAIL

COMPLETE THE FIGURE

SUPPORT TAIL WITH TOOTHPICK

FINISH THE FIGURE

PIPE HEAD AND BODY SEPARATELY

SUPPORT NECK WITH TOOTHPICK

ATTACH HEAD, PIPE LIMBS AND TAIL

FINISH THE FIGURE

144

FIGURE PIPED ANIMALS TRIM THE CUTEST CAKES

A PEACEABLE PAIR OF LIONS rest tranquilly on a two-layer 8″ round cake. Pipe drop flowers in royal icing with tubes 225 and 190, dry and mount a few on wire stems. Fill and ice the cake and roughen green icing on top with a damp sponge. Run a tube 12 line around base, then a tube 8 line. Do scalloped top border with tube 8 and trim with tube 4. Pipe tube 1 stems on cake side and add flowers and tube 65 leaves. Insert stemmed flowers, set Mr. and Mrs. Lion on cake top and add a few sprigs of tube 1 grass. Serve to twelve animal lovers.

TWO ALERT SQUIRRELS enjoy a marzipan lunch break. Make the acorn by forming a small ball. Shape a little circle of marzipan and press it over the top of the ball. Roll out marzipan thinly and cut several leaves with the small holly cutter and others with the oak leaf cutter. Dry within curved surface. Paint a 5½″ separator plate with thinned royal icing.

Bake, fill and ice a two-layer 9″ oval cake. Pipe ball border at base with tube 5 and trim with tube 4. Do reverse scroll border on side with tube 5. Top ball border is piped and trimmed with tube 4. Set separator plate on cake and edge with tube 4, add tube 2 dots. Attach squirrels and small leaves with icing, then add a cluster of larger leaves and acorns at base of cake. Serve to twelve —a lucky guest will claim the ornament!

A YELLOW WARBLER WELCOMES SPRING

Make an exquisite ornament, as lovely as a jewelled Fabergé egg. Use your figure piping skill to create a bird just alighting on a flowering branch. The ornate stand is made of gum paste.

FIGURE PIPE THE BIRD

Use royal icing for its lasting qualities to make this little golden songbird in three steps.

PIPE THE TWO WINGS separately on wax paper, doing outer curves with tube 1, feathered·space between with tube 1s. Dry within curved form.

PIPE UPPER BODY on wax paper with tube 6. Pull out a long pointed shell shape, then insert tube in rounded side and pipe neck and head. When dry, turn body over and pipe rounded tube 6 breast. Immediately insert a "U"-shaped wire, ends about 1¼" long. Dry again.

ATTACH WINGS with icing. Prop to dry, then over-pipe body and wings with feathery strokes of tube 000. Pull out a slender tube 1s beak and pipe dots for eyes with same tube.

MOLD THE EGG

GLUE THE TOP HALVES of two 3" plastic egg molds together to use as a mold. Dust with cornstarch. Roll out gum paste, drape and smooth over narrow end of mold and trim off about 2" down from top. Dry about 15 minutes, remove from mold and dry thoroughly. Mold the lower part of egg on wide end of mold the same way, trimming off about 1" from rounded base.

LEGS OF EGG STAND are molded in side extensions of Baroque Classic Shell molds. Mold twelve of these, then put them together, back to back, with royal icing to form six legs.

DECORATE THE EGG sections with royal icing and tube 1. Divide upper egg into six sections with triple lines. Transfer Wilton Way III tulip pattern to egg and outline. Complete icing trim as picture shows. When dry, fill in areas and pipe tube 1s dot trim with piping gel. Make finial with balls of gum paste, dried and attached with icing.

Divide lower egg section in sixths to indicate position of legs. Trim with royal icing in similar design to upper egg. Attach legs with tiny pieces of gum paste moistened with egg white. Dry, then add gel fill-in and dots.

MAKE THE TREE

TWIST FOUR 6" LENGTHS of cloth-covered florists' wire together to form trunk. Spread out wires from base to form beginning of roots. Form heavier branches with double twisted wire, branches at ends are single wire. Coat with royal icing and groove for bark effect. Pipe tube 23 drop flowers and dry.

ASSEMBLE THE TABLEAU

Fill lower egg to ½" of top with royal icing. Set in tree and pull up tube 1 grass with very light pressure. Attach bird by twisting wire legs around branch. Pipe claws and fill in feathered legs with tube 1s. Secure flowers with dots of icing and pipe tube 65s leaves. Pipe tube 1s piping gel "dew," dry, and spray completed ornament with acrylic spray glaze.

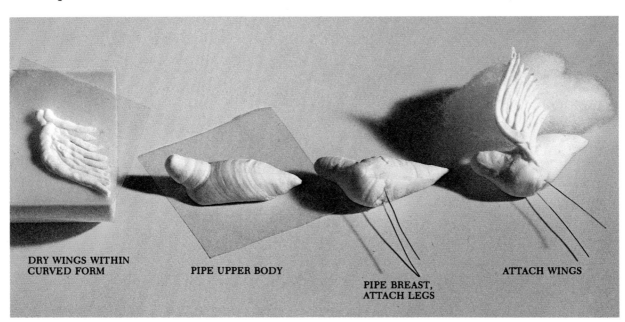

DRY WINGS WITHIN CURVED FORM   PIPE UPPER BODY   PIPE BREAST, ATTACH LEGS   ATTACH WINGS

The picture above shows ornament in actual size.

147

ROUND TUBES SET DUCKLINGS AFLOAT ON A POND

Use large round tubes and your upright figure piping skill to create these engaging little ducklings in their springtime setting.

PIPE DUCKLINGS FIRST on wax paper, using stiffened buttercream or royal icing. Pipe broad bodies with tube 1A and heavy pressure, relaxing as you move back to pointed tail. Pipe round head with the same tube. To pipe wings, tuck tube 3 into side of body and make a pointed shell shape. Do beak with tube 67, then outline with tube 1. Add tube 2 beady eyes. Dry thoroughly.

PIPE DROP FLOWERS with tube 225 and royal icing. Add tube 2 centers. Pipe daffodils with tube 101 petals and form ruffle-edged center with a tube 2 spiral. Mount on wire stems. Pipe long tube 65s leaves on wire. Dry.

BAKE AND FILL a two-layer 10″ round cake. Ice with buttercream, sides yellow, top white. Divide side into sixteenths and mark about 1″ up from base of cake. Mark an 8″ circle on top of cake with a cake circle.

Pipe a bottom ball border with tube 6. Following marks, drape a row of tube 6 strings, then drop two more rows above them. Add balls at points of strings. Spread blue-tinted piping gel over cake top within marked circle. Insert two Flower Spikes in top of cake near one edge. Twist stems of leaves and daffodils together and place in spikes. Pipe a tube 3 top bulb border, then fill in area from border to marked circle with tube 233 "grass". Scatter with drop flowers. Set ducks on pond and serve to 14 enchanted guests.

CHAPTER EIGHT

Oval and Multiple Opening Tubes

In this chapter we explore an interesting group of tubes that are close relatives of the plain round tubes. The two oval tubes, tubes 55 and 57, pipe forms in two sizes that are subtly flatter or higher than those piped with round tubes. Other tubes in the group have two or more round openings in the tip instead of one. Use them for many exciting and time-saving effects.

A BRILLIANT HARVEST CAKE
Warm rich color and the oval tubes pipe simple but very effective designs on a cake that welcomes the autumn season.

BAKE AND FILL a two-layer 10″ round cake. Ice sides with chocolate buttercream, top in pale yellow buttercream. Divide into twelfths and mark midway on side of cake. Using marks as guide to placement, transfer Wilton Way III patterns. Set cake on serving tray.

DO ALL DECORATING IN BUTTERCREAM and a cone striped in orange and filled with golden yellow icing. Hold tube 57 with flatter side against cake and run a line around base. Holding smaller side of tube against line, pipe a bulb border on it, then one on either side for a bevel effect. Do side design with tube 55, flatter side of tube against cake. Pipe curving stems, then fill in with "leaves" to form heart shapes.

Pipe a spray of tube 55 stems on top of cake, holding flatter side of tube against surface. Add leaves to form heart shapes just as you did for side design. Holding smaller side of tube down, pipe a crisp bow where stems join. Finish with a tube 57 top bulb border, holding smaller side of tube against cake. Serve this handsome treat to 14 at a fall party.

149

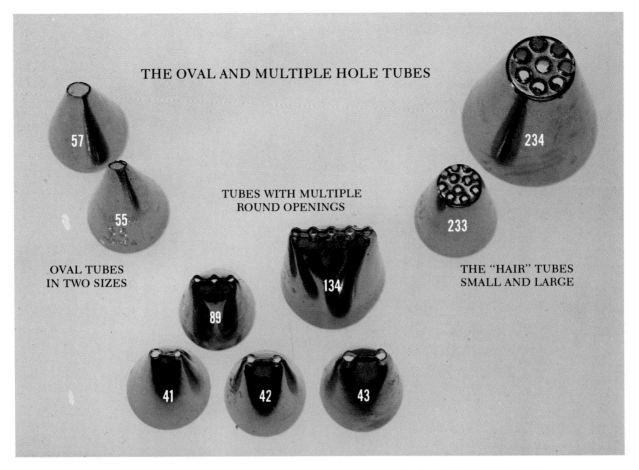

THE OVAL AND MULTIPLE HOLE TUBES

57

55

TUBES WITH MULTIPLE
ROUND OPENINGS

234

233

OVAL TUBES
IN TWO SIZES

134

THE "HAIR" TUBES
SMALL AND LARGE

89

41   42   43

USE THESE TUBES FOR FASCINATING DECORATIVE EFFECTS

These tubes pipe many of the forms done by the plain round tubes, their close relatives, but with intriguing differences.

THE OVAL TUBES, tube 55 and its larger version, tube 57, do forms that appear at first glance to have been done by round tubes, but the oval tubes add a new dimension to piping. When held with their flatter side against the cake they pipe lines subtly rounded, ideal for branches, vines and bunches of grapes. When held with the smaller side of the tube against the cake, they pipe outstanding bulb borders and very sharply defined lines. Because of the oval shape of these tubes, you can use them to pipe bold script with an attractive thick-and-thin effect. Hold the tube with the flatter side against the cake. Experiment with them for small-to-mid-size borders, too—or weave a wicker basket.

THE TUBES WITH MULTIPLE ROUND OPENINGS each have a special use, but are best known for their time-saving qualities. With these tubes you can pipe an intricate looking border or trim in one-half to one-fifth the time it would take to get the same effect with a small round tube.

The tubes with two openings, 41, 42 and 43, pipe double, accurately spaced lines that are progressively larger. Use them also for double bulb borders, dotted designs, scallops, curves and "plaid" lattice.

Tube 89, with three openings, can be used in the same ways as the two-opening tubes but with fancier effects. Tube 134, with five openings, is known as the "musical scale" tube and can quickly pipe a scale around a cake with all lines evenly spaced. Pipe a straight scale or a curving one, or pipe quick borders and designs as you would with the other multiple opening tubes but with even more lavish effects.

THE "HAIR" TUBES, 233 and 234, are fun and fast to use! Each has a cluster of round holes on its flat tip. With just a series of quick squeezes, you can fringe an afghan or poncho, make a fuzzy dog or cat, pipe spiky hair on a clown or grow grass on a garden cake. You can even pipe a very realistic shag rug. Experiment with them also for intricate borders. All these effects are done effortlessly by the hair tubes, and piped much faster than with a plain round tube.

150

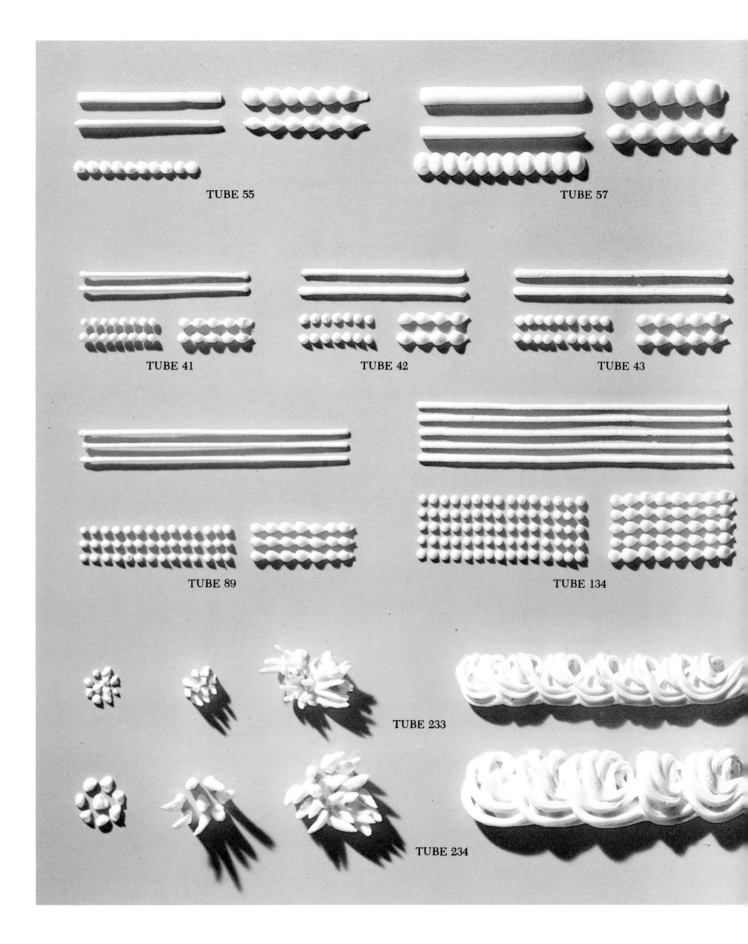

TUBE 55

TUBE 57

TUBE 41

TUBE 42

TUBE 43

TUBE 89

TUBE 134

TUBE 233

TUBE 234

151

GARLANDS ARE QUICK TO PIPE WITH
A MULTIPLE-HOLE TUBE

Want a show-off holiday cake in a hurry? Here's a colorful answer. Plain round tubes join the multiple-hole tube 233 to drape festive della Robbia garlands of piped fruit around an easy-to-serve long loaf cake.

STEP ONE. Bake a cake in the 16″ loaf pan. Angel food is a good choice, but choose the recipe your family especially enjoys. For additional delicious flavor, chill the cake, split in two and fill the two halves with buttercream or your favorite filling. Assemble on foil-covered cake board, then ice smoothly with buttercream.

STEP TWO. Divide long sides of cake into fourths and drop string guidelines for garlands with tube 3. Garlands are 2″ deep. An even quicker way to do this is to mark the sides with a 4″ round cookie cutter. Transfer Wilton Way III pattern for greeting to cake top and pipe script with tube 3, or pipe the greeting freehand.

STEP THREE. The high relief figure piping technique makes the colorful fruits. Use buttercream in warm colors for all decorating. Following guidelines or marks, first pipe three large balls with tube 12 in center of each garland. Keep tip of tube buried in icing as the form builds up and stop pressure completely before drawing away. Fill in garland shape with more balls piped with tube 8. At the points of each garland, pipe a tube 8 red ball on top edge of cake.

Add evergreens to frame the fruit with tube 233. Hold tube straight out from side of cake and give a series of quick squeezes for clusters of needles. You'll be surprised at how quickly the garlands are finished. Complete the cake by piping a tube 8 ball border at base and a tube 6 ball border at top edge, filling in spaces between the red balls at points of garlands. Serve this merry treat at a Christmas party to 16 guests, cutting in uniform 1″ slices.

PIPE ROWS OF ANGELS WITH OVAL TUBES
SET THEM OFF WITH DAINTILY TINTED ICING

This unique little Christmas cake really shows what the oval tubes can do! Borders, flowers and stylized angels are all piped with oval tubes 55 and 57. These versatile tubes can even do relief figure piping.

STEP ONE. Bake and fill an 8″ square two-layer cake. Ice smoothly in buttercream, top white, sides pink, and set on doily-trimmed cake board. Divide each side of cake into fifths and mark 1½″ up from base. Make a second series of marks directly above first marks 1″, down from top edge.

STEP TWO. Do all decorating in buttercream. Pipe the angels with tube 55. Starting at a lower mark, pipe an upright shell, flatter side of tube against cake, then one on either side of it to form skirt. At apex of shells, pipe two more shells for wings. Pipe a heart shape for arms with one movement and add a dot for hands. Still holding flatter side of tube against cake, pipe a ball for head at upper

mark. Continue to pipe angels all around cake, with one at each corner. Drop tube 55 strings, starting the curves between angels. Top with dots piped with same tube.

STEP THREE. Transfer Wilton Way III pattern to top of cake, or make your own, basing the script greeting on a section of a 4½″ circle. Pipe script with tube 3. Holding tube 55 with flatter side against cake, pipe a spray of three stems, then add flowers formed by six shells. Finish with a center dot. Add streamers with tube 55, holding smaller side of tube against cake.

STEP FOUR. Use tube 57 to pipe comma-shaped shells around base of cake, flatter side of tube against cake. Run a tube 55 line around top edge of cake. Top it with a tube 57 bulb border, holding smaller side of tube down. Pipe tube 57 bulbs on either side of it for a triple border. Serve to twelve party guests.

TRIM A SPIRITED PATRIOTIC CAKE WITH OVAL TUBES

Oval tubes do all the piping on this quick-to-do, fun-to-do cake, and set off sparkling sugar stars. Make it for a Memorial day or Fourth of July picnic and listen for the "ooh's" and "ah's" of delight when you light the candles!

STEP ONE. Mold sugar stars in star candy molds and sprinkle with edible glitter as soon as they are unmolded. You'll need 17 stars, but make a few extra to use as patterns for piping.

STEP TWO. Bake and fill a 12″ round, two-layer cake, each layer about 1½″ high. Bake a single 2″ high layer in a 10″ star pan. Ice both tiers with buttercream and assemble on cake board. Divide round tier in twelfths and mark midway on side. Do all decorating in buttercream.

STEP THREE. Decorate round tier. Hold smaller end of tube 57 against tier and pipe a bulb border around base of tier. Following marks, drop string guidelines for garlands. With red icing and flatter side of tube 57 against surface, pipe an "e" motion garland, increasing pressure and lifting tube to let icing build up in center of garland. Pipe a white garland above it the same way. Hold smaller side of tube 55 against tier to pipe a fleur-de-lis at each point of garlands.

Press a sugar star within curve of garland to mark pattern for red side trim. Pipe a five-pointed star with tube 57, smaller side of tube against cake. Each point is formed with three shells. Immediately press a sugar star into piped star. Repeat within all garlands around tier. Use the same procedure to pipe five white stars on top of tier, but build up with a second layer of shells. These will be candle holders.

STEP FOUR. Pipe a bulb border at base of star tier with tube 57, holding smaller end of tube against tier. Pipe a tube 55 top bulb border. Pipe red five-pointed stars with tube 57 on top of tier, just as you did on side of round tier. Press in sugar stars, add a tall taper in center and ring with tube 55. Press birthday candles into white stars on round tier. Serve this showy treat to 27. Star tier provides five slices, round tier, 22.

SHAGGY MUM CUPCAKES
EASY AS ONE, TWO, THREE

A batch of cupcakes and tinted buttercream create a brilliant bouquet! Pack them for a picnic, surprise the children after school or brighten up any meal with these flowery treats. Tube 234 makes them extra-quick to decorate.

Just prepare cupcakes, allowing them to mound up as they bake. Swirl tops with icing and edge with tube 16 shells. Pipe four tube 67 leaves on each cupcake. Starting at outer edge of flower, pipe shaggy petals with tube 234, circling in to hold tube straight up for center petals. Arrange the bouquet on a serving tray.

A SUMMERTIME CAKE WITH LAVISH TRIM
PIPED WITH MULTIPLE-HOLE TUBES

Radiating rows of lacy scallops and double and triple beading trim this outstanding cake. The decoration looks intricate, but is quickly done by multiple-hole tubes. These time-saving tubes pipe two-, three- or five-part trims all at one time.

STEP ONE. Pipe nasturtiums in royal icing and tube 103 in a 1⅝" lily nail. Paint base of petals with thinned paste color and a small artist's brush. Pipe tube 5 dots in centers and insert artificial stamens. Pipe flat round leaves on a number 7 nail with tube 104 and add tube 1 veins. Dry. Mount seven or eight of the flowers and an equal number of leaves on wire stems. Set aside to dry thoroughly.

STEP TWO. Bake a two-layer 12" hexagon cake. Fill, then cover with rolled marzipan and again with rolled fondant. This smooth covering gives a perfect background for piping trims. Mark a 4" hexagon in center of cake with Wilton Way III pattern, or cut your own pattern. Mark the center of each side at top edge and base of cake. Set cake on foil-covered board cut in hexagon shape. Insert a Flower Spike in center of cake.

STEP THREE. Decorate in buttercream. Pipe tube 1D lines from small marked hexagon on cake top down to base of cake, using marks as guide. Edge lines with tube 2 beading. On both sides of lines, pipe five-part scallops with tube 134. Down the centers of the tube 1D lines, pipe a row of tube 89 triple beading. See how quickly the lacy design takes accurate form!

From corners of small hexagon to cake-top corners and down to base, pipe double beading with tube 42. Now edge small hexagon with the same tube. Add a tube 5 bulb border at base of the cake.

Twist stems of flowers and leaves together to form a bouquet and insert in spike. Attach a flower and a leaf to each side of cake at base with icing. Serve this little masterpiece to 20 guests.

"PLAID" LATTICE DRESSES UP A CAKE
WITH MULTIPLE TRIMS

Lattice gets a brand new look when it's piped in a plaid pattern with a multiple-hole tube. The tailored, but feminine, piping designs are set off by airy daisies.

STEP ONE. Use royal icing to pipe the daisies with tubes 101 and 102. Pipe tube 5 centers and flatten with a fingertip dipped in granulated sugar. Dry within curved surface.

STEP TWO. Bake a two-layer 10″ round cake, each layer about 2″ high. Fill and ice with buttercream and set on cake board or tray. Transfer Wilton Way III pattern for lattice area to top of cake or make your own. Cut an indented curve from each corner of a 5½″ square of paper. Divide side of cake into eighths and mark 1″ down from top edge. Make a second series of marks 1″ up from base of cake, midway between marks near top.

STEP THREE. Use buttercream for all decorating. Pipe a tube 7 bulb border at bottom of cake.

Above it pipe a row of double scallops with tube 42. Pipe diagonal lines of five-part beading on side of cake with tube 134, piping from upper marks to lower marks. This fancy effect is very quickly achieved. The design of the tube makes accurate spacing automatic.

Pipe lattice within marked area on cake top with tube 89. Start in the center of one side of the square and pipe a triple line to opposite side. Fill in with four lines on either side of first line, then pipe triple lines in the opposing direction. The three holes in the tube make the plaid pattern even quicker to pipe than lattice done with a plain round tube. Edge lattice area with double beading done with tube 42. Pipe a double bulb border at top edge of cake with tube 43.

Attach daisies with mounds of icing. First secure three flowers at each corner of lattice, then complete side trim with trios of daisies. Trim with tube 66 leaves. Serve to 14 guests.

CHAPTER NINE

The Versatile Star Tubes and the Handsome Borders They Create

The star tubes are the ones decorators turn to most frequently. The forms they pipe are baroque and sculptural and well suited to the ornate nature of decorating. As an added benefit, star tubes can trim a cake very quickly.

The tips of all star tubes are composed of a number of evenly spaced pointed teeth surrounding an opening. While the family is large, it falls easily into two main groups. The teeth of *the open star tubes* surround a rather broad circular opening. Within this group are two subgroups—the star tubes with numerous very finely-cut teeth, and a special group of tubes identical except for size—the Stellar tubes.

The closed star tubes have teeth bent sharply inward to pipe especially clear and well-defined forms. Tubes in both groups vary in size from tiny to large. All are shown in this chapter.

PIPING BORDERS IS THE MOST IMPORTANT FUNCTION of the star tubes. From the classic vocabulary of curves, shells, stars, rosettes and garlands, an almost infinite variety of beautiful borders can be created. As all decorators know, a border does much more than cover the edges of a cake. The rhythmic curves of skillfully executed borders can often be the only decoration of an outstanding cake. Within this chapter you'll see dozens of borders piped with star tubes. All will serve as inspirations for your own border designs.

BOLD BORDERS
TRIM A CHARMING CAKE

Pipe puffy stars and garlands, add curves and rosettes to set them off and you've created a centerpiece cake as pretty as a flower! Do it all with a few star tubes and boiled or buttercream icing—and show it off at any happy get-together.

BAKE AND FILL a two-layer 10" round cake, each layer about 2" high. Ice smoothly and set on cake board. Divide cake into sixteenths and mark at base. Pipe a tube 22 star at each mark, leaving a little space between each. Pipe a green curve below each star and a deep pink curve above, both with tube 13. Finish the border with a tube 19 star piped between each large star and a tiny tube 13 star at its point.

THE TOP BORDER IS BASED ON GARLANDS. Pipe 16 puffy garlands with tube 19 around top edge of cake, positioning them between large stars at base. With tube 13, pipe a deep pink "S" curve on top of each garland, extending onto cake top. Pipe tube 22 stars on garlands and center each with a tube 13 star. Pipe green curves with tube 13 to frame lower edge of garlands, and complete the border with tube 13 green rosettes. Serve your pretty cake to 16.

See how daintily contrasting color can bring out the design of a border. Skillful use of color will add charm to any cake.

159

THE OPEN STAR TUBES
ARE THE MOST POPULAR OF ALL

BELOW, IN ACTUAL SIZE, are the ten standard open star tubes, the ones you'll use again and again for beautiful borders—and for many other decorative effects. They range in size from tiny tube 13, used for dainty borders and accents, to tube 22, large enough to border a really big cake or tier.

All of the open star tubes pipe multi-pointed stars, shells and curved shells, curved and straight garlands, rosettes and fleurs-de-lis. Use them also to pipe grooved curves to frame a shape, zigzag trims, attractive heart shapes and upright shells that extend into a column of icing on a cake side. Smaller open star tubes can be used for dropped string work. Combine several of these forms to create simple but very effective borders, quickly done, or pipe one upon another for elaborate over-piped effects. Turn to page 234 to see arrangements of the pretty drop flowers these tubes can pipe also.

Pipe basic forms with the open star tubes, then use tubes from other families to complete a border. Pages 173 and 178 through page 181 give good examples of this technique.

BORDERS AND DROP FLOWERS are just the beginning of the uses of the versatile open star tubes. See Chapters Ten and Eleven for dozens of other uses. Pipe top and side designs, paint a picture on a cake, pipe three-dimensional filigree, cover a loveable animal with fluffy "fur", or create instant stylized flowers.

TO PIPE A PERFECT STAR, be sure to hold the decorating cone perpendicular to the surface—straight up, if you're piping on a cake top—straight out if you're working on the side of a cake. Then the center of the star will appear in the exact center of the form piped.

Tubes 13, 14 and 15, the smallest of the open star tubes pipe true five-pointed stars. Tubes 16 and 17 pipe six-pointed stars, tube 18 a seven-pointed star, tubes 19 through 21 eight-pointed stars and tube 22 a large 9-pointed star.

ON THE OPPOSITE PAGE, IN ACTUAL SIZE, are samples of what each standard open star tube can pipe. A star, a shell, a curved shell and a rope border are done with each tube. Study the page before piping a border to decide which tube to use.

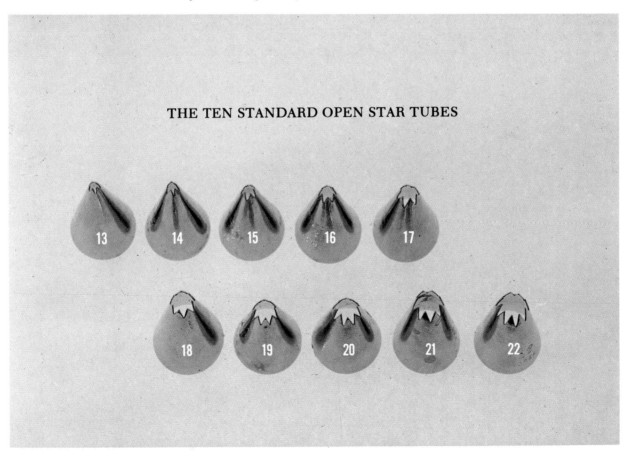

THE TEN STANDARD OPEN STAR TUBES

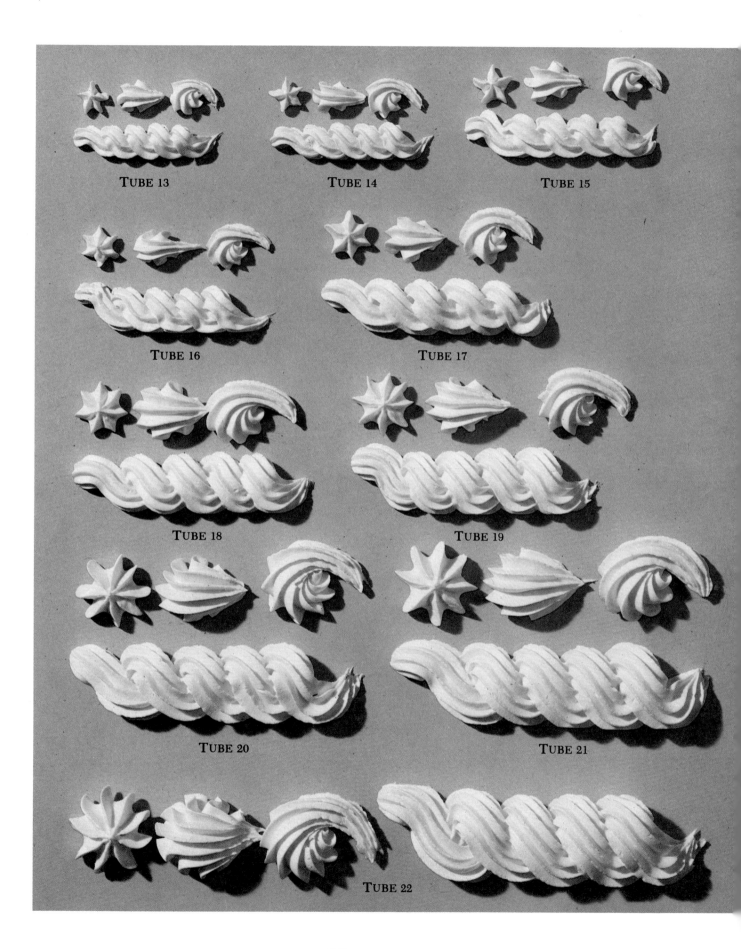

TUBE 13

TUBE 14

TUBE 15

TUBE 16

TUBE 17

TUBE 18

TUBE 19

TUBE 20

TUBE 21

TUBE 22

THE OPEN STAR TUBES
WITH FINELY-CUT TEETH

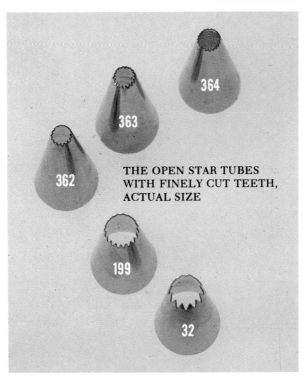

THE OPEN STAR TUBES WITH FINELY CUT TEETH, ACTUAL SIZE

These five tubes are shaped just like the standard open star tubes, but their teeth are much more numerous and very finely cut. This characteristic gives the forms piped with them a different, more refined effect. The curves are accented by the many closely spaced grooves.

The finely cut open star tubes can be used for any of the forms piped with standard open star tubes, but they have some special uses. The stars piped with them have a button-like shape much like that of a chocolate "kiss" candy.

Use these tubes for piping interesting stylized flowers and leaves like those shown in Chapter Eleven, starting page 202. The same chapter shows how they are ideal for some figure piping too, where a light texture is desired.

THE OPEN STAR TUBES IN THE ESSEX SERIES, tubes 362, 363 and 364 are very similar except for size.

TUBES 199 AND 32 are larger, with teeth not quite so finely cut as the tubes in the Essex series.

BELOW ARE ACTUAL-SIZE samples of forms these fine-cut tubes can pipe.

TUBE 362   TUBE 363   TUBE 364

TUBE 199   TUBE 32

162

THE WELL MATCHED
STELLAR OPEN STAR TUBES

Here is a unique and very useful group of star tubes, identical except for size. Each has ten sharply cut teeth curved slightly inward for piping very clear, well defined forms.

Use the Stellar tubes to decorate a many-tiered bridal or anniversary cake. By using these tubes, you may put the same borders and trim on each tier. Use the largest of the Stellar tubes, tube 508, for the largest, base tier—work up to tube 501, the smallest tube, for the top tier. You will achieve a very unified harmonious cake.

The Stellar tubes also make good-looking drop flowers in a range of sizes. Trim a cake with garlands of them as shown on page 234. And, of course, any of the shells, curved shells, fleurs-de-lis and other motifs piped with star tubes can be done with Stellar tubes too. Add dropped stringwork or other decorative accents.

BELOW, IN ACTUAL SIZE, are samples of stars, drop flowers and shells piped with the Stellar tubes.

AT RIGHT: the five matched Stellar star tubes, each shown in actual size.

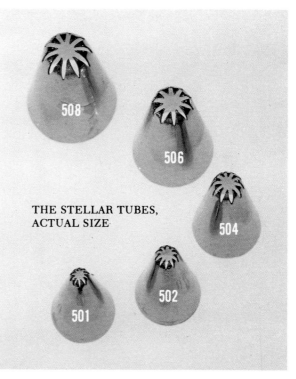

THE STELLAR TUBES, ACTUAL SIZE

TUBE 501

TUBE 502

TUBE 504

TUBE 506

TUBE 508

163

ACTUAL SIZE SAMPLES OF SOME OF THE FORMS PIPED WITH CLOSED STAR TUBES

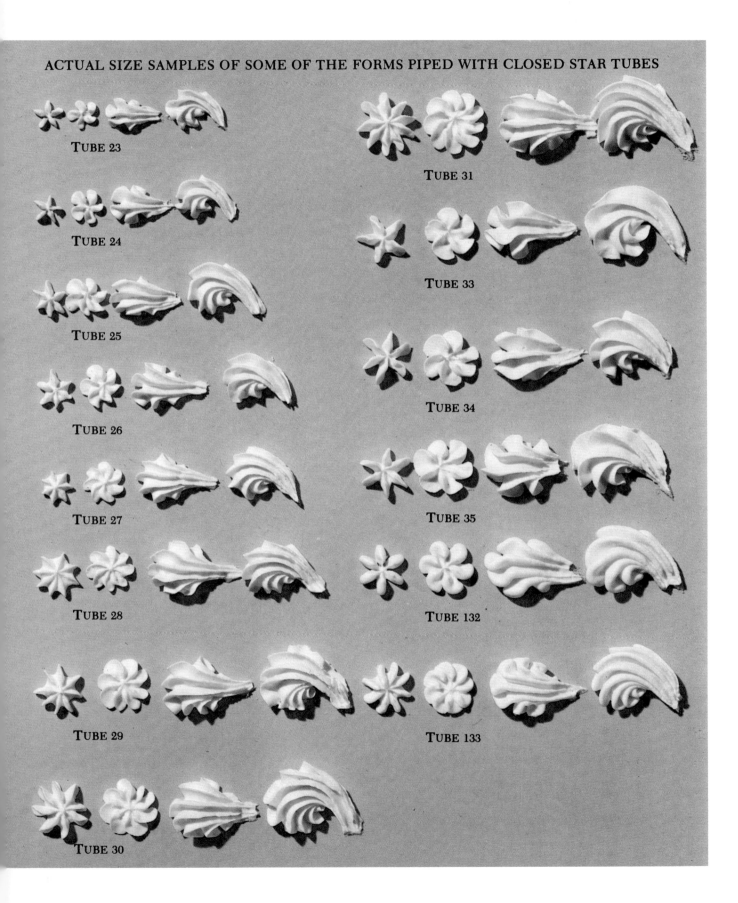

TUBE 23

TUBE 24

TUBE 25

TUBE 26

TUBE 27

TUBE 28

TUBE 29

TUBE 30

TUBE 31

TUBE 33

TUBE 34

TUBE 35

TUBE 132

TUBE 133

THE CLOSED STAR TUBES
PIPE DEEPLY CARVED DESIGNS

The fourteen closed star tubes pipe designs rather similar to those of the open star tubes and are sometimes used interchangeably with them. But there are important differences to the discerning cake decorator.

All of the closed star tubes have teeth that are bent sharply inward, narrowing the opening through which the icing passes. The result is a form more sharply grooved and sculptural. Stars, shells and fleurs-de-lis are more defined.

The closed star tubes have a very close range of sizes, much narrower than that of the open star tubes. They are useful for piping borders and motifs where careful measuring and attention to scale is necessary.

The number of teeth in closed star tubes vary. A sharp five-pointed star is formed by tiny tubes 23 and 24, but a larger version is formed by tube 33. The clear-cut six-pointed stars are made with tubes 25 and 26 and tubes 34 and 35, a seven-pointed star with tube 27. Tubes 28 through 30 make eight-pointed stars, tube 31 a nine-pointed star. The teeth of tubes 132 and 133 are rounded, rather than pointed, and they create rounded differently shaped stars of six points and eight points respectively.

USE THE CLOSED STAR TUBES for any of the borders in this chapter. Experiment with them in piping some of the richly decorative top and side trims in Chapter Ten, starting page 185.

ALL OF THE CLOSED STAR TUBES pipe nicely formed drop flowers to be arranged in dozens of pretty ways. See the page at left for examples, or turn to page 234 for flowers in arrangements.

Take time to experiment and practice with the closed star tubes. They'll add a new finesse and subtlety to your decorating.

BELOW, ACTUAL SIZE PICTURES of the closed star tubes. At left, actual size samples of some of the forms they pipe.

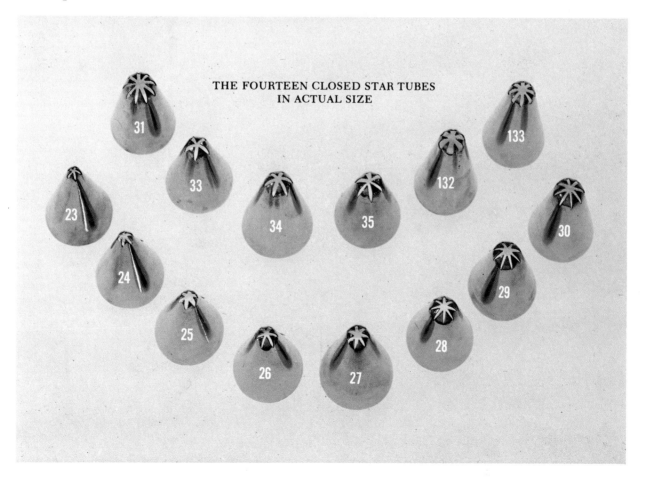

THE FOURTEEN CLOSED STAR TUBES
IN ACTUAL SIZE

ATTRACTIVE STAR TUBE BORDERS
OFTEN START WITH SIMPLE SHELLS

THE SHELL is the most classic and traditional form in decoration, and one of the most beautiful. When piped in icing, it is possible to vary it in innumerable ways. Curve the shells, pipe them upright in vertical position, add trims to make a unique border. Let color add its charm to the basic shape. Observe and practice these quick variations of the shell border, then go on to design new shell borders of your own.

VARIATIONS ON A THEME. Pipe a series of spaced upright shells around the top edge or side of a cake, drape with string and add bulbs and dots. The results will be completely different depending on the tube you are using to pipe the upright shells. In the first unit of three, round tube 8 was used to pipe the upright shells. In the middle, or second unit, open star tube 18 was used, and in the third and last unit at right, finely cut open star tube 364 was used. All upright shells were draped with tube 3 strings and trimmed with tube 3 bulbs and dots.

CURVED SHELLS MAKE A PRETTY BORDER for top or base of a cake. Use only open star tube 18. Start with a row of curved shells, evenly spaced. Below it pipe a second row of shells, curved in the opposite direction. Change to a contrasting color of icing and pipe a row of simple shells. Result is a feathery, plume-like border.

DRESS UP A SIMPLE SHELL BORDER three ways with varied trims. First pipe a row of neat shells with tube 22. Tube 14 is used for all contrasting trims. In version one, the shells are framed with a tight zigzag. Version two shows the effect of over-piped "C" shapes in opposing directions. In version three, the basic shells are trimmed with graceful "S" curves. Any of these borders may be used for either the top or bottom edge of a cake.

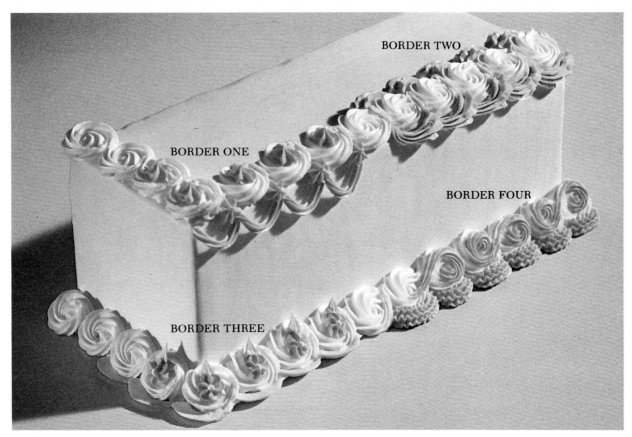

Many attractive borders start with a flower-like rosette. The four borders shown above all begin with a row of tube 18 rosettes. Hold the decorating cone straight up and make a quick circular motion, starting in the center. Continue for an evenly matched row. Now trim the rosettes in any way your imagination dictates.

BORDER ONE. Top each rosette with a tube 16 star. Drop curves of tube 13 string and add tube 16 stars where the curves meet.

BORDER TWO gets its charm from color contrast. Above each rosette pipe a curved tube 16 shell. Change the tint of icing and pipe curved shells below the rosettes in the opposing direction.

BORDER THREE makes a dainty trim on a cake for a girl. Ahead of time, pipe tube 34 drop flowers in royal icing, add tube 2 centers and dry. Add a ribbony curve at the base of each rosette with petal tube 102. Attach the flowers with dots of icing and pipe perky tube 65s leaves.

BORDER FOUR has a formal, ornate appearance. First frame the base of each rosette with zig-zag piped with tube 13. Pipe a "C" curve on each rosette with the same tube, starting each in the opposite direction from the one preceding it.

HERE'S ANOTHER BORDER that shows the versatility of the basic rosette piped with an open tube. Pipe a row of rosettes with tube 15. Pipe scallops above them with tube 13, then add tube 13 upright shells where the scallops meet. Use this border as pictured at the base of a cake.

167

PIPE A ROW OF LARGE UPRIGHT SHELLS with open star tube 22. On each, pipe a "question mark" scroll with tube 13 and add a "C" curve at its base. Drop tube 13 string below them and trim with inverted upright shells and stars piped with the same tube. Frame the tops of the large shells with tube 14 zigzag garlands. This imposing border will add beauty to the tiers of a wedding cake or any cake for an important occasion.

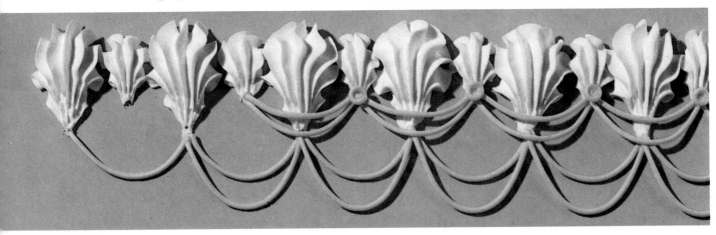

PIPE UPRIGHT SHELLS with star tube 22 and smaller ones between them with tube 17. Drop double tube 3 strings from the tails of the large shells, then from the tails of the smaller shells. Finish this top border with little twirls below the smaller shells.

FORM A HEART SHAPE by piping two tube 16 upright shells at angles, sides touching. Emphasize the shape by over-piping two curved shells with tube 13. Drop double strings with the same tube and finish with a tiny shell.

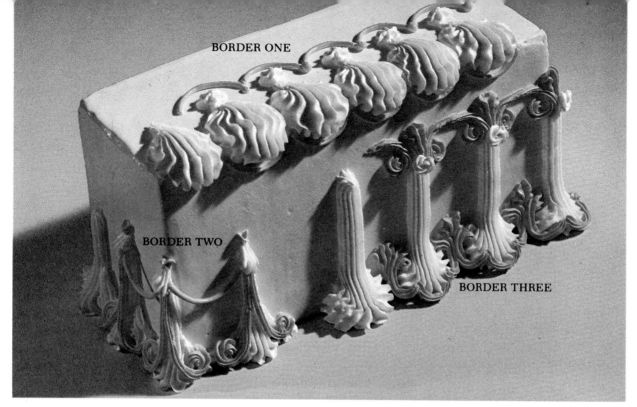

BORDER ONE

BORDER TWO

BORDER THREE

BORDER ONE. Pipe a row of tube 32 puffy shells curving over the top edge of a cake. Frame them with tube 4 scallops and dropped strings. Add a tube 13 star on the tail of each shell.

BORDER TWO. Start by piping an inverted upright shell with tube 18. Let the shell build up, then relax pressure and draw it smoothly up the cake side to form a column. Pipe a shorter tube 18 shell on each side of it. In contrasting color, over-pipe with tube 13. Pipe tube 4 string, then

add a tube 13 shell and star.

BORDER THREE. Pipe a row of tube 32 inverted upright shells to form the columns. Do contrasting trim with tube 13. Pipe an upright shell between each column at the base. Add a curved elongated shell on either side of it and join with a scallop. Pipe an upright shell at the top of the column and join with two curved shells. Finish with a tube 13 white rosette.

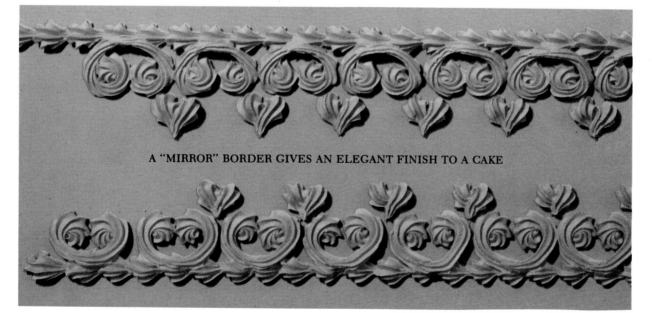

A "MIRROR" BORDER GIVES AN ELEGANT FINISH TO A CAKE

Just tube 17 pipes intriguing matching borders for top and base of a cake. Use only tube 17. For base border, start with a row of shells. Above them pipe two sharply curved shells, joining for

a scallop effect. Between each scallop, pipe a heart—two touching upright shells. Do top border the same way.

169

AN OPEN STAR TUBE FRAMES A CAKE
IN BOLD BAROQUE SHELLS

Only a tube in the star tube family can decorate a cake so lavishly—and in such a short time! The next time you need a showpiece cake in a hurry, try trimming it this way.

PIPE THE FLOWERS FIRST. We chose brilliant nasturtiums to set off the snowy whiteness of the cake, but you can use any of the pretty made-ahead flowers you've stored away. You might even decide to center the cake with a little bouquet of fresh flowers from your garden.

For the nasturtiums, use royal icing, a 1⅝" lily nail and tube 103. Directions are on page 13. Dry the flowers, then paint deeper color in the centers with food color. Pipe a tube 5 center dot and insert artificial stamens. Pipe round flat leaves with tube 124 on a number 7 flower nail. Add veins with tube 1. When flowers and leaves are completely dry, mount on florists' wire stems.

PREPARE THE CAKE. Bake and fill two 10" square layers and ice smoothly in buttercream. Set on a 14" square foil-covered cake board. Insert a Flower Spike in center of cake. To guide the decorating, transfer Wilton Way III pattern to cake top. Or you may pipe freehand. Mark each side in the center at top edge and base.

PIPE THE LAVISH BORDERS in meringue boiled icing. If you are using the pattern, outline it first with tube 3. Use tube 20 for all shells. Starting at center mark on cake top, pipe four sharply curved shells to reach the corner. Continue until cake-top border is complete. Repeat the pattern of curved shells on side of cake at top edge. Pipe a single shell at each corner, then pipe curved shells down to base.

At base of cake, pipe a bold fleur-de-lis at center mark. Flank it with two shells, then pipe curved shells to reach corner. Complete base border in the same way. Add stars at base of fleurs-de-lis and at corners. Emphasize the border designs by outlining with tube 3. Insert flowers in spike and accept the compliments of your guests. Serve to 20.

A FINELY CUT STAR TUBE MAKES A FLOWER-LIKE BORDER

Pipe simple shell shapes in sunny colors to make a cake bloom with a border of daisies. Pipe four radiating shells with tube 362. Just above them pipe a tube 13 upright shell. On top of the first four shells, pipe five tube 362 shells. Add a tube 13 rosette in the center and the daisy's in bloom! This is a highly decorative border, very quickly piped, for the base of a cake. To put it around the top, just turn it over. Add more petals on the cake top to make a complete circular flower.

STAR TUBE GARLANDS START SOME OF THE PRETTIEST BORDERS

IT'S EASY TO PIPE A PERFECT GARLAND. For a curved cake-side garland, *always drop a string guideline first* to guide the curves. For perfect proportions, it's wise to measure and mark the cake. Keep the cake at eye level. Hold decorating cone straight out, perpendicular to the cake, and start with a very light pressure and an up-and-down zigzag motion. Increase pressure and lift the tube as you near the center of the garland to let the icing build up. Gradually decrease the pressure as you approach end of curve. Embellish the garlands in scores of lovely ways.

PIPE A ROW OF SHELLS with tube 19, add a puffy tube 19 garland and tube 3 trim.

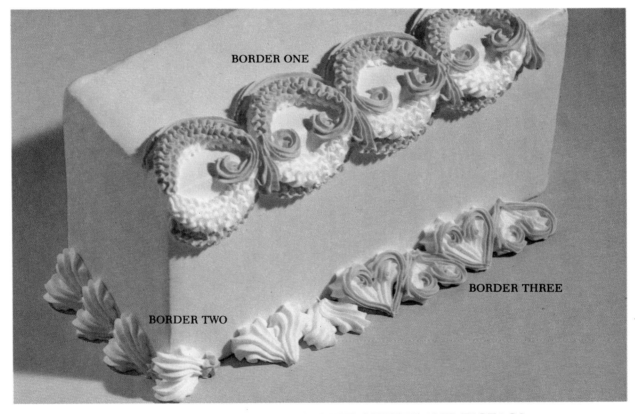

BORDER ONE

BORDER THREE

BORDER TWO

TRIM STAR TUBE BORDERS WITH CURVES AND ZIGZAGS

BORDER ONE is a double garland border for cake top. Mark the cake every 2″. Drop string guidelines for side garlands and mark curves for cake-top garlands. Pipe white side garlands with tube 16 and frame with contrasting tube 13 zigzags. Pipe white tube 13 garlands on top of cake, then over-pipe with contrasting 13 zigzags. Finish by outlining the cake-top garlands with tube 13 and add curves and inverted upright shells with the same tube.

BORDER TWO is based on tube 18 shells. Pipe two shells to form a heart shape, add a tube 13 star.

BORDER THREE uses the heart motif again. Pipe heart shapes in opposing directions, then over-pipe with elongated curved shells done with tube 13 in contrasting color.

172

PIPE SHELL EDGING and rosettes with tube 13, add leaves and dots with tube 3.

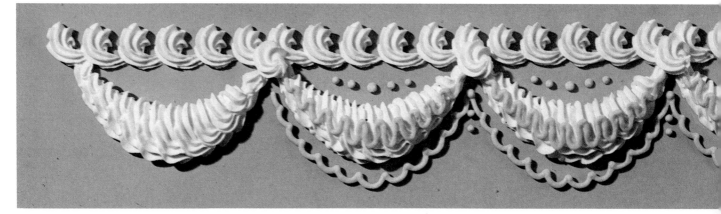

CURVED SHELL BORDER is tube 17. Zigzags, scallops and dots are done with tube 3.

OVER-PIPE GARLAND and pipe shells with tube 17. Add contrast trim with tube 3.

ADD A SMALL GARLAND with tube 16, rosettes with tube 17, leaves with tube 65.

PIPE SPACED STARS with tube 32, add tube 362 curves and stars.

PIPE PUFFY STARS with tube 362, pile more on top. Color gives it charm.

TUBE 363 FLEURS-DE-LIS and stars alternate with tube 32 stars.

PIPE FRAMES with tube 28, top with tube 199 stars.

STAR BORDERS . . .
QUICK AND VERY PRETTY

Simplest and one of the most attractive forms piped by the star tubes is the star itself. Just a row of neat stars makes an attractive border. Add trims for more fanciful effects. Since the star tubes vary so much in size and number of teeth, it's easy to achieve many different effects just by piping simple stars.

To PIPE A PERFECT STAR, hold the decorating cone perpendicular to the surface. Give a quick squeeze, stop pressure and pull away. If you have not held the cone absolutely perpendicular, the middle of the star will be off-center.

For a puffy star, or one built up to a cone shape, lift the tube as you apply pressure to let the icing build up. Stop pressure completely before moving the tube away.

When piping a row of stars for a border, work in a rhythmic manner, applying the same pressure for each star to achieve a neat, uniform effect.

STAR BORDER VARIATIONS

BORDER ONE looks like a row of little turbans. Pipe a star with tube 364. Stop pressure but do not pull away, then apply medium pressure as you lift the tube. Stop pressure and pull away for a neat pointed effect. Continue to form border.

BORDER TWO—a line-up of miniature Christmas trees! Pipe a row of stars with tube 199. On each, pipe a cone shape with tube 364, lifting the tube as you press. Add a tube 2 dot at top.

BORDER THREE is deliciously pretty. Hold tube 21 straight up and pipe a spiral, narrowing the circu-

lar motion to form a cone. Frame with curves done with tube 13.

BORDER FOUR starts with puffy tube 364 stars. Point the cone directly at the point where the cake meets the cake board or tray for a beveled effect. Pipe a contrasting tube 2 spiral on each star to give a bonbon look.

BORDER FIVE is a dainty, flowery finish for a cake. First pipe a row of tube 16 shells as a base. Cover the shells with tube 504 star daisies and add tube 2 dots in the centers. Pipe perky tube 65 leaves.

176

SHELLS DECORATE A SUNNY BIRTHDAY CAKE

Shells and strings, piped with a variety of finely cut and open star tubes surround the tiers of a cheerful cake to salute a birthday. We chose sunshine yellow accented with brilliant orange icing to decorate this show-off cake, but suit the color scheme to the wishes of the birthday child.

To achieve the crown effect of the upright shells on the top tier, start the shells just at the edge of the tier. Apply pressure to let the shell build up and curve over the top of the tier, then relax pressure and move down. Cover the cake and do all decorating in buttercream.

STEP ONE. Prepare the two-layer tiers. Bake lower tier in 12″ round pans, each layer 2″ high. Bake upper tier in 8″ round pans, each layer about 1½″ high. Fill and ice the tiers, then assemble on a 15″ or 16″ cake board or tray. To assure uniform placement of the shells forming top border of lower tier, divide the tier into twentieths and mark on top edge.

STEP TWO. DECORATE BASE TIER. Pointing decorating cone directly at point where cake rests on tray, pipe a tube 199 bottom shell border. This will give a bevel effect to the border. Frame each shell with a tube 13 zigzag. On top edge of tier, at each mark, pipe a tube 199 upright shell, letting it curve over top of tier. Between each upright shell, pipe a tube 199 shell on top of tier, letting it curve over tier edge.

Drop deep tube 13 string from tails of upright shells, then go back and drop shallower strings. Finish with tube 13 rosettes. Frame shells at top of tier with tube 13 zigzags.

STEP THREE. DECORATE TOP TIER. Write message on tier top with tube 3. Pipe a tube 364 base shell border. Pipe orange rosettes at tails of shells on top of base tier with tube 13. Do shells at top of tier with tube 199, letting them curve over top edge of tier.

Connect shells with tube 13 dropped string in interlaced effect. Frame shells with tube 13 zigzags on top of tier. Insert candles in push-in holders in side of tier.

This birthday showpiece will bring summer inside, even on the darkest day! Light the candles, start the birthday song and serve to 32 well-wishers.

Star tubes take naturally to the dimensional, deeply sculptural forms used in over-piping. A cake trimmed with over-piped borders has an elegant formal beauty suitable for the most important occasion.

Over-piped borders look elaborate, but are really not difficult to pipe, taken one step at a time. Basic forms are piped with a star tube. When these are completed all around the cake, the curves are repeated one or more times with smaller star tubes. The finishing touches are often done with a small round tube.

The borders on these pages are done in contrasting colors to show the succeeding steps. Try a few of them, then invent some over-piped borders of your own.

FLOWERED RIBBON BORDER is quick to do and very attractive. Pipe a pink ribbon of icing with tube 2B. Curve white tube 15 zigzags over it. Over-pipe with tube 13 pink curves. Add tiny tube 23 stars and accent the design with dropped strings and bulbs piped with tube 3.

FEATHER BORDERS. Mark top edge of cake every 2″ and drop string guidelines for garlands. Pipe a curved zigzag garland from mark to mark with tube 16. Build it up twice more to bring it level with cake top. Add scrolls on top of garlands with the same tube. Over-pipe the scrolls with green tube 14 scrolls. Finish the border by over-piping white tube 3 scrolls.

To pipe a matching base border, mark the cake every 2″. Pipe a tube 16 garland and "shelf" on the cake board, then build it up with a second garland. Over-pipe with white tube 16 scrolls, green tube 14 scrolls and white tube 3 scrolls.

For your convenience, patterns for these borders are in the Wilton Way III Pattern Book, but by studying the steps you can make your own, or do them freehand. These are planned for the base of a cake, but are equally imposing at the top edge. Just turn them upside down. All begin with a row of tube 15 shells.

"S" CURVE BORDER. Mark the cake every 3"—completed motif is 6" wide. Pipe white scrolls and inverted upright shells with tube 15. Over-pipe the curves in pink with tube 14, then in white with tube 13. Add tube 13 stars and upright shells, then a final piping with tube 3 in yellow.

BAROQUE CURVE BORDER. Mark the cake every 1¾"—completed motif is 3½" wide. Pipe first in white with tube 15. Over-pipe in pink with tube 14, then in white with tube 13. Add final yellow trim with tube 3.

FAN BORDER. Mark the cake every 2". Pipe a "C" scroll in white with tube 15. Over-pipe in pink and add a pink zigzag garland above it with tube 13. Add five upright shells in fan shape and over-pipe scrolls and garlands in white with tube 13. Finish with tube 3 in yellow icing.

Delicate, airy lattice gives a dainty look to any border, whether for base, side or top of a cake. To give firm support to its see-through beauty, decorators often use the versatile star tubes. Here are five outstanding borders featuring lattice, each framed or supported by piping done with star tubes. Careful measuring is needed for each.

CHRISTMAS TREE BORDER. Mark base of cake every 2″. On side of cake, 2″ up from base, make a second series of marks 2″ apart, midway between the first series. Pipe a zigzag tube 14 garland at base of cake between marks. Pipe a second, slightly smaller garland on top of it. Drop tube 2 strings from marks on cake side to garland to form a triangle. Fill in with lattice, then add tube 2 dots and a tube 14 star.

FAN BORDER is flowery and feminine. Measure and mark the cake and pipe a tube 14 garland at base the same as for the Christmas tree border, above. Drop radiating tube 2 strings from mark on cake side to edge of garland. Add a tube 14 upright shell at top and a dainty tube 2 bow. Trim base with drop flowers piped in advance with tube 24 and tiny tube 65s leaves.

180

CLASSIC BORDER is an old favorite given a new twist by being done entirely with star tubes. Mark top edge of cake every 2½". Drop string guidelines, then pipe tube 14 zigzag garlands. Build them out by over-piping with second garlands. Pipe lattice with tube 13 string. Drop contrasting string below and on edge of garlands, then pipe curves to form scallops on cake top. Finish with tube 13 shells on edge of cake.

CUSHION BORDER has a plush, Continental look. Cut a curved pattern from folded paper 2½" wide, 2" high. Transfer to cake, leaving ½" between each design. Do lattice with tube 1. Starting well within marked outlines, drop vertical strings, diagonal strings over them, then a second set of diagonal strings in the opposite direction. Moving closer to outline, drop a second series of strings, vertical and diagonal, piping the strings exactly on top of those piped in the first series. Finally add the third series of strings, starting and stopping at marked outline. Frame the lattice with curved tube 13 shells.

BRIDAL VEIL BORDER looks lovely on a wedding cake. Mark cake every 2½", 2" up from base. Drop string guidelines for garlands and shallower strings to define top of lattice. Pipe a tube 14 shell border at base of cake. Use the same tube for zigzag garlands. Pipe second garlands on top of the first. Complete the border with tube 1. Pipe lattice and edge with beading. Finally, drop double parallel strings above lattice and top these with dots and fleurs-de-lis.

181

182

SKY BLUE PINK ... A DREAM OF A BRIDAL CAKE

This exquisite cake displays everything a young bride dreams of! There's something old—the lovely traditional rope borders done with star tubes that drape and edge the tiers. There's something new—the never-before icing flowers, garden pinks. Something borrowed—the white satin ribbons, as lustrous as the bridal gown, that tie up the double ring ornament and festoon the pillars. And something blue—the delicate tints of the flowers.

Hexagonal tiers set off all the pretty trims and make decorating easy—the six sides make measuring almost automatic.

PREPARE TRIMS AHEAD OF TIME

PIPE THE FLOWERS. The pink is a cousin of the carnation so it is piped in a similar way. Use stiff royal icing to give a ragged edge to the petals, a number 7 flower nail and tube 102. Holding the decorating cone almost straight up, wide end in center of nail, pipe five ruffled petals, one overlapping the the other. Pipe five more ruffled petals on top of the first five, and pull out tube 1 stamens in the center. You'll need about seven dozen pinks. Mount about two dozen on florists' wire stems for bouquet. To pipe leaves for bouquet, insert lengths of florists' wire into a cone fitted with tube 65 and pull out the leaves.

FOR BETWEEN-TIERS ORNAMENT, glue two large plastic wedding rings to the plate of a petite ornament base. Tie with white satin ribbon. Prepare six more ribbon bows for pillar trim.

MAKE THE VASE FOR THE FLOWER BOUQUET. Remove the plate from a petite ornament base and glue the base to the plate in upside-down position. Glue four Angelinos to sides of vase. Dry, then fill with a styrofoam half-ball and arrange stemmed flowers and leaves.

PREPARE AND DECORATE THE CAKE

BAKE, FILL AND ICE three hexagonal two-layer tiers. Base tier is 15", each layer 2" high. Middle tier is 12", each layer 2" high and top tier is 9", layers 1½" high. Cover a 19" hexagonal cake board with silver foil and edge with a blue ruffle. Assemble the cake on it, using six 5" Corinthian pillars and 9" hexagon plates. Mark Wilton Way III oval patterns on base and top tiers and drop string guidelines for swags.

DECORATE BASE TIER. Classic rope borders done with open star tubes, and star tube tassels are the simple trim. Pipe base border with tube 19, ovals and swags with tube 13, top border with tube 16.

Do the tassels by piping a tube 19 inverted upright shell, a horizontal tube 13 shell for binding and a tube 16 shell at the top. Attach an Angelino within each oval with a mound of icing.

ON THE MIDDLE TIER, pipe top and bottom rope borders with tube 16. Pipe rope swags with tube 13. Do the tassels just the same as those on base tier. Edge separator plate with tube 16 scallops.

ON THE TOP TIER, pipe base rope border with tube 16. Pipe rope swags with tube 13, and outline ovals with the same tube. Pipe a tube 13 top rope border. Add tassels done the same as on base tier. Glue bows to underside of plate at corners.

TRIM THE CAKE WITH FLOWERS

Set vase with bouquet on top tier. Attach a flower with icing within each oval. Set ornament within pillars and trim with a spray of flowers. Form garlands of flowers on side of middle tier and frame Angelinos on base tier with flower clusters. Set off all the flowers with tube 65 leaves.

Serve two lower tiers of Sky Blue Pink to 116 guests. The top tier serves 22, but is usually frozen for the couple's first anniversary.

CHAPTER TEN

Star Tubes Pipe
Lavish Top and Side Trims

NOTHING GIVES BEAUTY, rich texture and design to a cake as much as top and side trims—and these are most quickly and easily accomplished with the convenient star tubes. This technique of trimming a cake with piped designs on top and side was widely practiced by culinary artists in the past century and the early years of this one, but is sometimes overlooked today.

Many of these trims start with simple measuring as you can see on pages 194 and 195—then the areas are filled in with stars, curves and shells for a lavishly decorated cake.

Apply this technique to cakes for any occasion. Add swirling designs to impressive tier cakes, pipe quick trims on layer cakes to give them a rich continental look. Trim birthday cakes with brilliant stylized flowers or geometric piping, even paint bright pictures on cakes—all with the familiar star tubes. Leaf through this chapter for ideas, then go on to decorate your own distinctive cakes with top and side trims.

BLOSSOM BROCADE

Ornate piped designs cover the sides of this handsome bridal cake and quickly piped filigree scrolls seem to support the tiers. Patterns for the scrolls and side trims are in The Wilton Way III Pattern book, but you can easily make your own. Design on bottom tier is based on a simple heart shape, the graceful design on middle tier is an embellished colonial scroll.

MAKE ROYAL ICING TRIMS in advance. Pipe twelve filigree scrolls and pieces for the top ornament with tube 13 on wax paper. When dry, turn over and pipe again. Cut a 4½" circle from rolled gum paste, or make one with the Color Flow technique for base of ornament. Assemble ornament on base with icing, then pipe upright shells

for top finial. Pipe daisy petals with tubes 102 and 103, add tube 5 centers and dry. Pipe tube 66 leaves on wire, mount most of the flowers on wire stems and arrange in four ribboned bouquets to place on base tier.

PREPARE THE TWO-LAYER TIERS—14", 10" and 6". Layers for two lower tiers should be 2" high, for top tier 1½" high. Ice smoothly in pastel buttercream to set off the snowy side trims. Assemble with clear twist legs and 10" and 6" separator plates. Divide base tier into tenths and mark about 1" down from top edge. Divide middle tier in tenths and mark about 1" up from bottom. Divide top tier in eighths and mark midway on side. Transfer patterns to tier sides.

ON BASE TIER, pipe side design with tube 16. Do design on side of middle tier with the same tube. Add simple shell borders. On base tier use tube 18 for bottom border, tube 16 for top. On middle tier, pipe top and bottom borders with tube 16. Form a cluster of daisies and leaves and place in center of middle tier.

DECORATE TOP TIER with tube 14. Pipe bottom and top shell borders, then drop string from mark to mark. Top points of string with shell petals and rosettes. Pipe garlands at base of tier, using string above as guide for placement, then drape with more string.

Secure ornament to top of cake and trim with daisies. Attach filigree scrolls to middle and top tier—one at each pillar and one in space between each pillar. Attach four scrolls to base tier, using pillars as guide to position. Set daisy bouquets between scrolls.

Serve two lower tiers of Blossom Brocade to 140 wedding guests. Top tier serves 16. Present the daisy bouquets to the bridesmaids.

185

QUICK-TO-DO TOP AND SIDE DESIGNS TRIM PARTY CAKES

The simplest of designs piped in fresh pastels on the top and side of a cake can turn it into a real conversation piece! Each of these charmers is quickly decorated with the speedy star tubes.

A ROSY VALENTINE *below*

Wreath it with hearts piped in pretty tints of pink. Ice a two-layer 9" heart cake and mark sides with a line about 1" down from top edge. Make a second line 1" below the first. Mark a heart shape on top about 1½" in from edge.

Pipe a tube 16 bottom shell border, then add dropped tube 13 strings. Using marked lines as guides, pipe tube 19 shell-motion hearts on side of cake, then tube 13 hearts between them. Pipe tube 13 scallops around top of cake, then pipe the wreath of hearts with tubes 19, 16 and 13. Do largest hearts first and fill in with smaller ones. Serve your pretty love cake to twelve.

GREET A NEW BABY *at right*

Stripe the side of a tailored cake in delicately tinted pastel icing. Bake, fill and ice a 10" two-layer cake. Mark an 8" and a 6" circle on top by pressing lightly with cake circles. Pipe message with tube 14 in center of cake.

Cover the cake side with tube 4B stripes in alternating colors. (Each stripe is ½" wide.) Now top the stripes with tube 32 shells in matching colors, letting them curve over the edge of the cake. Let the tails of the shells touch the outer marked circle. Pipe a tube 16 star between each shell. Pipe a second circle of tube 32 shells in white, tails touching the inner marked circle. End with tube 16 stars. Finish the cake with tube 18 rosettes at base. Serve to 14.

TULIP TIME *at right*

Colorful stylized tulips bloom all over this flower-shaped cake. Bake a two-layer cake in 12" petal pans. Each layer should be 2" high. Fill and ice, then transfer Wilton Way III patterns.

Star tube 16 does all the decorating. At bottom of cake, pipe curved scrolls first, then fill in base of cake with shells. Pipe tulips and over-pipe center teardrop shapes for raised effect. Pipe stems and leaves, then pipe a rosette at ends of stems. Do curved scrolls at top edge of cake, then pipe tulips on cake top the same as those on side. Serve this springtime treat to 24.

186

ARCHES OF FLOWERS. This is a large design, so measure and mark the cake side before piping. About 1½″ up from base of cake, make a mark every 3½″. Now mark a 2″ circle at each of these points, base on mark. (A cookie cutter makes quick work of this.) Pipe the circle with four tube 27 curves, joining smoothly in the center. Continue piping circles, then go back and connect them with tube 27 curves. Trim with tube 24 drop flowers and tube 65 leaves.

HEARTS AND FLOWERS. Measure first. Make a mark every 2¾″, 1″ down from top edge of cake. Make a second series of marks 1⅝″ below the first marks. Use these marks to guide the piping of two tube 30 "C" curves, joined in the center. Add an upright shell and two curved shells with tube 26. Top with a star. Pipe this design all around the cake, then pipe pink tube 18 hearts at the base of the curves. Complete with tube 24 drop flowers and tube 65 leaves.

FRAMED FLOWERS. This is a variation of the graceful colonial scroll. To keep your work even, mark the cake side. Main curves are 3″ apart, 2″ deep. Pipe the scrolls with tube 26, then go back and add feathery trim with the same tube, blending in smoothly. Pipe a stylized daisy within curve, six tube 27 radiating shells. Add a tube 26 rosette in the center.

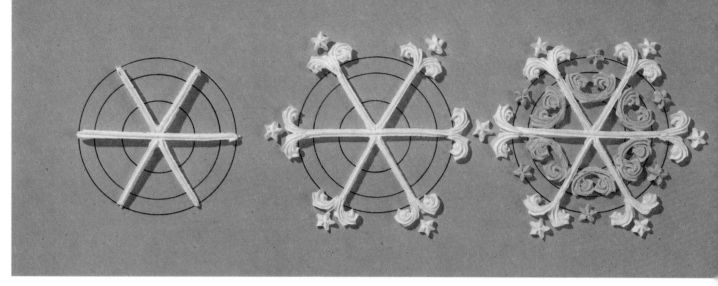

SNOWFLAKE is a very festive trim for the side of a large cake or tier. Round cookie cutters make the pattern easy. Press side of cake with a 3″ cutter, keeping the circles 1″ apart. Within each circle mark two smaller circles with 2½″ and 1½″ cutters. Use only tube 13 to pipe the design. Pipe a six-pointed star, points extending to largest circle. Add two curved shells and a star at each end. Use smaller circles to guide you in piping green curves. Finish with green stars.

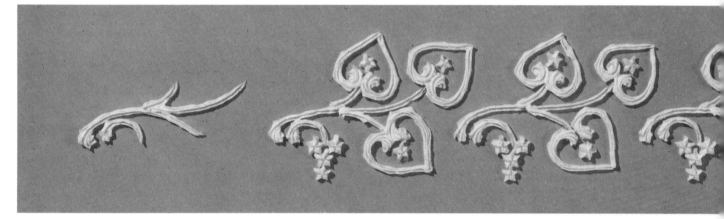

FLOWERING BRANCH looks lovely on side of any cake. Tube 13 pipes this design. First pipe a series of shallow "S" curves, each about 2½″ long. Add two short branches, then a curve below each. To complete the design, press icing with a 1″ heart cookie cutter. Pipe the heart shapes with two curves, then add dainty stars. Experiment with other small cutters to make interesting side trims. It's fun—and easy!

EMBROIDERED RIBBON is a showy side trim. Cut a 1½″ strip of rolled fondant and wrap around the cake side, securing with icing. Mark the pattern by pressing with a 1½″ heart cookie cutter. Pipe the hearts with tube 16. With tube 13, pipe short curves between the hearts. Color contrast makes this trim especially pretty. The design can be done without the fondant ribbon, if you wish.

FRAMED LATTICE looks lovely on a wedding cake. Cut a 1¼" x 2" oval from folded paper. Mark it on the cake every 6½", tops of ovals 1" below top edge. Fill in ovals with tube 2, then use tube 24 for rest of design. Frame ovals, then add sweeping "S" curves and flourishes as pictured. Complete with tube 24 drop flowers.

CLASSIC VASE. Mark the cake side every 5", 1½" down from top edge. Mark again 1½" below first marks. Pipe an upright tube 32 shell from upper to lower mark. Over-pipe with a tube 16 shell and add curves on either side. Pipe two curves, a shell and a rosette with tube 13 at base. Pipe branches and stars with tube 13 and heap with tubes 27 and 30 drop flowers.

PLUMED CASCADE. Mark the cake side every 3", 1½" down from top edge. Pipe a tube 19 upright shell, top of shell at mark. Continue piping upright shells, then frame each with a tube 13 curve at top. Connect the shells with tube 16 curves and pipe the "plumes" with tube 16 fleurs-de-lis and rosettes. Form the cascades with tubes 502 and 504 drop flowers.

DIAMOND SIDE TRIM is shown actual size. Mark points of diamonds on cake side or use a 2" diamond cookie cutter. Pipe the shape with tube 16 starting with a quick curve. Add shells at top and bottom for fleur-de-lis effect. Add a tube 13 green rosette where diamonds meet and four green shells in flower formation. Finish with a tube 16 star.

FERN SIDE TRIM. Make a series of marks 1½" down from top edge of cake, 1⅜" apart. Mark a second time, 1½" down from first marks to define ferns. Stripe a decorating cone, fitted with tube 362, on both sides with green icing, fill with white. Pipe shells from bottom to top, then add tube 13 "C" curves. Picture is actual size.

CURVE-AND-BRANCH TRIM, shown actual size, is piped entirely with tube 13. First make a series of marks 2¾" apart, midway on side of cake. Stripe the decorating cone on both sides with green icing, fill with white. Starting at marked points, pipe the "C" curves and add a curved shell at the ends. Pipe "branches" with long curved shells. Finish with a rosette and stars.

QUICK STAR TUBE TRIMS TURN CAKES INTO SHOWPIECES

Start with a simple cake, add bright colored trims on top or side—you've made a celebration!

STRAWBERRY CUPCAKES

Nothing could be quicker—or prettier! Bake a batch of cupcakes and swirl on boiled icing. Press a green star with tube 35 on each, then add the strawberry—a puffy tube 364 star.

A CIRCLE OF POSIES

Bake, fill and ice a two-layer 10″ round cake, tint buttercream in sunny colors and you're ready to plant the garden. Divide cake into sixteenths and mark on top edge. Use tube 18 for all decorating. Pull stems from marks to base of cake, then join with shell "leaves." At top of stems, pipe eight-petal daisies, half of petals on top of cake, half on side. Pipe center rosettes. Finish with puffy shells at base of cake. Cluster candles on top of cake and serve to 14 birthday guests.

"CROCHET" AN AFGHAN CAKE

Bake a layer in a 14″ base bevel pan, one in a 10″ round pan and top layer in a 10″ bevel pan. Fill and ice. Mark a 7″ circle and a 4½″ circle on cake top to define message and pipe with tube 13. Divide cake into twelfths and mark vertical lines on side above base bevel. Tint buttercream in four bright colors and use tube 18 to pipe the afghan. Starting at mark, about 1″ above bevel, pipe a "V" to next mark. Work your way up the cake, piping two "V's" with each tint of icing. Continue until cake side and top bevel is completely piped. Pipe rosettes and leaves with tube 18 and also the base shell border. Push in a tall taper. Serve to 20 (bevel layer serves six).

192

INVENT YOUR OWN PRETTY CAKE-TOP DESIGNS

Create a cake that's really *decorated* in the old world Continental style—but do it with efficient time-saving methods. You won't need a pattern—just start with careful measuring of the cake using the folded paper technique. Then star tubes and contrasting icing will do the trim.

A CAKE FOR A GALA

Rich chocolate is a perfect background for the intricate-looking design. Start with scallops, then fill in with shells, hearts and stars. First fill and ice a 10″ two-layer round cake.

FOLD A 10″ PAPER CIRCLE into sixteenths. While circle is still folded fan-fashion, snip the center point and cut notches on both sides of fan, first 1½″ in from open edge, then 2½″ in. Open circle and transfer notches to cake top with a toothpick.

Pipe tube 19 shells from edge of cake to first series of marks. Connect tails of shells with tube 17 scallops and stars. Connect inner marks with tube 16 scallops and border with tube 13 stars. Pipe tube 17 hearts between scallops.

ON SIDE OF CAKE, pull up tube 199 columns, using shells on cake top as guide. Connect with tube 13 string. Add tube 16 rosettes and hearts. Complete bottom border with tube 16 shells and do top shell border with tube 19. Pipe four tube 70 leaves on cake top and finish with a big yellow rose. Serve this impressive treat to 16. Scallops serve as guide for slicing.

STUDY THE PRETTY CAKE TOPS on the opposite page, then dream up some striking designs of your own. *All the cake tops are 10″ round.*

FLEURS-DE-LIS AND FERNS. Divide the cake top into eighths and mark ½″ and 2¼″ in from edge and in center. Pipe fleurs-de-lis with tube 19, starting and stopping at marks. Add stars with same tube. Pipe ferns with tube 16 shells, extending to center of cake. Add a tube 19 rosette in center and a border of tube 17 stars.

RING-AROUND. Divide cake into twelfths and mark at edge. Use a 2″ cutter to define circles. Pipe the circles with tube 19, adding a rosette at side of each, then a tube 65 leaf. Pipe tube 68 leaves pointing toward center. Pipe tube 68 center leaves, then a tube 19 rosette. Fill in top edge with tube 32 upright shells.

SUNBURST. Fold a 10″ circle in eighths, cutting notches on both sides of the folded fan shape 2″ and 4″ in from open edge. Cut a notch on the open edge in center. Mark cake. Pipe an eight-pointed tube 17 star from edge of cake to outer marks. Pipe elongated shells from inner points of star to inner marks. Connect with short curved shells. Complete the trim with tube 16.

LATTICED HEARTS. Begin by dividing cake into eighths and marking on edge. Mark with a 2½″ heart cutter. Mark a 3¼″ circle in center. Fill in areas with tube 2 lattice and frame with tube 17. Edge circle with tube 19 shells and tube 16 stars. Add tube 21 shells at edge of cake and pipe a tube 17 shell border. Accent with drop flowers and tube 65s leaves.

CORNUCOPIAS CURVE ON A BOLDLY BEAUTIFUL CAKE

Pipe cornucopias on a cake top, add plume-like curves and borders done with star tubes—then accent with dainty drop flowers. You've trimmed a cake you'll be proud to show off!

PIPE DROP FLOWERS IN ADVANCE with tubes 193, 190 and 225. Add tubes 1 and 2 centers and dry. Bake, fill and ice a two-layer 12″ petal cake. The shape makes measuring the cake unnecessary. Transfer Wilton Way III cornucopia pattern or make your own. Curved shapes are 4″ long.

PIPE A TUBE 16 SHELL BORDER at base of cake. Use tube 18 to pipe elongated curved shells in plume effect over it. Pipe a long curved shell on each petal on top edge of cake with the same tube.

Decorate the cake top with tube 20. Pipe a rosette in center, then outline cornucopia shapes. Pipe cornucopias in spiral fashion, then insert tube into each cornucopia and press to fill space inside. Pipe shell borders around openings. Attach the flowers on dots of icing and trim with tube 65 leaves. Serve to 24, cutting each petal into three slices.

FRAME A BOUQUET WITH STAR TUBE SWIRLS

Compose your own lavish trim for a cake top with a Stellar star tube. We centered our cake with a cluster of tube 104 roses, made ahead and stored, but other varieties of flowers you have on hand would be just as pretty. Fresh garden flowers arranged in a Flower Spike are lovely too!

BAKE, FILL AND ICE a 10″ round two-layer cake. For a delicious Continental touch, press sliced toasted almonds into the side. To start the design, lightly press a 9″ oval pan on the cake. Do all cake-top trim with tube 504.

First outline the oval. At top narrow end of oval pipe curving swirls, blending in to the outline. Add more swirls to the bottom narrow end. Lastly, add swirls and curved shells to each side to fill out the frame. Be sure to blend all curves smoothly into the original outline.

PIPE THE BOTTOM SHELL BORDER with tube 506. Finish the top edge of the cake with tube 501 shells. Arrange the flowers on the cake top, tilting each on a mound of icing. Pipe tube 67 leaves. Serve this Continental creation to 14.

STAR TUBES PAINT A BRIGHT PICTURE ON A CAKE

Brighten a party with this brilliant peasant-art cake! It's sure to be the center of attention. Star tubes and icing in vivid colors paint the picture and pipe heart designs on top and sides.

BAKE AND FILL a two-layer 9" x 13" cake. Be sure the layers are about 2" high. Ice smoothly in

buttercream, then transfer Wilton Way III patterns to top and sides. Refer to this picture as you pipe the designs.

OUTLINE THE BIRDS with tube 1. Pipe stem and curving branches with tube 13. Join tube 14 shells to stems. Outline the large center flower with tube 13, then fill in the petals with tube 15 shells. Pipe petals of small pink flowers with tube 13 shells and a star.

Pipe birds with tube 13. Fill in heads with orange stars, bodies with shells. Pipe green stars for eyes and surround with a fan of shells. Outline wings and tails twice, then fill in spaces with tube 15 shells. Pipe legs, feet and shell beak.

For the yellow-orange flowers, pipe tube 13 scallops, tube 15 rosettes. Pipe small pink-orange tulips with tubes 14 and 13 shells. Frame the oval and all heart designs with tube 17 stars.

Within hearts on cake top, pipe tube 16 shells and top with tube 14 shells. Within side hearts, pipe tube 13 scallops and outlines. Pipe orange hearts with tube 16 shells and add tube 13 shells above them.

COVER THE ENTIRE CAKE, up to designs, with tube 16 stars. Serve your masterpiece to 24.

LIGHT UP A LOAF CAKE
WITH A CHRISTMAS CANDLE (below)

Decorate this cheery, easy-to-serve cake for the centerpiece of a happy holiday get-together. Star tubes pipe the design in a hurry.

BAKE THE CAKE in a 16″ long loaf pan and ice smoothly in buttercream. Transfer Wilton Way III pattern to top and sides.

PIPE THE CANDLE with one stroke of giant star tube 6B. Fill a cone with half yellow, half orange icing and pipe a tube 195 shell for flame. Do scalloped circles and stars with tube 13, then add tube 13 rays. Fill in holly leaf shapes with tube 13 stars and add tube 195 rosettes for berries. Finish the cake with a tube 18 curved shell border at bottom. Serve neat 1″ slices to 16 guests.

199

LACE KERCHIEF
...AS PRETTY AS THE BRIDAL GOWN

This little wedding cake is a perfect example of how simple star-tube trims can pattern a tier and give the cake an elaborate effect very quickly. Here the pastel tiers are engraved with butterfly designs that look like the points of a lace handkerchief. Delicate roses and buds complete the enchanting picture.

MAKE FLOWERS IN ADVANCE

PIPE ROSES AND BUDS with tubes 103 and 101 and dry. Pipe some tiny tube 101s roses to trim the cupid figures. Mount about a dozen of the largest flowers and buds on florists' wire stems. Pipe tube 66 leaves on wire. Dry, then twist stems of leaves and flowers together to form a nosegay. Cut a hole in the center of a 6″ paper doily, insert stems, tape securely and tie with a ribbon bow.

PREPARE AND DECORATE
THE CAKE

BAKE AND FILL the two-layer tiers. Lower tier is 12″ square, each layer 2″ high. Upper tier is 8″ round, each layer 1½″ high. Ice in pastel buttercream and assemble on a 16″ square ruffle-edged cake board. Use the Harvest Cherub separator set. The four little seated cupids enhance the daintiness of the cake.

Transfer Wilton Way III pattern to side of base tier. On top of tier, mark lines from edges of triangular areas on sides to indentations on separator plate. Transfer pattern for side of upper tier to cake.

DECORATE LOWER TIER. Pipe a tube 18 bottom shell border, then drape tube 13 scallops and stars over it. Pipe butterfly pattern at corners of tier and edge area with scallops using tube 13. Continue scallops on top of tier, following marked lines. Add stars at points of scallops. Fill in area in polka dot fashion with tube 13 stars. Do top shell border with tube 16 and edge plate with tube 13 stars.

DECORATE UPPER TIER. Pipe a tube 16 bottom shell border, then drape with tube 13 scallops and stars. Pipe butterfly design on side with tube 13 and continue scalloped edge on top of tier to center. Add stars with same tube. Pipe top border with tube 13.

COMPLETE THE TRIM

Attach tiny roses to seated cupid figures with dots of royal icing. Attach roses to hands of a standing cupid figure and trim all the tiny roses with tube 65s leaves. Secure standing cupid within pillars with icing. Attach tube 101 roses and buds to tier sides and trim with tube 65 leaves. For the final beautiful touch, set the nosegay on the top tier.

Serve lower tier of Lace Kerchief to 72 guests, top tier to 30.

CHAPTER ELEVEN

More Amazing Uses of Star Tubes

Borders and trims for tops and sides of cakes are just the beginning of the long list of uses of the star tubes. Use these handy tubes to figure pipe, make pretty stylized flowers, pipe fuzzy "fur" on a pet, fill in designs or create a just-like-real bachelor button. They'll even weave a basket or spell out a message!

This chapter is a treasure trove of ideas for happy-go-lucky cakes decorated with star tubes. You'll think of many more ways to put these helpers to use.

A BIRTHDAY CAROUSEL

Here's just the brightest, happiest cake ever for a youngster's birthday! Star tubes pipe the high relief ponies, make the tent-like filigree roof and print the birthday message.

FIRST MAKE CAROUSEL ROOF. Tape Wilton Way III pattern to a stiff surface, tape wax paper over it and pipe the six triangular sections with tube 13 and royal icing. Pipe tube 16 shells at the top points of the triangles. Dry. Pipe a dozen or more tube 225 drop flowers on wax paper to trim ponies. Pipe tube 199 drop flowers and push a birthday candle into each. Dry.

BAKE THE TIERS. Base of carousel is a single-layer 12″ round. Upper tier is three layers baked in 9″ hexagon pans, filled and assembled to a height of 5″. Ice tiers smoothly and assemble on serving tray. Mark a vertical line in center of each side of hexagon tier. Press a 3″ high horse cookie cutter into each side for ponies or use pattern. Mark

lines on side of round tier ½″ above base and ½″ below top edge. This will define lettering.

AT BOTTOM OF ROUND TIER, pipe a tube 16 rope border and a shell border at top with the same tube. Pipe message with tube 362.

Pipe tube 16 shells down each corner of the hexagon tier and around base of tier. Pipe orange rope borders down marked center of sides for poles and finish with rosettes.

The ponies are figure piped with tube 364. Start at nose with light pressure, turn sharply and pipe neck, then body, all without lifting tube. Tuck tube into body and pull out legs. Pipe a tube 13 ear. Trim with drop flowers, tube 13 curved shells for mane and tail and a tube 1 saddle. Complete saddle with a tube 13 star.

ASSEMBLE THE ROOF. Insert a long cocktail stirrer into top center of cake. Make a mark on stirrer 2½″ up from cake surface. Pipe tube 16 lines on stirrer from mark to cake. This will form a "ledge" to support roof. Pipe small mounds of icing on top of cake at two adjacent corners and on "ledge." Place one section of roof in position. Secure a second roof section to opposite side of cake in the same way. Fill in with remaining sections, piping lines of icing on sides to secure. Trim roof with tube 13 shells where sections are joined, then with dropped string to form scallops. Pipe the birthday child's name with tube 1 on a paper banner and glue to stirrer. Serve to 22 —hexagon tier serves twelve, round tier ten.

FRIENDLY LION CUBS PEER THROUGH A GREEN JUNGLE

This cake is as much fun as a tropical safari—and doesn't cost nearly as much! An open star tube pipes the jungle, a finely cut star tube figure pipes the cute cats.

PREPARE THE CAKE. Bake a layer in a 10″ round pan and one in a 10″ top bevel pan. Fill, then swirl on boiled icing and set on serving tray. Use boiled icing for the leaves, too. Pull up long slim shapes with tube 16 all around the cake, letting them drape over the bevel and top.

NOW FOR FIGURE PIPING FUN! Pipe the lions right on the cake with tube 362 as the diagram shows. Use boiled icing. First pipe an oval, then two puffy stars for cheeks, and a third, smaller one for chin. Pull out a straight nose and pipe two quick curves for ears. With tube 1 and piping gel, pipe two dots for eyes and a little heart shape at end of nose. Pipe a few more curving tube 16 leaves and present this enjoyable creation to 14.

BASKETS OF CHIRPING CHICKS

PIPE THE CHICKS on wax paper with boiled icing. Pipe a pointed shell with tube 364 for body, then pull out wings with star-cut tube 98. A tube 364 puffy star makes the head. Add eyes and beak with tube 2 and dry.

BAKE CUPCAKES, allowing them to mound up at top. Ice, then cover sides with basket weaving, using tube 3 for vertical lines, tube 13 for horizontal strokes. Pipe a tube 13 shell border at top. Attach chicks, then fill in tube 233 "grass."

. . . and to all a good night . . .

Santa relaxes in his easy chair after his arduous night-long flight. The children will love this little tableau so much they'll want to make a Christmas tradition of it—so use lasting royal icing to pipe the little figure.

MAKE THE WING CHAIR from rolled gum paste and Wilton Way III pattern. First cut the styrofoam block as pattern directs and cover smoothly with wax paper. Construct the chair over the block, brushing seams with egg white to join. Dry the chair on its back, propping wings in position and rolling arms over pencils. When dry, cover all over with tube 1s cornelli lace and trim edges with tube 1 beading.

MAKE BOOTS, BAG, CAP AND CARPET. Mold the feet and lower part of legs with gum paste in a 10-year old child People Mold. When dry, paint with egg white and cover smoothly with rolled gum paste, butting seam at back and trimming smoothly at top. Cut a 2" x 3" piece of rolled gum paste and fold to 2" x 1½" to make bag. Trim with tube 1 laces. For cap, pipe an upright shell with tube 199 on wax paper and add tube 13 trim. For braided round carpet, cut a 5" circle of gum paste, dry, then cover with tube 13 zigzag circles, starting at outer edge.

FIGURE PIPE SANTA in royal icing with finely cut star tubes. Make a facsimile of the chair in light cardboard and cover front and inner surfaces with wax paper. Pipe Santa on this chair. Pipe two upright cylinders for socks with tube 363. Insert tube into ankle and pull out pointed feet. Pipe a tube 364 "doughnut" on chair seat. With the same tube, pipe extended shells, curving over the edge of the seat, for upper legs. Pipe two upright shells against back of chair with tube 199, then add a third shell for torso.

Add "fur" trim down front of jacket, around hem and around socks with tube 13 zigzags. Pipe arms with tube 199. Add trim at cuffs and collar. Pipe a tube 11 oval for head and add tube 4 cheeks and nose. Use the same tube to pipe hands. Pipe a ball, flatten it, and pull out fingers.

Pipe eyes, mouth and eyebrows with tube 1. Finish Santa with tube 13 mustache, beard and hair. Attach figure to gum paste chair, chair to carpet with royal icing.

BAKE, FILL AND ICE a 10" round two-layer cake. Divide side in eighths and drop string guidelines for garlands. Pipe a shell border at base with tube 18, at top with tube 16. Pipe zigzag garlands with tube 18 and cover with tube 233. Lightly mark an 8" circle on cake top as guide for script. Pipe message and tie up garlands with tube 2. Place a 5" circle of plastic wrap on cake top and set Santa on it. Arrange his boots and bag nearby. Lift off the tableau before serving the cake to 14.

207

A SURPRISE FOR EASTER MORNING

Here's a cake as bright as spring sunshine that says "have a happy Easter" without a word! The children will adore this sweet surprise—it's a portrait of their favorite friends, Mr. and Mrs. Bunny. It shows the versatility of the star tubes, too. They weave the baskets, form the Easter eggs and figure pipe the cute bunnies.

STEP ONE. Pipe drop flowers in advance. Use royal icing in bright pastels and tubes 225, 35 and 13. Pipe centers with tube 2 and set aside to dry.

STEP TWO. Prepare the cake. Bake two layers in 8" square pans. Be sure the layers are about 2" high. Fill and ice smoothly with buttercream and set on cake board.

Make a stencil from a piece of light cardboard by cutting a 6" square opening. Lay stencil lightly on cake top, opening in center, and stroke blue icing over upper area with a spatula, green icing over lower area. Remove stencil and roughen green area with a damp sponge.

STEP THREE. Pipe a ribbon of icing around base of cake with tube 2B. If icing looks rough at corners, don't be concerned, flowers will cover it. Transfer Wilton Way III basket pattern to center of each side, or make your own pattern from folded paper. Basket is 1½" high, 1¼" wide at base, 2½" wide at top. Build up rounded shape by piping several layers of zigzags with tube 15, piping first across, then up and down. Smooth with a spatula. Cover the rounded shape with basket weaving, using tube 3 for vertical lines, tube 13 for horizontal strokes. Pipe a tube 13 rope border at top.

Pipe tube 101 triple bows on each side of baskets. Fill each with eggs by piping puffy stars with tube 362

STEP FOUR. Figure pipe the bunnies. Transfer Wilton Way III pattern to blue-green area on cake top, or save time by pressing with a bunny cookie cutter, 3½" high. Use boiled or buttercream icing and tube 364.

First pipe a puffy ball-shaped star for head. On it, pipe two balls for cheeks with light pressure. Below it, pipe a shell, then a second shell, to form body. Tuck tube into body just above second shell and pipe lower leg. Without lifting tube, turn sharply to pipe paw. Repeat for lower leg on other side.

Pipe upper legs by tucking tube just below head and piping two quick curves. Change to tube 353 and pipe ears, decreasing pressure to draw to points.

Pipe tube 1 pink eyes and mouth. Paint center area of ears with pink icing. Pipe a few tube 1 stems on Mrs. Bunny and attach flowers with dots of icing. Pipe tube 362 Easter eggs between Mr. Bunny's paws.

STEP FIVE. Complete the decorating. Pipe a tube 48 frame on cake top and edge with tube 2 beading. Pipe mounds of icing at corners of frame and secure flowers. Attach a few flowers around bunnies and pipe tube 1 "grass." Pipe mounds of icing at base of cake at corners and press in flowers. Trim all the flowers with tube 65 leaves. Cut this Easter portrait into twelve servings.

FIGURE PIPE THE BUNNIES WITH A FINELY-CUT STAR TUBE

BEARDED IRIS

ROSEBUDS

DAY LILY

TULIP

CHRYSANTHEMUM

DAISY

GERANIUM

PIPE SPEEDY CAKE TOP FLOWERS WITH STAR TUBES

When you want flower trims in a hurry, turn to the handy star tubes! Use buttercream or boiled icing and pipe them right on the cake top in just a few minutes. Try these showy blooms, then create some star-tube flowers of your own. All the flowers shown above are in actual size, all have a realistic three-dimensional look.

BEARDED IRIS is piped with tube 32. For lower part of flower, pipe a shell, then two curved shells, one on either side. Pipe two sharply curved shells for upper part of flower and add the beard with tube 2.

ROSEBUDS are just rosettes piped with tube 19. Trim with tube 16 shell leaves.

DAY LILY gets its two-tone effect by fitting a cone with tube 364, striping it with orange icing, then filling it with pink. Pipe a long shell for base of flower, then pipe five shells on top of it for petals. Add tube 2 stamens.

TULIP is quickest of all to pipe—just a tube 364 shell with a curved shell on each side.

CHRYSANTHEMUM stems, leaves and petals are all piped with tube 13. Pull out stems and top with a green shell. Petals are curved shells, leaves just tight zigzags for lobed effect.

DAISY is fresh and perky. Mark center, then pipe a circle of tube 14 shells, tails touching center mark. Add a tube 13 yellow rosette.

GERANIUM is a show-off flower done with tube 13. Pipe stem, then a few green shells for buds. Pipe many five-petal blossoms with shells, piling one on another in center for rounded look. Pipe center stars with light pressure. To pipe two-tone leaf, start with four or five loops, then add repeated outlines.

GERANIUMS BLOOM ON A SHEET CAKE

Pipe these scarlet flowers on a cake that's as cheerful as a sunny kitchen!

CUT PATTERNS FOR CAKE TOP from folded paper. Oval is 6½" x 9½", basket is 3" wide at base, 4" wide at top, 3" high.

BAKE AND FILL a 9" x 13" cake and ice smoothly with buttercream. Transfer patterns to cake top and mark position of flowers. Pipe the cute "rickrack" border at base of cake with tube 16 and two tints of green. Pipe zigzags, then fill in spaces with rosettes.

PIPE STEMS, FLOWERS AND LEAVES on cake top with tube 13 as described above. Weave basket with tube 3 vertical lines and tube 13 horizontal strokes. Finish top and bottom with tube 13 rope. Use tube 13 again for zigzags around oval and fill in with stars. Serve your cheery treat to 24.

DAY LILIES BLOOM ON A PARTY CAKE

If you're looking for an idea for a quick cake for a summer celebration, here's the answer!

BAKE AND FILL a 10" round, two-layer cake. Ice smoothly in buttercream. Now tint icing in two shades of green and in orange and pink. Stripe a decorating cone fitted with tube 13 with deep green icing and fill with light green. Pipe curving stems on top and side of cake. Change to tube 364 and pipe the long lily leaves.

Fit a decorating cone with tube 364, stripe with orange icing and fill with pink. Pipe the lilies just as explained on page 211, then add tube 2 stamens. Buds are formed with tube 364, too—shells drawn to a point.

AT BASE OF CAKE, pipe a tube 4B shell border. Frame shells with tube 13. Pipe a reverse shell border at top of cake with tube 16. Serve to 14.

A PARASOL FILLED WITH FLOWERS FOR A SHOWER

Star tubes pipe the parasol, blossoms and borders on this carefree cake—even the message!

BAKE, FILL AND ICE a two-layer 9″ oval cake. Transfer Wilton Way III pattern for message and parasol to cake, or make your own. Letters are about 1¾″ high.

PIPE CURVED SHELLS at base of cake with tube 17. Do block letters with tube 13 and frame with a few tube 13 drop flowers. Outline areas of the parasol with tube 3, then fill in with tube 14 stars. Pipe handle with the same tube. Tie with a tube 13 bow. Pipe tube 13 scallops around top edge.

Pipe the flowers as described on pages 210 and 211. Pipe iris first with tube 18, then tube 17 rosebuds, blue daisy-like blossoms with tube 13 and tube 13 drop flowers. Use tube 13 for all leaves. Serve this flowery treat to twelve.

TWIN PANDAS BRING BIRTHDAY GREETINGS

To a panda, bamboo leaves are better than candy. To a youngster, this is the best birthday cake ever! The "fur" on the pandas is done with the star fill-in technique—closely set stars that completely cover an area. This quick technique is convenient for piping simple designs on a flat surface, and indispensable for covering three-dimensional areas.

BAKE, FILL AND ICE a 9″ x 13″ sheet cake. Bake two cakes in 5″ panda molds. Paint bottom of paws with thinned icing, then cover the pandas with tube 13 stars, using chocolate and white buttercream. Pipe eyes and noses with tube 3. When icing sets, glaze with corn syrup.

PIPE "BAMBOO" BORDERS on cake. First run a line around bottom of cake with tube six, then cover it with tube 353. Use even pressure, pausing every 2″ or less, to allow icing to build up. Do top border the same way. Pipe tube 2 stems for bamboo at corners of cake, extending on to top. Pipe slender tube 65 leaves and do tube 3 greeting.

Set the pandas on the cake top and fill their paws with tube 65 bamboo leaves. Arrange an appropriate number of tall tapers behind them. Serve the sheet cake to 24 guests. Save the pandas for the birthday child.

214

A BIRTHDAY BALLOON FLOATS IN TO THE PARTY

CUT THE RIBBON for the message from rolled gum paste, using Wilton Way III pattern. Dry over pencils, then pipe tube 1 message. Pipe royal icing drop flowers with tubes 17 , 34. Paint 4½" lengths of thin spaghetti with thinned icing for ropes. Cut 1" long banners from colored paper and attach to 1½" lengths of spaghetti.

BAKE, FILL AND ICE a 9" x 13" two-layer sheet cake. Also bake and ice a half-ball in a 6" ball pan and a cupcake for the basket. Set half-ball on a 6" cake circle and divide in fifths with a taut thread. Mark free-hand curved design, outline areas with tube 3 and fill in with tube 14 stars.

CUT CUPCAKE IN HALF, secure to its own cardboard base, prop upright and figure pipe the passengers. Use tube 10 for bodies and hats, tube 7 for arms and heads. Add tube 2 hands and tube 1 features. Weave basket with tubes 3 and 13.

AT BOTTOM OF SHEET CAKE, pipe groups of tube 2 stems and attach drop flowers. Pipe tube 65 leaves and tube 233 "grass." Do top ball border with tube 8. Set message ribbon on cake, then secure basket and balloon. Attach ropes and banners with icing and arrange candles. Serve sheet cake to 24, balloon to six.

A BASKET OF BACHELOR BUTTONS

Decorate a little square cake in a sweet and simple way, then crown it with a basket of blue bachelor buttons. Pipe the basket and flowers with star tubes in royal icing, then the guest of honor can keep it as a lasting souvenir.

PIPE THE BACHELOR BUTTONS

To pipe a bud, first pipe a tube 5 ball of royal icing on a wax paper square. Insert a length of florists' wire and brush the icing onto the wire to form a cone for calyx. Stick wire in styrofoam to dry. Peel off paper. Thin the icing slightly and pipe a cluster of tube 13 stars on the calyx, then surround with a few petals with the same tube. Cover the calyx with tube 65s green leaves.

To pipe a flower, use thinned icing, nail number 1 and tube 13. Pipe a cluster of stars and pull out pointed petals around them. Continue forming circles of petals, turning your hand so the final row is almost flat. Prepare calyx with a wire stem as you did for bud. Dry, then attach flower to calyx with a dot of icing. Pipe long slender leaves directly on wire with tube 65s.

MAKE THE BASKET

Tape Wilton Way III pattern to largest Flower Former and tape wax paper smoothly over it. Use the basket weaving technique and royal icing. Pipe radiating lines with tube 3 and cross with tube 13 short strokes. Add a rope border at edge. When dry, pipe a 1″ circle of tube 13 shells on bottom. Dry again. Tape handle pattern to a stiff surface and cover with wax paper. Pipe the handle like a rope border with tube 13. When dry, turn over and pipe other side.

Twist stems of flowers, buds and leaves together and place in basket. Now attach the handle with mounds of icing. Add the final pretty touch with a ribbon bow.

DECORATE THE CAKE

Simple but very effective star tube borders trim the cake and make a perfect background for the basket of flowers.

Bake and fill two 8″ square layers. Ice smoothly with buttercream and set on cake board. Lightly mark a 5″ circle on cake top. Divide each side of cake into fourths and mark 1″ down from top.

Pipe a rope border at bottom of cake with tube 16. Drop double tube 16 strings from mark to mark on cake side. Pipe upright shells with the same tube, then add tube 13 rosettes.

Pipe a tube 16 shell border on top of cake. Pipe scallops around marked circle with the same tube and finish with radiating shells and tube 13 rosettes. Place a 3″ circle of plastic wrap on cake and set basket on it. Add a few more flowers and serve to twelve guests. Present the basket to the guest of honor.

217

CHAPTER TWELVE

The Fascinating Star-Cut Tubes

These tubes are a very large and interesting sub-family of the familiar star tubes. Like the star tubes, each of the 22 star-cut tubes has a serrated opening, and some of them may be used to pipe the same designs as those done with the star tubes. But the basic forms and borders done with star-cut tubes are distinctly different.

The star-cut tubes fall into three groups. The eight cross tubes each have four teeth and pipe deeply grooved borders, four-pointed stars and four-petal drop flowers. A second group of eight tubes have unusual, even fancifully cut openings. They pipe fancy garlands, flat or swirled shells and three- or four-petal flowers. The third group of six star-cut tubes have asymmetric cuts and create boldly carved borders.

THE STAR-CUT TUBES PIPE FLOWERS, TOO. The pretty lilies on the cake at left were piped with an asymmetric star-cut tube. For holiday cakes, they are indispensable. They create the foliage on a miniature Christmas tree and make very realistic poinsettias.

A LOVELY EASTER CENTERPIECE

Shiny poured fondant sets off the curves of this springtime cake and provides a perfect background for decorating. Borders and flowers are piped with asymmetric star-cut tubes.

STEP ONE. Pipe the lilies in advance in royal icing. Follow the directions on page 225, and use tubes 74 and 75 for two sizes. Dry before inserting stamens and paint inner parts of petals with thinned yellow icing. Pipe center star, insert stamens and dry again.

Pipe long leaves with tube 66 in royal icing on wax paper. Dry on curved surface.

STEP TWO. Bake a single-layer tier in a 12″ round pan and one in the basic ring pan with swirl insert. Ice each tier with buttercream, then cover with poured fondant—white on ring tier, yellow-tinted on 12″ tier. Assemble on serving tray or foil-covered cake board.

STEP THREE. Pipe a shell border at base of both tiers with tube 73. See how the shells come out with three deep grooves when piped with this tube. Pipe tube 2 curves and dots on top tier, following indentations of tier. Push a tall taper into cake, then surround it with the smaller lilies and leaves, attaching each with a dot of icing. Attach larger lilies to top of lower tier, using curves in upper tier as guide for placement. Trim with more leaves. Ring tier serves twelve, 12″ tier serves ten.

219

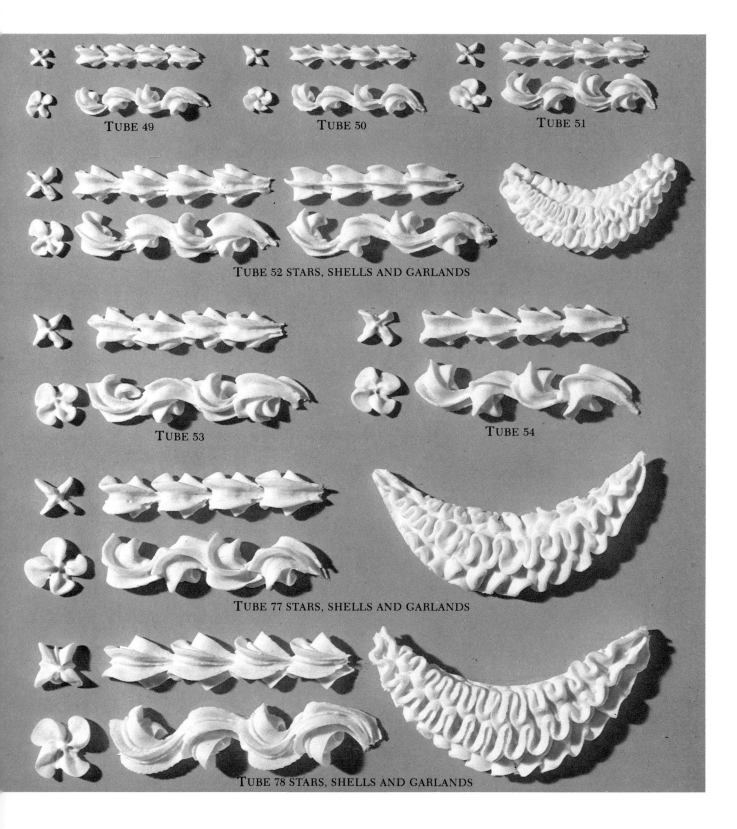

TUBE 49

TUBE 50

TUBE 51

TUBE 52 STARS, SHELLS AND GARLANDS

TUBE 53

TUBE 54

TUBE 77 STARS, SHELLS AND GARLANDS

TUBE 78 STARS, SHELLS AND GARLANDS

THE EIGHT STAR-CUT CROSS TUBES
PIPE SHARPLY CUT FORMS

While they vary somewhat in shape and in the sizes of forms they pipe, all of the cross tubes have four deeply cut teeth in the characteristic cross pattern.

Because their teeth are so few, the shells and curves they pipe are very boldly carved. Hold the tube with the cross straight up for a high center ridge—turn the cross on the bias for a double ridge. A reverse shell border piped with a cross tube shows this effect very clearly.

Garlands piped with the star-cut cross tubes have a deeply ruffled look. The double and triple ruffles look so distinct that they appear to have been piped individually. By holding the tube in different ways you can pipe a double ruffle with a third reverse ruffle at top (see tubes 52 and 77 at left) or a triple ruffle garland with a smoothly curved top (see tube 78).

Tube 78 has four additional little cuts. Curves and shells piped with it have more ornate detail.

ALL OF THE STAR-CUT CROSS TUBES pipe neat four-pointed stars, and very pretty drop flowers in the swirled version. Cluster the flowers on a cake for a bouquet or garland.

The cross tubes combine very well with other tubes in handsome borders. See page 230 for a beautiful example.

AT LEFT, IN ACTUAL SIZE are samples of what each star-cut cross tube can pipe. Experiment with all of them to add variety, speed and dramatic flair to your decorating.

**THE EIGHT STAR-CUT CROSS TUBES
IN ACTUAL SIZE**

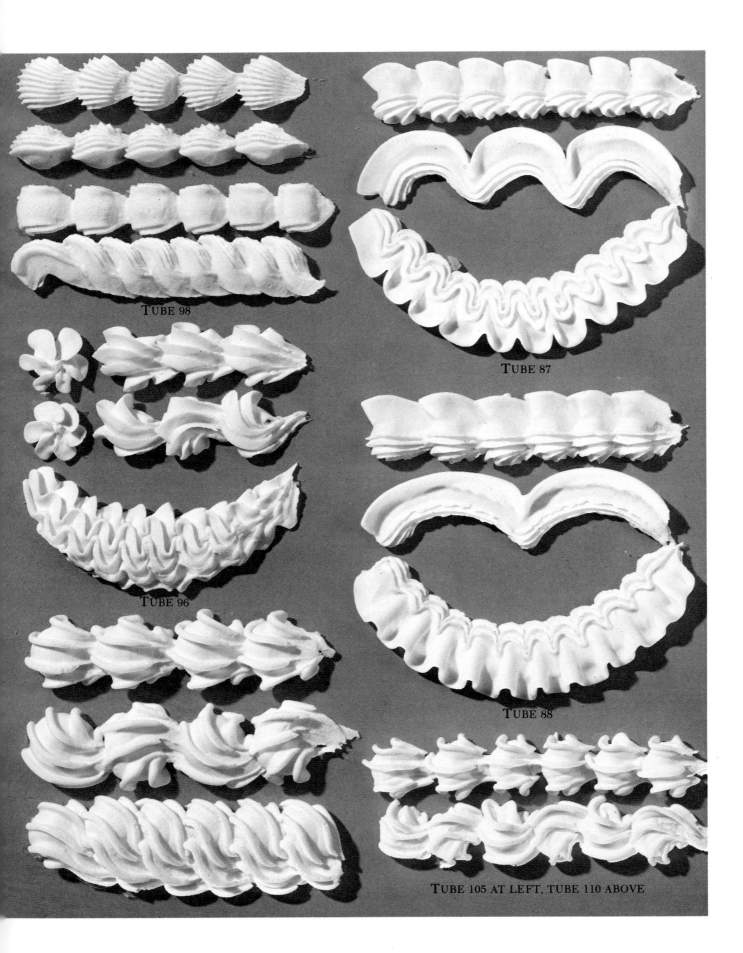

TUBE 98

TUBE 96

TUBE 87

TUBE 88

TUBE 105 AT LEFT, TUBE 110 ABOVE

THE STAR-CUT TUBES WITH
UNUSUALLY ARRANGED TEETH

These eight tubes are included in the star tube section because of their serrated openings. However their teeth are not cut in the even circular order of the star tubes, but rather in unusual, even fanciful arrangements. Each pipes clear distinctive forms.

SAMPLES OF PIPING WITH TUBES 98, 96, 105, 87, 88 and 110 are shown in actual size on the opposite page, with the tubes themselves shown at right.

TUBE 98 COULD BE CALLED A HALF-STAR tube. With the plain curved side down, it pipes a shallow, fan-shaped shell. Hold the tube in different positions for completely different effects. The teeth of tube 96 are cut in a swirled pattern. This tube pipes attractive drop flowers and sculptured borders and garlands.

TUBE 105 AND ITS SMALLER VERSION, tube 110, have square-cut teeth. Try piping shell borders with them, then filling the grooves with contrasting lines piped with a small round tube. The cake on page 230 shows this effect.

TUBES 87 AND 88 HAVE SERRATED OPENINGS combined with straight projections like that of a petal tube. Use them for decorated shells and scallops and rickrack-trimmed garlands.

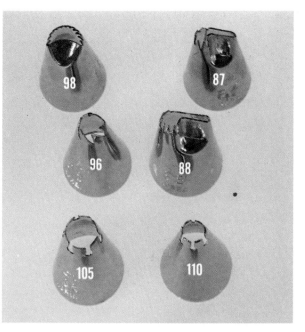

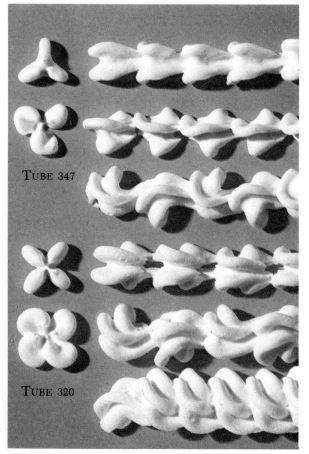

TUBE 347

TUBE 320

TUBES 347 AND 320, shown below, have three and four teeth respectively. Examples of what they pipe, in actual size, are at right. Use their neat three- and four-pointed stars as accents. Borders are very deeply carved. Experiment with them for unusual fleurs-de-lis and other curved forms. Tube 320 makes a pretty drop flower in the swirled version.

Turn to pages 228 and 229 for several striking borders based on forms piped with these tubes.

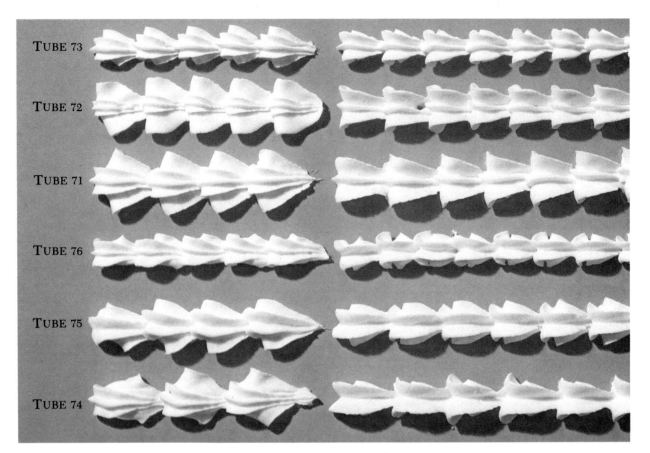

TUBE 73

TUBE 72

TUBE 71

TUBE 76

TUBE 75

TUBE 74

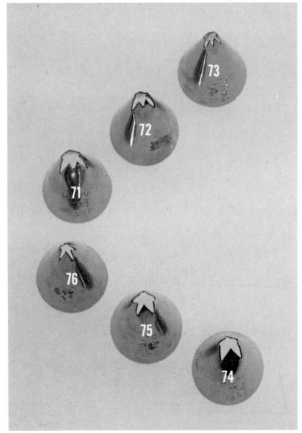

THE SIX STAR-CUT TUBES WITH ASYMMETRICALLY-CUT TEETH

Like the standard open star tubes, each of these star-cut tubes has an opening surrounded by sharply cut teeth. These tubes differ, however, in that their teeth are of uneven sizes and placement. Because of this, any of these tubes will create completely different forms depending on the position in which it is held when piping.

TUBES 74, 75 AND 76 are identical except for size. Each has five teeth arranged in a somewhat distorted star shape. Hold the tube with the two longest teeth up and pipe simple shells or slender pointed petals and leaves. The icing forced through the remaining three teeth will give support to these forms. Turn the tube over to pipe more complex curves, shells and garlands.

TUBES 71, 72 AND 73 have additional cuts to pipe more elaborate forms. Experiment with them. Pipe shells, curves, fleurs-de-lis, garlands. Turn the tubes in different positions, pipe the same forms and see how different they appear.

ABOVE IN ACTUAL SIZE, are samples of what the asymmetric star-cut tubes can pipe. Simple shells are shown with each tube held in two positions. At left tubes pictured in actual size.

224

ASYMMETRICALLY CUT TUBES
PIPE HOLIDAY TRIMS

Tubes 74, 75 and 76 pipe these flowers quickly
and easily. Since the petals are well supported
by icing, the result is a very strong flower. Buttercream or meringue boiled icing may be used,
but royal icing is best for flowers made well in
advance. Pipe spikes on the backs of royal icing
flowers to be used on cake sides, or mount them
on wire stems for bouquets.

PIPE A SCARLET POINSETTIA

Tube 74 makes quick work of piping this realistic
flower of Christmas. On a number 7 flower nail,
pull out four evenly spaced petals, leaving an
open space in the center. Hold the tube with the
two longest teeth up. On top of these, pipe four
more petals, placing them in between the first
four. Then, with light pressure, add five short
petals in a star shape. In the center of the flower,
pipe a cluster of tube 1 green dots. Use the same
tube and yellow icing to pipe dots on top of them.

Vary the size of the flower by piping it with
tubes 75 or 76. Pipe poinsettia leaves with the
same tubes.

PIPE AN EASTER LILY

Pipe this beautiful bloom in three sizes, using
either tube 74, 75 or 76 for petals. Line a 1⅝″
two-piece lily nail with foil. Holding the two
longest teeth up, insert the tube deep into the
nail and pull out three long petals, evenly
spaced, with pointed tips. Pipe three more petals, one between each of the first three. Press a
tube 14 star in the center and push in a circle of
six artificial stamens and a seventh stamen in the
middle. Lift out foil to dry.

PIPE A CHRISTMAS TREE

This realistic little tree makes a cheerful trim for
any holiday cake. Pipe it in royal icing for a
lasting decoration.

Push two marshmallows into an ice cream
cone, then attach a third one for base of tree with
icing. Cover the base with long zigzags piped
with tube 74. Ice the cone, then pipe spaced tube
74 shells on it. This will give the tree a lifelike
irregular shape. Starting at the bottom, pull out
long tube 75 "needles" over the entire cone,
making them shorter as you move up. You'll be
surprised at how quickly the tree takes form.

If you wish, trim the tree with brightly colored
dots of icing piped with a round tube.

TUBE 74

TUBE 76

TUBE 75

TUBE 74

225

TUBES 74 AND 75

WREATH A CHRISTMAS CAKE WITH POINSETTIAS

Snowy poured fondant sets off the scarlet flowers, a fat red candle lights the scene, asymmetric star-cut tubes do the simple decorating.

PIPE THE POINSETTIAS in advance according to the directions on page 225. Pipe poinsettia leaves the same as the flower petals with tube 73. Pipe circles of seven leaves in flower formation. Dry flowers and leaves.

BAKE THE CAKE in a hexagon ring pan. Ice with buttercream, then cover with poured fondant and set on cake board cut to hexagon shape. Pipe the base shell border with tube 75, holding longest teeth down. Crumple foil and insert in hole in center of cake, then set in candle. Pipe tube 14 shells around hole.

ARRANGE LEAF CLUSTERS in a wreath on cake top, attaching each with icing. Pipe a dot of icing on the back of each poinsettia and set on leaf clusters. Add more leaves and flowers to corners of cake at the base. Center the table with your Christmas treat, light the candle and serve to twelve appreciative guests.

MERRY CHRISTMAS AND A HAPPY NEW YEAR!

Center the cake with a Christmas tree and heap little presents around it! This cake is a special delight for children.

MAKE A STAND-UP CHRISTMAS TREE as described on page 225. For presents, dip sugar cubes in red and white thinned royal icing and dry. Tie the presents with tube 1 ribbons.

BAKE, FILL AND ICE a two-layer cake in 12″ hexagon pans. On sides of cake, about 1″ up from base, mark 1″ away from each corner. Connect with corner at top edge for triangular tree shapes. Pipe

tube 73 shell borders at base and top of cake, holding longest teeth down. Pipe the holiday message with tube 2.

DO THE SIDE TREES within marked shapes just as you piped the stand-up tree. First press miniature marshmallows into corners of cake for bases and cover with tube 73 zigzags, then pipe trees. Attach stand-up tree to cake top, then trim all trees with tube 2 balls. Arrange the presents around tree and at base of cake and present your holiday creation to 18 guests.

EYELET EMBROIDERY BORDER begins with a row of tube 347 stars, adds a tube 3 scalloped frame.

LAUREL WREATH. Cover a tube 347 line with tube 74 leaves, finish with tube 3 balls.

ZIGZAG BORDER is piped with tube 98, trimmed with tube 3 scallops and curves.

CORNUCOPIA is formed with tube 98 curves, filled with tubes 30 and 23 drop flowers.

CRISS CROSS BORDER. Pipe a tube 74 rope, cross it with tube 3 and contrasting icing.

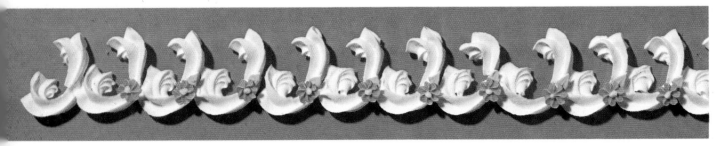

FLOWER SWIRL. Do opposing curves with tube 74, trim with tube 30 flowers, tube 65 leaves.

TOPSY TURVY BORDER. Pipe fleurs-de-lis with tube 320, add tube 27 flowers, tube 65 leaves.

OCEAN WAVE. A series of tube 98 "C" curves, over-piped with contrasting tube 3 curves.

BUTTERFLY IN FLIGHT. Tube 320 curved shells, tube 3 accents. Tube 30 flowers, tube 65 leaves.

SEA SPRAY BORDER begins with tube 347 "S" curves, adds tube 3 accents.

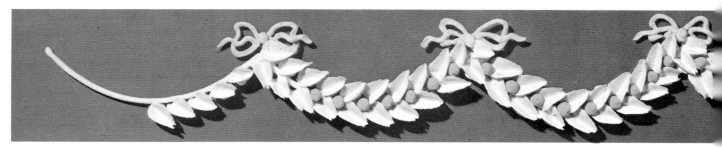

LEAFY GARLAND BORDER. Pipe tube 3 guidelines and bows, tube 74 leaves and tube 3 berries.

230

A SPLENDID CENTERPIECE FOR AN ANNIVERSARY GALA

A cake with all the drama and dignity of a bridal cake—but decorated to celebrate 25 years of wedded life. Star-cut tubes do all the flounced garlands, fleurs-de-lis and curving borders, even the blue forget-me-nots. Beautiful glow roses are heaped on the tiers.

MAKE FLOWERS IN ADVANCE

Pipe the roses and buds with "left-handed" petal tubes 61, 121, 122 and 123. Use pale yellow royal icing for the center petals, white for outer petals. The forget-me-nots are swirled drop flowers done with star-cut tubes 52 and 53, centered with tube 2. Set all flowers aside to dry.

For the between-tiers ornament, remove the base from a numeral ornament, leaving only the plate. Trim with forget-me-nots and purchased silver leaves.

PREPARE AND DECORATE THE CAKE

BAKE AND FILL the two-layer square tiers, 16", 10" and 6". Layers for two lower tiers should be 2" high, for top tier 1½" high. Ice smoothly and assemble on a 20" square cake board with 5" Corinthian pillars and 7" square separator plates.

Starting 1½" in from corners, divide base tier into fifths, mark on sides and drop guidelines for garlands. On middle tier, drop garland guidelines at each corner. Mark curved frame freehand in center of each side. Divide top tier into thirds, starting 3/4" in from each corner. Drop garland guidelines.

ON BOTTOM TIER pipe a tube 105 rope border at base, then trim with tube 2 contrasting string. Pipe ruffled garlands with tube 78, showy fleurs-de-lis with tube 320 and dropped string with tube 2. Do top border with curved shells piped with tube 96.

ON MIDDLE TIER pipe a tube 96 shell border at base. Do frame with tube 78 curves and corner garlands with tube 77. Accent with tube 2 string and write names with the same tube. Pipe a tube 96 curved shell top border.

PIPE BASE SHELL BORDER ON TOP TIER with tube 53, ruffled garlands with tube 52. Finish with tube 2 contrasting string. Pipe the decorative fleurs-de-lis with tube 320, the curved shell top border with tube 88.

FINISH WITH FLOWERS

Trim an anniversary couple ornament with forget-me-nots and secure to cake top. Form a spray of the smallest roses and buds at the base of ornament and accent with forget-me-nots and silver leaves.

Set numeral ornament within pillars and arrange a spray of roses, forget-me-nots and silver leaves on top of middle tier. Add forget-me-nots at points of garlands.

Make a cluster of roses, forget-me-nots and leaves on each corner of base tier. Trim the fleurs-de-lis on tier sides with forget-me-nots and leaves. Serve two lower tiers of this gala cake to 178 guests, top tier to 18. Slices are wedding-cake-size.

CHAPTER THIRTEEN

Pipe Instant Blossoms with Star and Drop Flower Tubes

Piping quick drop flowers is the prettiest use of the star tubes. Both open and closed tubes pipe good-looking flowers. Experiment with the star-cut tubes, too, for interesting petalled forms.

THE DROP FLOWER TUBES compose another large sub-family of tubes. See them and the flowers they pipe on pages 236 through 239. These tubes are basically closed star tubes that have been specifically designed to pipe well-formed drop flowers. Many of them have a center rod, so the flower drops out with an open center to be filled with piped stamens.

TO PIPE A PRETTY FLOWER, hold tube straight up, touch lightly to surface, press, stop, move away. Result is a star-like flower. For swirled petals, turn your hand as far as possible to left. As you press, turn your hand to extreme right, stop pressure and move away. You can pipe hundreds of drop flowers in royal icing on wax paper in just a short time. Then they're ready at any time to arrange in sprays, bouquets and garlands on beautiful cakes.

PINK HARMONY

Cascades, clusters and curving garlands of drop flowers in varied rosy tints circle this delicate bridal cake, set off by baroque curves.

PIPE DROP FLOWERS in advance with star tubes 25, 30 and 34. Pipe tube 2 dots for center stamens and dry thoroughly.

BAKE, FILL AND ICE the three two-layer tiers—16" round, 12" and 9" hexagon shapes. Layers for two larger tiers should be 2" high, for top tier, 1½"

high. Assemble on cake board using 5" Corinthian pillars and 9" hexagon separator plates. On base tier, mark two points, 4" apart, on side, directly below each side of the 12" hexagon tier above. Drop string curves from these marks to define small and large garlands. Cut a pattern from folded paper for frames on sides of middle tier. Frames are 2½" high, 1½" wide.

DECORATE BASE TIER. Pull up a tube 32 inverted upright shell below center of each small garland guideline to form a column. Add scrolls at top with tube 17. Complete bottom border with tube 17 rosettes, then outline entire border with tube 13 zigzags. Pipe a tube 18 reverse shell top border. Pipe tube 17 curved shells at points of garland guidelines. Outline separator plate with tube 13 curves.

ON MIDDLE TIER, pipe a tube 17 shell border at base and top. Pipe curved frame and add scrolls with tube 16. Pipe an inverted upright shell at each corner with tube 22.

ON TOP TIER, pipe a tube 16 shell border at base, reverse shell border at top. Pipe the curved scrolls with the same tube.

ADD THE FLOWERY TRIM. Set cherub and bell ornament on top of cake and cherub musicians within pillars, attaching with icing. Now, working from top to bottom, trim the whole cake with flowers, including ornament and tops of pillars. Attach each flower with a dot of icing. Add a few tube 65 leaves and Pink Harmony is complete. Serve two lower tiers to 178, top tier to 22 guests.

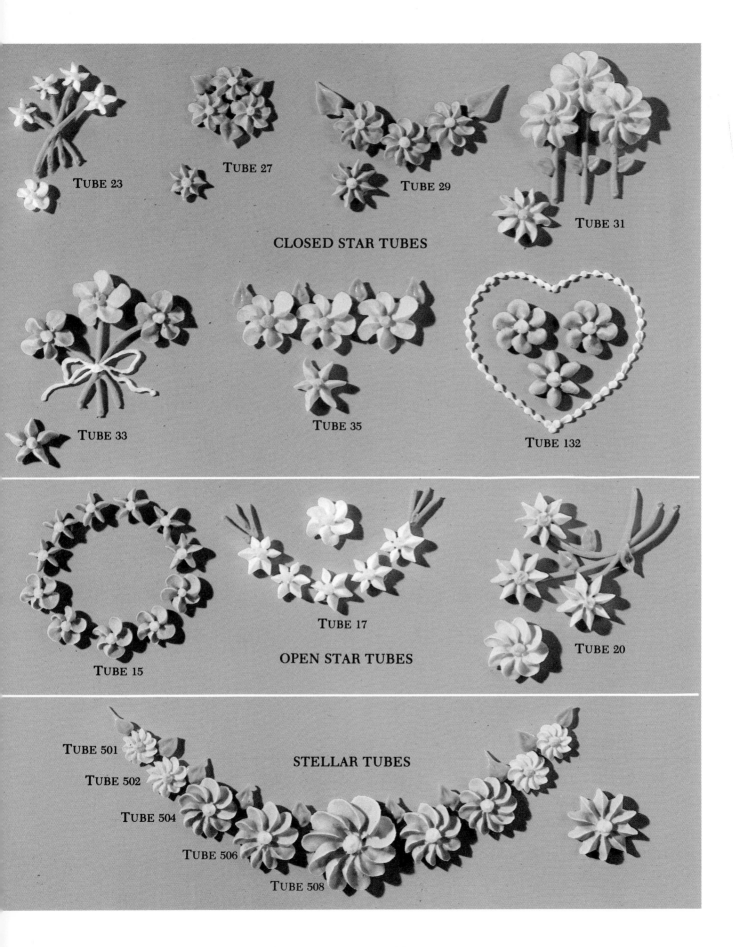

TUBE 23

TUBE 27

TUBE 29

TUBE 31

CLOSED STAR TUBES

TUBE 33

TUBE 35

TUBE 132

TUBE 15

TUBE 17

OPEN STAR TUBES

TUBE 20

TUBE 501

TUBE 502

TUBE 504

TUBE 506

TUBE 508

STELLAR TUBES

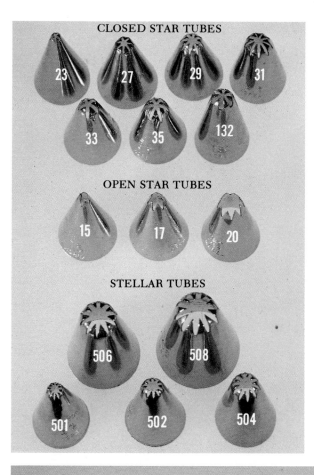

CLOSED STAR TUBES

23 27 29 31

33 35 132

OPEN STAR TUBES

15 17 20

STELLAR TUBES

506 508

501 502 504

STAR TUBE DROP FLOWERS

Study the opposite page to see how sweet the flowers piped with star tubes can be. All are actual size. We put them in little arrangements to give you just a sampling of their decorative possibilities. The flower made with each tube is shown both in its simple star and swirled-petal version.

Experiment with all of the star tubes by piping drop flowers with them. These versatile tubes make piping flowers fun—and very fast!

BELOW: SOME STAR-CUT TUBES make very pretty drop flowers, too. Compose the flowers in many attractive ways to border a cake or add quick, distinctive trims. All are shown actual size.

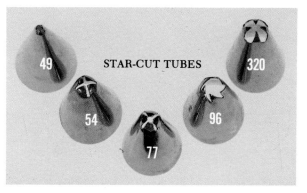

STAR-CUT TUBES

49 320

54 96

77

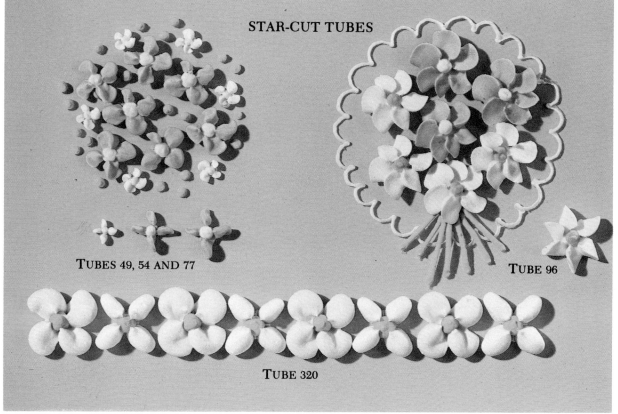

STAR-CUT TUBES

TUBES 49, 54 AND 77

TUBE 96

TUBE 320

THE SMALLER DROP FLOWER TUBES
MAKE DECORATING QUICK AND COLORFUL

Below are shown in actual size the 16 smaller drop flower tubes. Look at the opposite page to see the stunning and varied flowers they pipe—pretty enough to adorn any cake, even a formal wedding cake.

All the tubes have a design similar to closed star tubes, but the teeth are curved even more sharply inward, almost touching in the center, to pipe very clear-cut petals. All of these drop flower tubes, except tubes 106 and 108 have a center rod which keeps the flower centers open and the petals well separated. The number and shape of the teeth make it possible to pipe a really wide variety of decorative blossoms. The range of sizes is wide too—from tiny tube 225 flowers to rather large blossoms piped with tubes 108, 191, 190, 109 and 193.

By piping the flowers in the simple star version, or turning your hand for the swirled version, even more variety is possible.

Tube 220 pipes a surprising bell-shaped flower with a center cone, sometimes called a "pop" flower. Use it only in the star version.

THE CHIEF ADVANTAGE of the use of the drop flower tubes is, of course, the speed in which the flowers are piped. You can pipe dozens and dozens of them in a very short time, then use them lavishly on showpiece cakes. After the flowers are piped, add clusters of tiny dots for stamens, or center each with a small ball. Do it all in assembly-line fashion on wax paper.

THE BEST ICING TO USE for drop flowers is royal icing. Then you can make the flowers ahead and store them in covered boxes to use whenever you need to decorate a pretty cake in a hurry. The flowers will soften somewhat as they rest on the buttercream surface of the cake. A mixture of half royal icing, half meringue boiled icing is also practical for piping drop flowers.

Take advantage of the magic of color, too, when you pipe the flowers. Tinted icing brings out the beauty of the flower forms.

THE SMALLER DROP FLOWER TUBES, ACTUAL SIZE

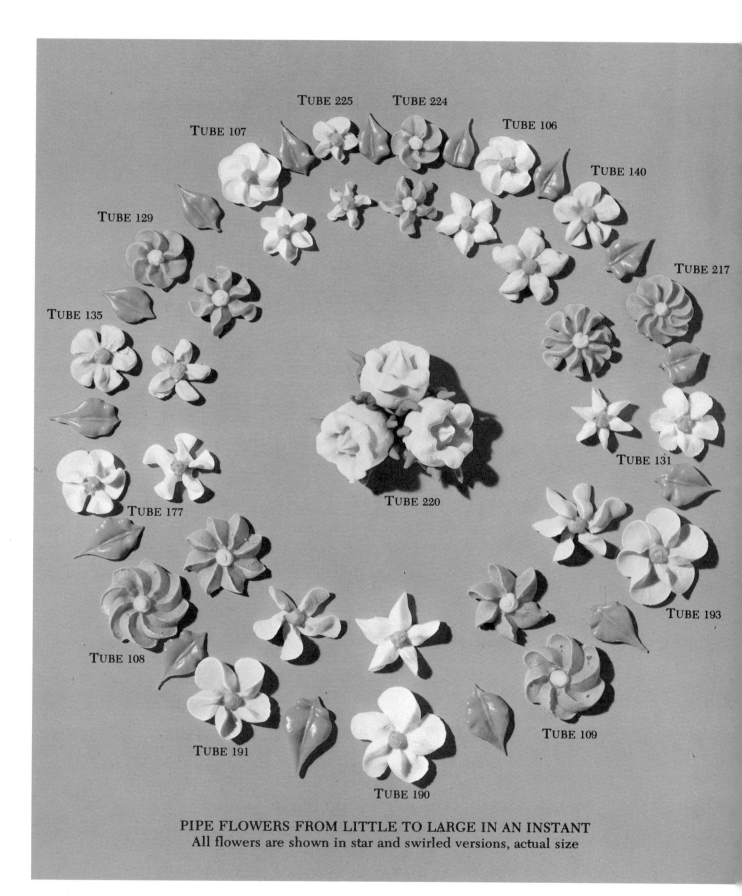

TUBE 225   TUBE 224
TUBE 107   TUBE 106
TUBE 129   TUBE 140
TUBE 135   TUBE 217
TUBE 177   TUBE 131
TUBE 108   TUBE 220   TUBE 193
TUBE 191   TUBE 109
TUBE 190

PIPE FLOWERS FROM LITTLE TO LARGE IN AN INSTANT
All flowers are shown in star and swirled versions, actual size

TEN TUBES THAT PIPE SUPER-LARGE DROP FLOWERS
FOR BOLD DRAMATIC TRIMS

When you'd like to add show-off flower trim to a cake in a hurry, turn to these tubes! They range from large to giant and you'll see some of them in the chapter on giant tubes, pages 288 and 289.

With the exception of tube 194, these tubes are all named by letter. Those with the prefix "1" are even larger than those prefixed "2."

Tube 194 has swirled angled teeth and pipes flowers with swirled petals. Tubes 1F and 2F have notched teeth. Each pipes a flower with five notched petals in the star version, double petals in the swirled version. All the tubes have deeply cut teeth and create clearly formed blossoms with varying numbers of petals. Though the flowers are large, they can be very effective on even small cakes. See the cake on page 240 for an outstanding example.

USE ROYAL ICING to pipe a variety of these super flowers, then store them well covered, for future decorating. For a stand-up bouquet, mount them on florists' wire stems and add royal icing leaves piped on wire. Meringue boiled icing, or a mix-ture of royal and meringue boiled icing, also produce clear-cut blooms. Even buttercream is acceptable to pipe flowers for the cake top. Freeze them, then arrange them on the cake top just before serving.

Experiment with the super-large drop flower tubes for piping borders, too, on very large cakes or tiers. They'll do the decorating in next-to-no time—with ease.

ON THE OPPOSITE PAGE are samples in actual size of flowers piped with super-large drop flower tubes. The flowers on the tips of the stems are done with the swirl method, those on the lower branches are piped with the star method. Mix and match them for beautiful cake trims.

TUBE 194   TUBE 2C   TUBE 2D   TUBE 2E

TUBE 2F   TUBE 1B   TUBE 1C

TUBE 1E   TUBE 1F   TUBE 1G

239

BASKETS OF FLOWERS

PIPE THE BIAS-WEAVE BASKETS in buttercream. Tape Wilton Way III pattern to a stiff surface, cover with wax paper and pipe with tube 44. Freeze. When ready to put on the cake, lay the cut-out pattern on the basket and trim off rough edges with a sharp knife. Pipe flowers ahead with tubes 1E, 1C, 2D, 108, 109 and 129.

BAKE, FILL AND ICE three 6″ square layers, each layer 2″ high. Attach frozen baskets to sides and pipe tube 7 lines at tops and bases. Do bottom shell borders and "S" scrolls on sides with tube 15. Attach flowers and trim with tube 66 leaves. Insert the taper and serve to ten.

A SUNBURST OF FLOWERS

PIPE FLOWERS with tubes 224 and 107 in advance.

BAKE, FILL AND ICE a two-layer 10″ round cake. Divide cake into tenths and mark on top edge.

Mark a 3″ circle in center of top of cake. Lightly mark lines from exact center of cake top to marks on edge. Drop tube 2 string guidelines on cake side for upper scallops. Mark corresponding scallops on cake top.

ALL LINES ARE PIPED with tube 2. Drop vertical lines from string guidelines on cake side to base of cake. Drop a second, lower series of string guidelines from the first series and drop lines from it to base, centering each line between two lines already piped. Do bottom ball border with tube 7, top border with tube 5.

Pipe radiating lines on cake top, from circle to scallops. Pipe along marked lines from circle to points of scallops first. Then pipe a line from circle to center of scallop and fill in on either side. Add tube 2 beading.

Cover all curves with flowers. Trim cupid with flowers and tube 65 leaves. Serve to 14.

241

DROP FLOWER TUBES PIPE THE PRETTIEST BORDERS

Flowers sweeten any cake trim and drop flowers are so quickly piped you can use them in profusion on curving borders. Most drop flower tubes, as members of the star tube family, can be used to pipe the basic structure of the border, too. *All the white shells, curves and garlands in the borders on these pages were piped with tube 106.*

FORM FLOWERY GARLANDS with tubes 224, 225 and 190 blossoms, add tube 3 bows, tube 2 dots.

ACCENT BOLD REVERSE CURVES with flowers piped with tube 190.

PIPE STRONG DOUBLE CURVES, add tubes 224, 225 and 190 flowers, tube 2 buds, tube 65 leaves.

OVER-PIPE CURVED SHELLS with tube 4, trim with sprays of tubes 2, 224 and 225 flowers.

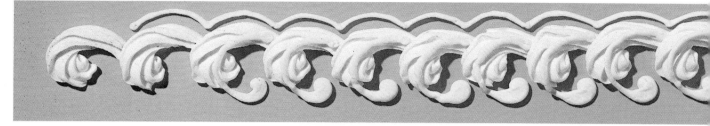

ADD TUBE 3 "C" CURVES to curved shells, finish with a tube 2 scalloped frame.

DAINTY FLOWER SPRAYS are formed of tubes 224 and 225 flowers, tube 2 buds.

TRIM A GARLAND with tube 4 wedding bells, tube 224 flowers and tube 65s leaves.

SET TUBE 190 FLOWERS in swirled oval frames, trim with tube 65s leaves.

Festooned with curving garlands and crowned by a little summer house, Edwardian Garden looks elaborate, but is really quite easy to decorate. Drop flowers in profusion add a beautiful and time-saving touch.

MAKE TRIMS IN ADVANCE

PIPE A VARIETY OF DROP FLOWERS in royal icing with tubes 23, 106, 107, 129, 225, 193, 501 and 504. Pipe centers with tube 1 and dry.

PIPE THE SUMMER HOUSE ORNAMENT. For base, roll gum paste ⅛″ thick and cut a 3½″ circle. Dry. For side arches, tape stiff paper around a juice can, 3″ in diameter. Tape Wilton Way III pattern to it and cover smoothly with wax paper. Pipe the arches in rope border effect with royal icing and tube 13. Note that sides are done in two sections. Dome is piped on half of a 3″ ball mold. Transfer the six curves of the pattern to the *inside* of the mold with a felt tip pen. (This is easily washed off later.) Grease the outside of the mold and pipe the dome on it with tube 13 rope.

Assemble the pieces on the gum paste base with royal icing. Secure a cupid figure inside with icing and trim the ornament with flowers and tube 3 pink hearts.

DECORATE THE CAKE

To give firm support to the tiers, we sugar-molded the base bevel in a 16″ base bevel pan. Dry thoroughly, at least overnight, then ice smoothly with royal icing.

BAKE, FILL AND ICE the tiers. Bottom tier is two layers, one baked in a 12″ round pan and one in a 12″ top bevel pan. Two-layer top tier is baked in an 8″ round pan and an 8″ top bevel pan. Assemble on the sugar-molded base bevel with clear pillars and an 8″ separator plate. Divide both tiers in twelfths and mark for garlands. Drop string guidelines for garlands. On top bevel of base tier, mark scallops to connect the garlands.

DECORATE BASE TIER. Stellar tubes are featured in all decorating. Pipe a tube 501 shell border around outer and upper edges of base bevel. Pipe the fluffy garlands with tube 502, then drape with tube 3 strings. Do bows with tube 2.

On top bevel, pipe garlands and marked scallops with tube 502. Drape garlands with tube 3 string and add fleurs-de-lis below them. Circle pillars with tube 13 shells.

DECORATE TOP TIER. Pipe tube 501 garlands at base of tier and around top bevel. Do top shell border and fleurs-de-lis with the same tube. Drape gar-

lands with tube 2 string.

ADD THE FINISHING TOUCHES. Attach ornament to top of cake with icing and secure sprays of flowers at its base. Cover the garlands at the bottom of the top tier with flowers, then drop double tube 2 strings from separator plate.

Set a little cherub figure within pillars, then cover the scallops on top of base tier with flowers. Add clusters of flowers on base bevel. Trim all flowers with tube 65s leaves. Your elegant little showpiece is complete!

Serve lower tier of Edwardian Garden to 68 guests, upper tier to 30.

CHAPTER FOURTEEN

Leaf Tubes Pipe Beautiful Cake Trims

The leaf tubes are most familiar to the decorator when used for their primary purpose—that of piping leaves. Since these tubes have such a broad range of sizes, leaves can be piped in a size to complement the flowers they trim—from a tiny tube 101s apple blossom to a giant rose piped with tube 127R.

SUIT THE LEAF TO THE FLOWER. Remember you are imitating nature. Observe that roses have smooth oval leaves in groups of three or five. Use a larger leaf tube for the broad wavy leaves of the tulip, a smaller one for the narrow long leaves of the narcissus or lily. Study the plants in your garden, or refer to seed catalogues or flower books. Flowers on your cakes will look more beautiful if they are set off by the proper leaves.

IN ADDITION TO PIPING LEAVES, many other decorative effects can be achieved with leaf tubes. Use tubes in this family to pipe a dainty bluebell or a large dramatic lily. Trim a cake with ferns and field flowers. Use leaf tubes, alone or in combination with other tubes, to pipe dozens of outstanding borders. They can create double ruffles, smooth curves, star-like trims and perky accents that really dress up a cake. A simple leafy vine piped around a cake is one of the most beautiful traditional side trims.

THE LEAF TUBES FALL IN THREE GROUPS. The seven *standard leaf tubes* range from tiny tube 65s to large tube 70. Each pipes deeply veined leaves in variety. The four *super-large leaf tubes,* tubes 112 through 115, are cut the same as the standard leaf tubes, but pipe much larger leaves and dramatic trims. The *Essex leaf tubes*, tubes 326, 349, 352 and 355, pipe grooved or finely veined leaves in small to medium size.

A LEAFY TIER CAKE

The standard leaf tubes are featured in this lovely cake, circled with ruffled leaves.

BAKE AND FILL the two-layer tiers, 10″ and 6″ round. Layers for base tier should be 2″ high, for upper tier 1½″ high. Ice smoothly in buttercream and assemble on cake stand.

BALL BORDERS support the leafy trim. Pipe a row of slightly spaced tube 11 balls around base of lower tier. Pipe all the leaf-tube trim in two-tone icing. Color-stripe the cone with green icing, fill with very pale green icing. Pipe a ruffled tube 70 leaf over each ball, then top each leaf with a tube 8 ball in contrasting color. Pipe a shell-motion border at top of tier with tube 68.

BASE BORDER ON TOP TIER is similar to that on bottom tier. Pipe spaced tube 9 balls around base of tier, cover with ruffled tube 68 leaves and add tube 8 contrasting ball trim. Pipe tube 7 balls around top of tier, add tube 67 leaves and tube 6 contrasting trim. Pipe a 2″ circle with tube 7 in top center of tier and cover it with six tube 68 leaves. Add tube 6 balls between each leaf. Serve this dainty creation to 20.

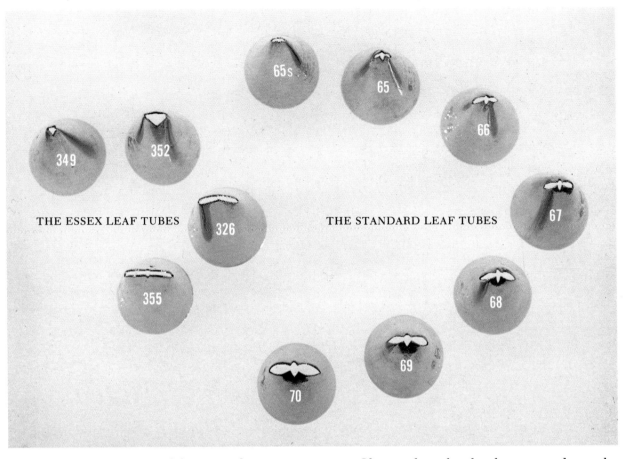

THE ESSEX LEAF TUBES

THE STANDARD LEAF TUBES

The leaf tubes can be used for many decorating purposes, but they are usually used, as their name denotes, for piping leaves. Decorators turn to them again and again to set off piped flowers with natural looking leaves in just the right size.

THE STANDARD LEAF TUBES. This series, from tube 65s to tube 70, consists of seven tubes identical except for size. Each has an opening in a shallow arc shape with pointed ends, and a notch in the center. The pointed ends give the leaves they pipe thin crisp edges. The notch creates the strongly marked center vein of the leaf. The standard leaf tubes can pipe many varieties of leaves—smooth pointed ovals, leaves with ruffled edges, or long slim leaves to set off daffodils, irises or day lilies. Their close range of sizes makes it easy to pipe a leaf in the right size to complement the flower trims.

THE ESSEX LEAF TUBES. Tube 349 and tube 352 are identical except for size. They pipe strongly formed leaves with a deep center groove rather than a vein. Tube 326 pipes a similar, somewhat larger and thinner leaf. Tube 355 pipes the largest leaf in this series with a very fine center

vein. Choose the tube that best reproduces the look of the natural leaf.

HOW TO PIPE A PERFECT LEAF

ALWAYS THIN THE ICING for leaves. Do this by mixing a small amount of piping gel or corn syrup into the icing. Thinned icing will produce perky looking leaves with nice pointed tips.

PRESSURE CONTROL IS IMPORTANT in piping leaves. Hold the tube at a 45° angle. Touch it to the surface and apply light, even pressure. Move the tube along and when the leaf is half formed, stop pressure completely and lift the tube to draw the leaf out to a point.

For long leaves, like those of the daffodil, be sure to keep a light, even pressure as you move along. Stop pressure entirely and lift the tube to form the pointed tip.

For leaves with ruffled edges, use a push-pull motion as you pipe.

PLACE FLOWERS IN POSITION FIRST in almost all cases. Then tuck the leaf tube under the petals and pipe the leaves.

248

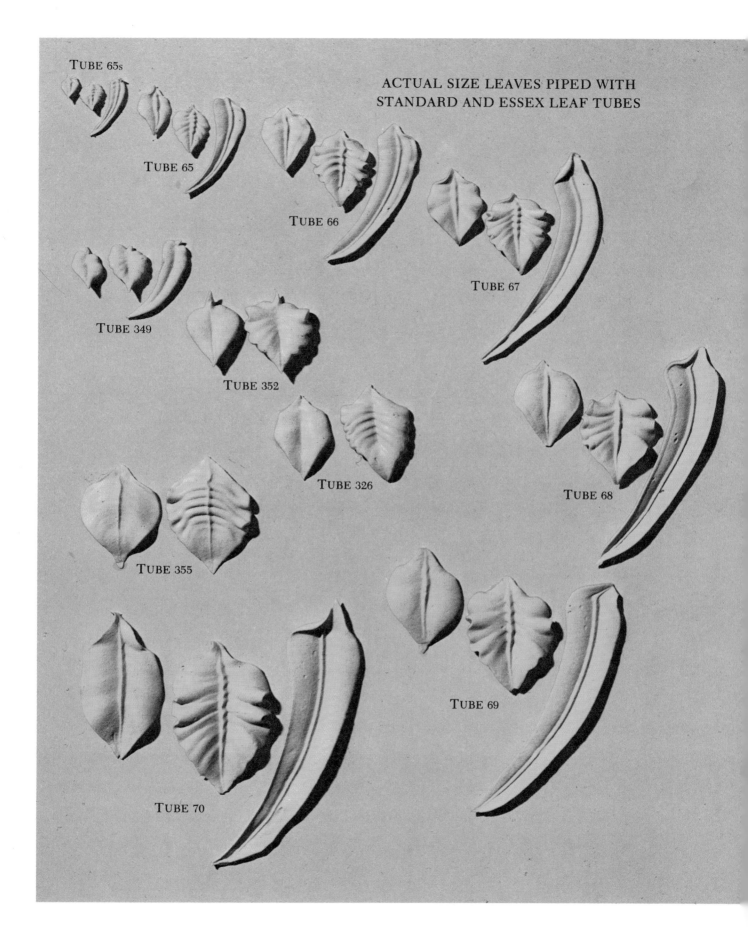

TUBE 65s

TUBE 65

TUBE 66

TUBE 67

TUBE 349

TUBE 352

TUBE 326

TUBE 68

TUBE 355

TUBE 69

TUBE 70

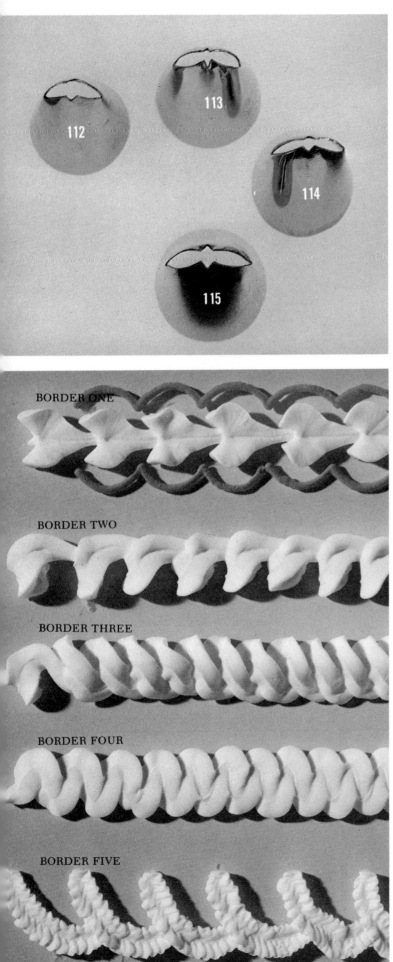

THE SUPER-LARGE
LEAF TUBES

These big tubes, cut exactly like the standard leaf tubes, pipe really big leaves and bold dramatic borders. Tubes 114 and 115 are classified as giant tubes and may even be used to pipe cookie dough, butter or whipped cream in pretty ruffly shapes. See examples on pages 297 and 298.

The super-large leaf tubes are also convenient for piping the long leaves of tulips, daffodils and that tiniest of flowers, the lily of the valley. See page 278 for a beautiful lily of the valley cake. Use thinned icing for piping leaves with these tubes, just as you would when piping with the standard leaf tubes.

AT LEFT, IN ACTUAL SIZE, the super-large leaf tubes. On the opposite page are pictured the leaves they pipe.

PIPE SIMPLE BORDERS
WITH ESSEX LEAF TUBES

Try using a leaf tube just as you would a star tube. You'll be surprised and delighted with the borders you pipe.

BORDER ONE. Use tube 352 and a shell motion for this curvy border. Emphasize the curves with tube 3 scallops.

BORDER TWO. Pipe a row of curved shells with tube 352, holding the tube just as you would when beginning to pipe a leaf.

BORDER THREE. Join shallow "S" curves piped with tube 352 to make a rope border.

BORDER FOUR. It would be hard to tell just which tube piped this interesting interlocked border. It's tube 352 again, this time piping a tight zigzag border.

BORDER FIVE. Use tube 349 and a push-pull motion to create this dainty double ruffled garland border. Drop string guidelines first to define the curves.

250

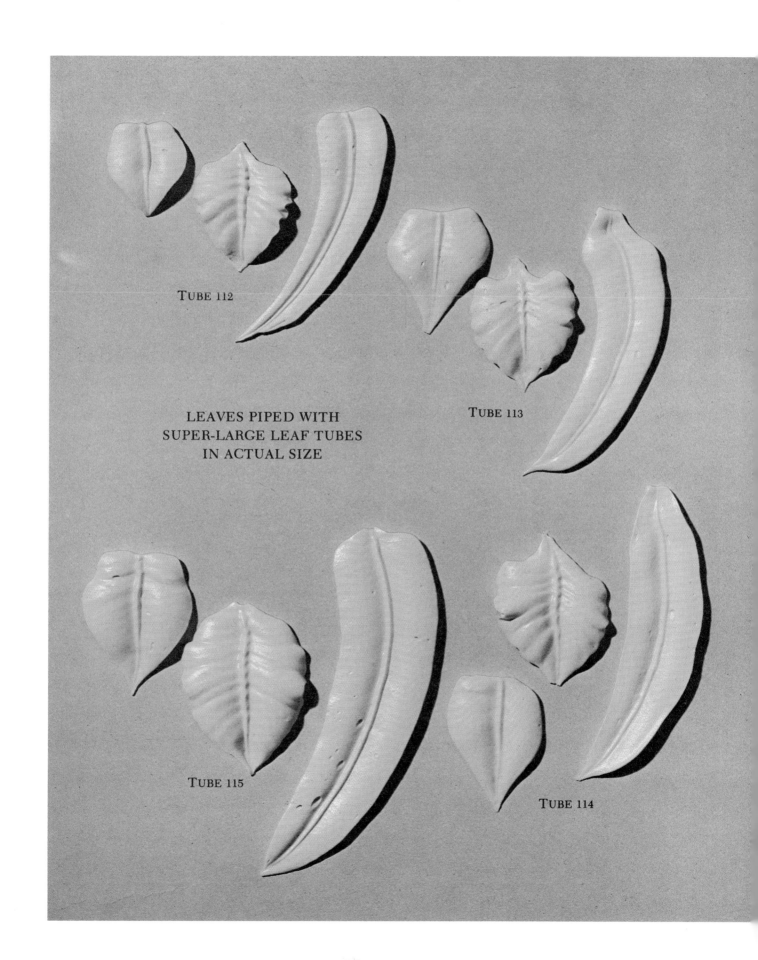

TUBE 112

TUBE 113

LEAVES PIPED WITH
SUPER-LARGE LEAF TUBES
IN ACTUAL SIZE

TUBE 115

TUBE 114

BAGUETTE. Begin by piping four tube 4 balls. Add a single ball separated by a tube 2 dot. Pipe a quartette of tube 66 leaves and finish with a tube 2 spike in the center. Continue around top or side of cake.

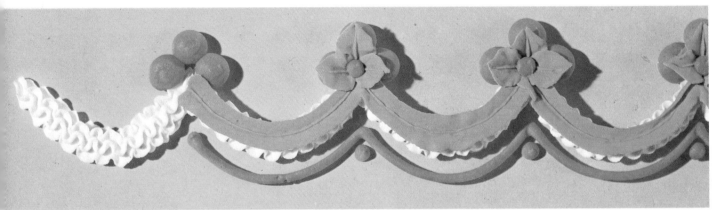

BUNTING. Drop guidelines, then pipe tube 16 zigzag garlands. Cover garlands with tube 66 curves and pipe tube 4 balls at the points. Pipe tube 66 leaves over balls, centered with a tube 4 dot. Use tube 4 again for strings and dots.

CRESTED HEARTS. Pipe a row of tube 67 leaves. Use tube 4 for all white trim. Frame leaves with curves and add fleurs-de-lis above them. Finish the border with double zigzags and balls below hearts. This border is very showy on the top edge of a cake.

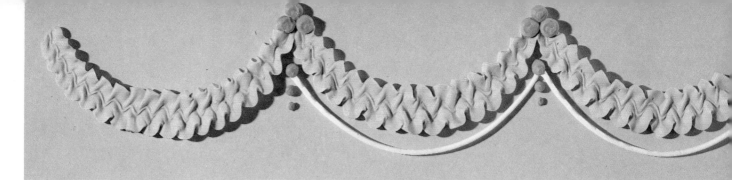

DOUBLE RUFFLE. Drop guidelines, then pipe zigzag garlands with leaf tube 67. Top the garlands with tube 4 balls. Accent the curves by dropping tube 3 string below them and adding dots piped with the same tube.

LEAVES AND BERRIES. Drop string guidelines for curves, then cover with tube 66 leaves, half pointing left, half right. Pipe tube 4 berries and tie a bow in the center with tube 3. For a wedding cake, pipe it all in white.

FLOWERING VINE. Pipe a wavy tube 3 vine around side or on top of cake. Add short stems, then tube 66 ruffled leaves in groups of three. Add clusters of made-ahead drop flowers piped with tube 33.

CHAIN OF HEARTS. Pipe heart shapes with two touching tube 20 shells. Continue around cake, then go back and trim with tube 66 leaves. Finish with tube 4 dots. This quick-to-do border is pretty on cake top or base.

HOLLY LEAVES CROWN A CHRISTMAS ELF

Here's the merriest little helper that ever came to a Christmas party! He's all dressed up in a ruffled collar with a red bow atop his holly hair.

PIPE THE HOLLY IN ADVANCE

Realistic holly leaves are easy to pipe and are the favorite trims on holiday cakes. Use boiled icing or a mixture of royal and boiled icing and tube 70. Pipe the leaves on squares of wax paper and pull out the points with a damp artists' brush. Lay the squares on or within a curved form to dry.

DECORATE THE CAKE

Once the holly leaves are made, the decorating is fast and easy.

BAKE A SINGLE-LAYER 8″ round cake and one in a 6″ ball pan. Ice side of 8″ cake green, top white. Set on serving tray. Cover the side with stripes piped with ribbon tube 2A. Pipe a tube 8 ball border at bottom, a tube 6 border at top.

FILL THE BALL CAKE and trim base to level it. Set on 3″ cardboard circle. Ice thinly, using flesh-color icing for face and lower head, green for top and back of head. Mark circles for nose and cheeks. Use the star fill-in method and tube 14 to cover ball. First do cheeks and nose, piping star upon star for rounded effect. Fill flesh-color area with stars, then pipe tube 10 balls for eyes and flatten with a finger-tip. Pipe a tube 4 smile.

ASSEMBLE ROUND AND BALL CAKES. Fit a decorating cone with giant tube 127R. Stripe inside of cone with a line of red icing piped with tube 10. Fill with white icing and pipe the double ruffle collar. Glaze eyes with corn syrup. Attach the dried holly leaves with icing and finish with a ribbon bow. Cut ball cake into twelve servings. Round cake serves five guests.

BORDER ONE

BORDER TWO

ADD LEAF TUBE TRIMS
TO PUFFY GARLAND BORDERS

The simplest straight garland border becomes a striking decoration when you trim it with leaf tubes and contrasting icing. Either border may be piped at top or bottom of cake.

BORDER ONE. Pipe a row of puffy garlands around cake with star tube 17. Go back and pipe two slender curved leaves on each garland with tube 66—one pointing left, one right. Add tube 3 twirls in contrasting color.

BORDER TWO. Pipe a row of puffy tube 17 garlands. Frame each with a ruffled tube 67 leaf, using a push-pull motion. Accent with elongated tube 4 bulbs. Just as pretty all in white.

LEAF TUBES PIPE
DELICATE FLOWERS

BLUEBELL. For this fragile flower, improvise your own lily nail. Insert a ¼" dowel rod into the small opening of tube 10, to serve as stem. Line the tube with foil. Thin royal icing with piping gel—we used 1½ teaspoons to one cup of icing.

Insert tube 65 deep into nail, and pull out five petals, using light pressure. Pull out three tube 1 stamens. Lift foil out of nail to dry flower. Turn flower on its face and pipe a five-pointed calyx with tube 1 on back. Dry again.

EASTER LILY. While this flower may be piped with star-cut tubes as shown on page 225, lilies made with standard leaf tubes have thinner, more delicate petals. The leaf tubes, with their wide range of sizes, give you more flexibility, too, in piping lilies from tiny to large.

Line a 1⅝" two-piece lily nail with foil and thin royal icing with piping gel—about 1½ teaspoons of gel to a cup of icing. Insert tube 68 into nail and pipe three evenly spaced petals, pulling them out over the edge of the nail to points. Pipe three more petals, one between each. Clip off tips of artificial stamens. Pipe a tube 4 dot in center of flower and push in a circle of six stamens. For center stamen, insert a short length of fine florists' wire. Pipe three tube 1 dots on center stamen and top the other six stamens with the same tube. Lift out foil to dry.

For a specially realistic touch, pipe the six petals, dry and paint the center of the lily with thinned yellow icing. Then add the stamens.

DAINTY BLUEBELLS
WREATHE A BIRTHDAY CAKE

PIPE THE BLUEBELLS just as described above with tube 65 and thinned royal icing. Set aside to dry.

BAKE AND FILL a two-layer cake baked in 12" petal-shaped pans. Be sure layers are about 2" high. Ice smoothly in buttercream. Lightly mark an 8" circle on the cake top by pressing with a cardboard cake circle.

ON SIDE OF CAKE, at each curve of petal shape, pipe a spray of tube 1 stems. *Tube 16 does all the two-tone trim.* To achieve this delicate color effect, drop tube 16 into a decorating cone, then, with a second cone, pipe a double tube 7 line of pastel green icing on the inside of the first cone. Fill with white icing. Pipe a shell border around base of cake.

The shape of the cake guides the decorating. At each indentation on side, pipe an upright shell. Starting just below shell, pipe curved scrolls as pictured. Over-pipe the scrolls, then connect them with a rosette.

PIPE SCROLLS AT TOP EDGE and over-pipe, following curves of cake. Pipe rosettes at center. Using marked circle as guide, pipe eight curved scrolls in scallop effect.

Attach pairs of bluebells in spaces between scallops. Secure bluebells to side of cake and pipe slender tube 65s leaves. This dainty birthday tribute serves 24.

258

EASTER LILY . . . A CAKE FOR A SPRINGTIME WEDDING

This tiered confection fairly sings spring! Snowy curves, garlands and draped strings make a perfect setting for the Easter lilies.

PIPE FLOWERS IN ADVANCE

Pipe the lilies as described on page 256 in royal icing and three sizes. For big lilies on base tier use tube 70 and a 2¼″ two-piece lily nail. For lilies on middle tier, use a 1⅝″ nail and tube 67. For ornament and top tier, pipe flowers with tube 66 in a 1¼″ nail. When flowers are dry, pipe royal icing spikes on backs of eight of the smallest lilies for tier side. Mount about eight of the smallest lilies on calyxes and wire stems for ornament. Pipe tube 65 leaves on wire stems.

MAKE THE ORNAMENT

Form heavy florists' wire in the shape of a heart, about 4″ high. Twist together the ends of the wire extending from point of heart. Wrap wire with white florists' tape. Make a hole in the plate from a petite ornament base with a heated nail. Position hole near one edge of plate. Attach stemmed lilies and leaves to heart by wrapping with florists' tape. Assemble ornament when cake is on the reception table.

DECORATE THE CAKE

BAKE AND FILL the two-layer tiers—15″ petal shaped, 10″ and 6″ round. Make layers for two lower tiers 2″ high, the layers for top tier 1½″ high. Ice smoothly and assemble on an 18″ cake board. Use clear pillars and 12″ and 6″ separator plates. Divide middle tier in twelfths and mark about 1″ down on side. Divide top tier in eighths and mark 1″ up from base on side.

DECORATE BASE TIER. The petal shape of the tier serves as a guide for decorating. Pipe a boldly curved reverse shell border at bottom with tube 2D. Pipe a tube 16 fleur-de-lis in each indentation on cake side. Pipe a zigzag garland with tube 16 on each side curve, starting and ending about 1″ away from indentations. Repeat twice more to bring garland up to top of cake. Drape garlands with double tube 3 strings, then drop three parallel strings below them. Pipe tube 13 stars at ends of string. Pipe curved scrolls on top edge of cake with tube 16. Circle pillars with tube 13 shells.

ON MIDDLE TIER, pipe a tube 19 curved shell border at base. Pipe fleurs-de-lis at marks with tube 16 and do reverse shell top border with same tube. Pipe tube 3 strings and tube 13 stars.

ON TOP TIER, pipe tube 16 zigzag garlands from mark to mark. Trim with tube 3 string, tube 13

stars. Pipe tube 16 curved shells at tier top. Note: it is best to pipe the string suspended from base of tier when the cake is in place at the reception.

ADD FLOWER TRIM. On top tier pipe tube 3 curved stems and tube 65 leaves above each garland. Push in spiked lilies on mounds of icing. Secure lilies on top of middle tier and add tube 65 leaves. Pipe eight tube 4 curved stems on top of base tier, pipe tube 65 leaves and attach largest lilies. Set ornament plate on top of cake and push wire stem on flowered heart through hole and into cake. Secure a petite bridal couple to plate in front of heart. Easter Lily is complete!

Serve two lower tiers to 110, top tier to 16.

There's no prettier use of the leaf tubes than piping ferns. Their lacy open foliage makes an especially graceful cake trim. Standard leaf tubes pipe them on this cake quickly and easily in two varieties and do the field flowers and borders too.

Nature's colors are used for the decorating. Tint buttercream in pastel blue-green and yellow-green and in a deeper yellow-green. Tint very small amounts of icing in bright orange, yellow and green for the flowers and stems.

BAKE AND FILL a two-layer 9″ x 13″ sheet cake. Ice smoothly in buttercream and set on cake board. Starting about 1½″ in from corners, divide top of cake into sixths on long sides, thirds on shorter sides. Mark about 1″ in from edge for scallops.

Use giant leaf tube 115 for the ruffled base border. Color-stripe the cone in bright green and fill with yellow-green icing. The easy way to do this is to pipe the stripe on the inside of the cone with tube 9. Dig one pointed end of the tube into the base of the cake, other end of the tube pointing up at a 45° angle. Apply even pressure as you move along. *Do not* move your hand up and down as you would when piping a petal tube ruffle—the leaf tube forms the ruffle by itself. You'll want to use this border often, on many types of cakes.

MARK CURVED LINES on cake top to define yellow-green ferns. Pipe stems for flowers and blue-green ferns with tube 3.

Do yellow-green ferns first. Starting at top of fern, pipe short leaves with tube 67 on either side of marked line. Increase pressure as you move down the fern to pipe larger leaves. Pipe a curled frond at top.

Pipe tube 65 ruffled leaves with a push-pull motion on stems of blue-green fern. Make the leaves longer as you move to base of fern.

PIPE THE FIELD FLOWERS with leaf tubes, too. For yellow flowers, pipe a tube 66 leaf on cake top. Cover it with three over-lapping leaf shapes. Add tube 3 sepals, blending them into the stems.

For orange flower, pipe a circle of nine over-lapping curved petals with tube 66. Heap tube 3 dots in the center and add tube 65 slender leaves to stems of all flowers.

FRAME THE PICTURE with tube 66 scallops, piping from mark to mark. Finish with a tube 15 top shell border. Serve this charming treat to 24.

DECORATIVE WAYS WITH LEAVES

MOUNT LEAVES ON STEMS to add to a bouquet or ornament. Lay a length of florists' wire on wax paper. Anchor the tip of the wire with a dab of icing, then pipe the leaf right on the wire in royal icing. Vein of the leaf will rest on the wire. Dry, then peel off wax paper.

FOR A WIRED FERN, fit a decorating cone with tube 3 and fill with royal icing. Push a length of florists' wire through the tube and into the cone. Exert even pressure as you pull out the wire, curving as you pull. Lay the coated wire on wax paper and pipe royal icing leaves on either side of it, making them longer as you go down to base of fern. Use any small leaf tube. Dry, then remove the wax paper.

CURVE LEAVES for a natural look. Use royal icing or a mixture of royal and boiled icing. Pipe the leaves on squares of wax paper, then lay the squares on or in a curved surface to dry.

CHAPTER FIFTEEN

The Straight Ribbon Tubes

This family of simple tubes does just what its name denotes—pipes ribbons of icing. The ribbon tubes are divided into two sub-groups. The *curved ribbon tubes* pipe ribbons with up-turned, curled edges. Chapter Sixteen, starting on page 274, shows many of the magical effects these tubes can produce. This chapter is devoted to the *straight ribbon tubes*.

The straight ribbon tubes have simple slot-shaped openings, either smooth or grooved on one or both sides to give a texture to the ribbons they pipe. They come in a good range of sizes to pipe trims from tiny to large. A charming characteristic of the decorating done with these tubes is its trim tailored look.

Straight ribbon tubes can curve around tiers to finish the edges neatly, stripe the sides of a cake, pipe precise borders, lattice and even simple flowers. But these straight tubes are turned to most often for piping baskets. They are even called the "basket weaving tubes." Leaf through this chapter to see some versions of pretty baskets piped with these tubes, as well as more surprising and unusual decorations.

A BOUNTIFUL BASKET
FOR THEIR FOURTH ANNIVERSARY

Fruit and flowers are the favored gifts for a couple celebrating four years of wedded life. Straight ribbon tubes weave the basket and the fringed place mat, border the cake and pipe the perky daisies.

MAKE TRIMS IN ADVANCE. The luscious fruit heaped in the basket is hand modeled from marzipan. The pineapple is a rounded cylinder, 3″ high, scored with a stick. Roll out green-tinted marzipan and cut oval leaves 1″ long. Form into a crown by brushing with egg white, brush crown with egg white and press to pineapple.

To make the apples, roll red-tinted marzipan into a cylinder ¾″ in diameter. Cut into 1″ pieces and roll between your hands into balls. Indent with a stick and press a clove into each. To make the grape cluster, cut an oval base from rolled marzipan, 3″ long, 1½″ wide. Place over the edge of an inverted pan covered with wax paper. Model small balls of marzipan and attach to base with egg white. Dry all the fruit on wax paper, glaze with corn syrup glaze and dry again.

Pipe the perky daisies in royal icing. Pipe eight petals with straight ribbon tube 46 and fill center with tube 2 dots. Dry within curved surface for a natural look..

Cut a 2″ x 3″ card from colored paper and print message on it with tube 1.

BAKE AND FILL the cakes, a two-layer 10″ square and a two-layer 6″ round. Ice square cake with chocolate buttercream. Weave the placemat on top with tube 45 exactly as you would a basket. (See page 265.) Start 1″ in from edge of cake and leave edges "fringed." Use tube 45 again for base border in rope effect and double scallops on top edge of cake.

Ice round cake thinly. See page 265 for method and weave basket, piping vertical lines with tube 44, horizontal strokes with tube 45. Pipe top edge and handle with tube 6 bulbs.

PUT EVERYTHING TOGETHER. Set basket on square cake and arrange fruit and flowers, securing with a little icing as necessary. Attach card at handle and surprise the happy anniversary couple. Present the basket cake to them, and cut the square cake into 20 servings.

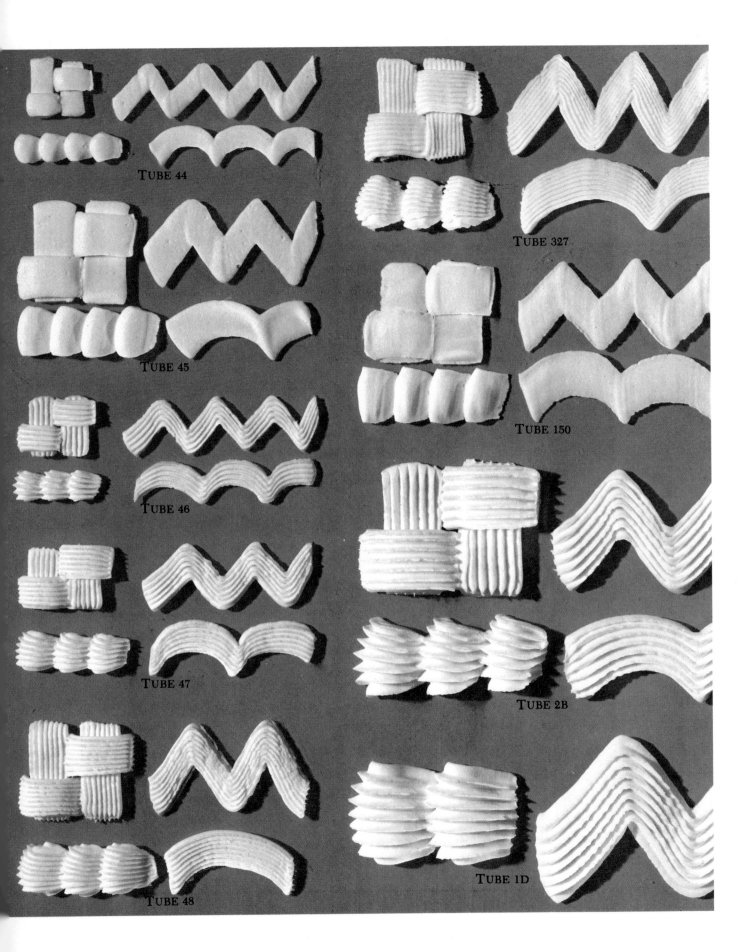

TUBE 44

TUBE 45

TUBE 46

TUBE 47

TUBE 48

TUBE 327

TUBE 150

TUBE 2B

TUBE 1D

264

THE STRAIGHT RIBBON TUBES
PIPE TAILORED TRIMS

The straight ribbon tubes are fun to experiment with because everything they pipe has such a neat trim appearance. Zigzags look like rickrack, curves are flat and even. Try them in some of the motions you'd usually use with a star tube. They'll pipe tidy shell borders and unusual curved shells as you can see on the cake on page 262. These tubes are especially useful for decorating a cake for a man.

Tubes 44, 45 and 150 have smooth openings, tubes 48 and Essex tube 327 have openings with notches on both sides. The others pipe smooth or textured ribbons, depending on which side of the tube is up. Tubes 150 and 327 are different from other straight ribbon tubes in having their openings placed on a slant. This makes it somewhat easier to pipe curves. Tube 1D is classified also as a giant tube, but can often be used on cakes of moderate size.

AT LEFT are samples in actual size of forms piped by the straight ribbon tubes. At right are the tubes, pictured in actual size.

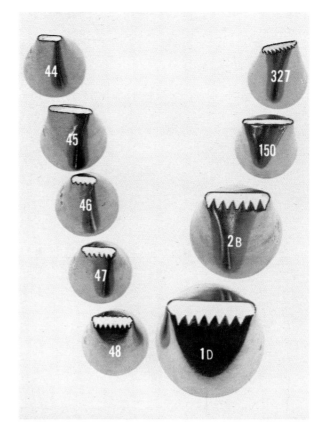

WEAVE A BASKET
WITH STRAIGHT RIBBON TUBES

Basket weaving is easy to do and never fails to bring forth admiration for its realistic effect. For this example, tube 46 was used. We picture the steps in actual size.

Pipe a smooth vertical line with notched side of tube held against the surface. Cross the line with short even strokes, holding the tube with smooth side against the surface for a textured effect. Keep the spaces between strokes about the width of the stroke.

Pipe a second vertical line and cross with short strokes. Continue piping vertical lines and horizontal strokes until the basket is complete. Vary the effect by using straight ribbon tubes in different sizes, or by piping the vertical lines with a round tube in an appropriate size.

TIPS ON BASKET WEAVING. For this technique to appear at its best, it is essential that the spaces be uniform and the vertical lines completely true. Mark the side of the cake at intervals to guide you in piping the lines, and work rhythmically.

For a basket whose base is smaller than its top diameter, remember that the lines must be set closer at the bottom in a radiating effect.

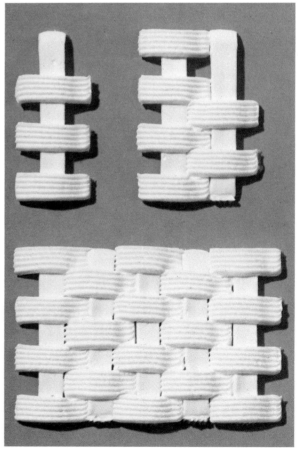

A golden cake for a golden party to honor the couple who have been married fifty years!

MAKE TRIMS IN ADVANCE

TAPE PATTERNS FOR DOUBLE HEARTS to a 14″ curved form and tape wax paper smoothly over them. Pipe hearts with tube 46 and royal icing, edge with tube 2 beading. When dry, join hearts with icing. Tape pattern for lattice hearts to a 10″ curved surface and cover with wax paper. Lay a length of stiff florists' wire down center of heart, end extending about 2″ below point of heart. Tape end of wire to steady it and pipe lattice and heart with tube 46 and royal icing. Tape "50" pattern to 10″ curved surface, cover with wax paper and pipe with tube 5. Dry, then attach to dried lattice with icing.

Pipe roses with tube 101. You will need 50 for base tier. Pipe larger roses and buds with tubes 103, 104, 124 and 127. Dry all roses.

DECORATE THE TIERS

BAKE TWO-LAYER TIERS—18″, 14″ and 10″ round. Layers for two lower tiers should be 2″ high, for 10″ tier, 1½″ high. Also bake two 6″ round layers, 2″ high for basket. Fill and ice the three tiers, then assemble. Set 18″ tier on a 24″ sturdy cake board. Secure 14″ tier to a 14″ separator plate, then set on base tier. Place 10″ tier on a 10″ separator plate and assemble with lower tiers with clear plastic legs. Chill the filled 6″ layers, then taper to a 5″ diameter at base. Ice and secure to 6″ separator plate.

DECORATE BOTTOM TIER. Divide tier into fiftieths and mark midway on side. Do this by first dividing into tenths, then making further divisions. Pipe a tube 1D ribbon around base of cake, a tube 1B ribbon on top of tier at edge and one joining it on side. To pipe ribbons on such a large tier, place cake on a turntable and have a helper slowly turn it as you pipe. Pipe a tube 127 ruffle around base of cake, letting it rest on cake board. Edge ribbons with tube 3 beading and drop tube 2 strings and dots over ribbon at bottom. Pipe double tube 2 strings from mark to mark on side.

DECORATE TWO UPPER TIERS, using tube 2B for ribbons, tube 125 for ruffles, tube 2 for string.

MAKE HANDLE FOR BASKET. Form stiff florists' wire into an arch using Wilton Way III pattern. Tape ends to a stiff surface covered with wax paper. Pipe a tube 7 royal icing line on wire, then one on either side of it. When dry, turn over and pipe a line on wire again. Weave the basket by piping tube 5 vertical lines and tube 48 horizontal strokes. Pipe a tube 14 rope border at bottom, a tube 16 border at top. Insert ends of handle into basket on mounds of icing. Pipe crisscross lines over it with tube 2. Add a ribbon bow.

COMPLETE WITH FLOWER TRIMS. Fill basket with roses first. Wrap wires on lattice hearts with floral tape and insert in cake in front of clear legs. Attach double heart to tier side with icing, propping if necessary with pieces of toothpick. Write names with tube 2 and trim the hearts with rosebuds. Attach roses to side of base tier within string curves. Trim with tube 65 leaves. Arrange roses on tiers and pipe tube 67 leaves.

Serve wedding cake-sized pieces to 288. Present the basket to the anniversary couple.

DAINTY PLACE CARD BASKETS

Pipe handle using Wilton Way III pattern the same way as you did the large handle, with tubes 4 and 1. Grease an Australian Basket nail and pipe the basket on it with tubes 3 and 46. Add tube 13 borders. Remove from nail and fill with marshmallows and icing. Attach handle and heap with roses and leaves.

REPEATED BORDERS TRIM A PRETTY BIRTHDAY CAKE

Rhythmic borders piped with straight ribbon tubes are the appealing trim on this festive cake. Measure the cake carefully to achieve a neat precise look.

BAKE, FILL AND ICE a 10″ round, two-layer cake. Make sure layers are about 2″ high. Divide cake into sixteenths and mark on top edge. Lightly mark top of cake with a card from center to marks. On each of these lines make marks 1″, 2″ and 3″ in from edge to guide top trim. Using marks on top edge as guides, mark side 1″ up from base.

PIPE A TUBE 16 bottom shell border. Drape tube 150 curves over it from mark to mark. Above curves, pipe tube 48 scallops. Above them pipe tube 47 zigzags. Trim with tube 2 dots and print birthday message with the same tube.

DO SHELL BORDER on top edge of cake with tube 16. Top trim mirrors trim on side. Pipe tube 150 curves from mark to mark, then tube 48 scallops and tube 47 zigzags. Finish with tube 2 dots and fleurs-de-lis. Insert a cluster of birthday candles and serve to 16, using borders to indicate slices.

TIE UP A SHOWER CAKE WITH RIBBON BORDERS

Dainty drop flowers trim a cake for a bridal shower. Edge the heart-shaped tiers with ribbons piped with straight ribbon tubes.

DO THE FLOWERS IN ADVANCE with tubes 224 and 225 and royal icing. Pipe centers with tube 2.

BAKE AND FILL THE TIERS—a 12″ two-layer heart and a 6″ single-layer heart. Ice smoothly and assemble on a heart-shaped cake board. Place doilies on the board to give a dainty touch. Pipe a tube 1D ribbon around base of lower tier, then a tube 6 bulb border. Edge ribbon with tube 2 beading and trim with tube 2 strings and dots. Pipe strings and dots above the ribbon and more strings and dots at top of tier. Pipe a tube 1D ribbon on top of tier at edge. Trim with tube 2 beading, scallops and dots.

ON 6″ TIER, use tube 2B for ribbon, tube 2 for string, scallops, dots and beading. Pipe the two wedding rings with tube 2 and tie a bow with the same tube. Finish this pretty treat with the drop flowers and tube 65s leaves. Lower tier serves 24, top tier three.

269

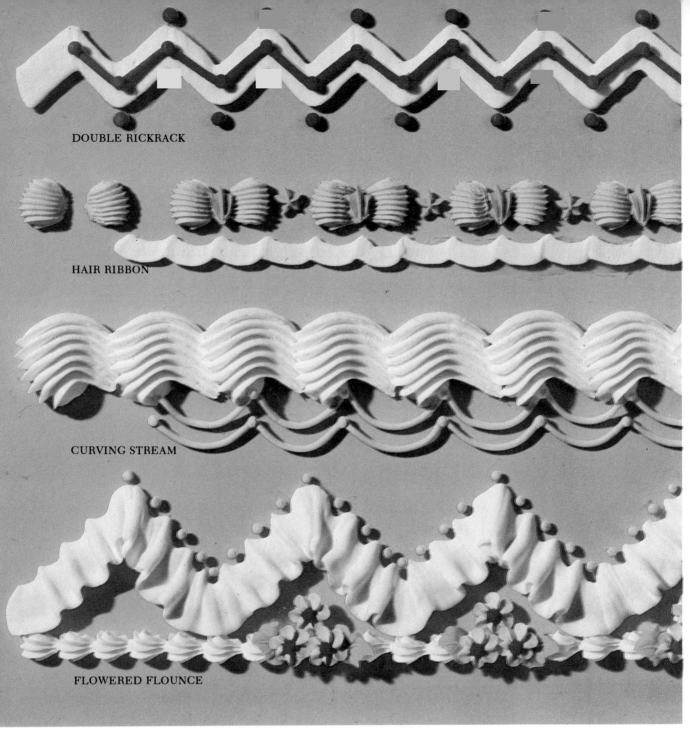

DOUBLE RICKRACK

HAIR RIBBON

CURVING STREAM

FLOWERED FLOUNCE

STRAIGHT RIBBON TUBES PIPE NOVEL BORDERS

Here are four quick-to-do borders done with straight ribbon tubes, all shown in actual size.

DOUBLE RICKRACK. Mark the side of the cake every 1″, and lightly mark a 1″ strip for the depth of the border. Use tube 45 to pipe rickrack from mark to mark. Pipe red rickrack and balls with tube 4.

HAIR RIBBON. Make a series of marks every 1½″. Pipe facing shells on either side of marks with tube 48. Pipe white scallops below shells with tube 44, then join the shells with a tube 14 upright shell. Pipe a star between each "bow".

CURVING STREAM. Pipe a row of curved shells with tube 2B. Drop tube 3 double strings below the shells, then add tube 3 dots.

FLOWERED FLOUNCE is dramatic at base of the cake. Mark the cake side every 2″ about 2″ up from base. Make a second series of marks 1″ down from first and midway between them. Pipe a row of tube 16 shells, then pipe tube 150 fluted ruffles from mark to mark. Trim with tube 3 dots, tube 26 drop flowers and tube 65 leaves.

WAVE A FLAG FOR THE FOURTH

. . . or make this cake for any patriotic occasion! Straight ribbon tubes pipe the stripes, flowers and waving flag.

BAKE, FILL AND ICE a 9″ x 13″ two-layer cake. Transfer Wilton Way III flag pattern to cake top. Mark top edge of cake every 1″ as guide for stripes. Make daisies in advance with tube 46 as described on page 263.

COVER SIDES OF CAKE with tube 2B, using marks as guides. Pipe a tube 2B shell-motion border at bottom. Drop guidelines for "rope", using stripes as guides. Pipe tube 14 rope and finish with tube 2 tassels.

PIPE STRIPES ON THE FLAG with tube 47. Fill in blue area with tube 13 stars. Lightly mark a 2″ circle in center of blue area and pipe thirteen tube 13 stars. Pipe a tube 47 flagpole and use tube 46 for the shell-motion border on top of cake.

Arrange the flowers on mounds of icing and trim with tube 65 leaves. Serve this stirring creation to 24 guests.

SUMMER HOUSE . . . A SENTIMENTAL TIER CAKE

Here's a sweet tier cake to decorate for any sentimental occasion—Valentine's day, an anniversary, a bridal shower—even for the wedding itself. Snowy lattice, piped with straight ribbon tubes, encloses the space between the tiers and gives an intriguing glimpse of little winged angels in the heart-shaped windows.

MAKE TRIMS IN ADVANCE

PIPE ROSES AND BUDS in royal or boiled icing with tubes 103 and 104. Set aside to dry.

DECORATE ORNAMENT. Cut two hearts from rolled gum paste or colored paper, using a 1″ heart cutter or Wilton Way III pattern. Attach to hands of a Card Holding Cherub with royal icing, then edge with tube 2 beading.

MAKE LATTICE PANELS with royal icing. You will need six. Tape Wilton Way III pattern to a stiff surface, tape wax paper over it and pipe lattice with tube 44. Edge with same tube. Dry thoroughly.

DECORATE THE CAKE

BAKE AND FILL the two-layer tiers, 12″ round, each layer 2″ high and 9″ hexagon with 1½″ high layers. Ice smoothly in buttercream. Also bake and ice a cake baked in a blossom pan. Assemble the tiers with 9″ hexagon separator plates and 5″ Corinthian pillars. Secure blossom cake to center of top tier.

Divide base tier into twelfths and mark at top edge. Make a second series of marks midway between first series, 1½″ up from base. Drop string guidelines for ruffles.

ON BASE TIER, pipe a tube 17 bottom shell border. Following guidelines, pipe ruffles with tube 104. Edge ruffles with tube 2 beading and add double strings above them with tube 2. Pipe ruffles from top edge of tier and add beading and string. Do top shell border with tube 16 and pipe scallops around separator plate with tube 13.

ON TOP TIER, pipe a tube 19 shell border at bottom and a tube 17 reverse shell border at top. In center of each side pipe a tube 17 heart (two shells touching) and outline with tube 2 beading. Pipe tube 13 shells around blossom cake.

ADD FINAL DECORATIONS

HANG ANGEL FIGURES. Put invisible thread through loops in backs of figures and tape securely to underside of upper separator plate. Be sure angels hang about 1″ in from edge of plate and are centered on each side.

ATTACH LATTICE PANELS. Pipe a line of royal icing on bottom separator plate, just within scalloped edge. Pipe small mounds of icing on top corners of a panel and set panel in position on piped line. Pipe a line of icing on one side of panel and on separator plate and attach second panel. Continue until all panels are in position. Cover seams with lines of tube 14 shells.

Secure cherub figure to top of blossom cake with a mound of icing.

TRIM WITH FLOWERS. Form clusters of roses and buds on top tier, letting buds hang down on corners of tier. Attach a rosebud at each window of lattice. Form flower clusters on top of base tier. Secure twelve roses at base of cake. Trim all flowers with tubes 65 and 66 leaves.

Serve dessert-size slices to 34 party guests. At a wedding reception, bottom tier serves 68, top serves 22 guests.

CHAPTER SIXTEEN

Curved Ribbon Tubes
Pipe Flowers and Graceful Borders

The five tubes in this little group are first cousins to the straight ribbon tubes. They range in size from little to large, each with a crescent or arc-shaped opening.

The piping done with the curved ribbon tubes looks entirely different than the trim tailored effects achieved with the straight ribbon tubes. The curved tubes pipe beguiling borders with sweeping curves and flounces, very realistic "feathers" for a bird cake and graceful fluted forms to edge a tier or cover the skirt of a doll cake in a hurry.

SOME OF THE LOVELIEST FLOWERS are piped with the curved ribbon tubes. They create the poetic water lily, especially fluffy daisies in the Philippine technique, dainty lilies of the valley and fall's own flower, the chrysanthemum.

CURVED RIBBON TUBES
TRIM AN AUTUMN FESTIVAL CAKE

This glowing cake is very quickly decorated with scalloped curves done with a curved tube. A curved ribbon tube pipes the flowers, too.

PIPE THE CHRYSANTHEMUMS in royal icing. First pipe a tube 10 ball on a number 7 nail, covered with a wax paper square. Starting at top center, pipe a cluster of upstanding petals with tube 81, holding the cone almost straight up. Surround this cluster with rows of petals, slanting the cone more with each row. The last row is piped with the cone held almost horizontal.

For an especially realistic look, pipe the center petals in a deeper tint of icing.

BAKE AND FILL a two-layer 10″ round cake. Ice in chocolate buttercream and place on serving tray. Fold an 8″ paper circle in twelfths, unfold, place on cake and mark folds with a toothpick. Using

marks as guide, mark side 1″ down from top.

PIPE A SHELL BORDER at base of cake with tube 18. Now pipe the furled scallops from mark to mark on cake side with tube 79. Pipe a tube 18 upright shell at points of scallops and finish with a tube 17 rosette. Accent the curves by dropping tube 3 strings above scallops and adding dots at ends. Pipe a tube 17 top shell border.

Pipe scallops on cake top from mark to mark with tube 79. Accent with tube 3 strings and dots and tube 17 rosettes.

Ice two or three marshmallows to center of cake top to give the flowers a lift. Arrange the flowers on small mounds of icing, tilting them to show off at their best. Pipe leaves with tube 67. Serve this luscious treat to 14.

THE FIVE CURVED RIBBON TUBES

Tubes 81, and 80 and 79 are the same except for size. In tubes 401 and 402, the ends of the crescent openings are sharply pointed to pipe forms with very crisp edges. There is a third tube in this series, giant tube 403. See it on page 286.

Use the curved ribbon tubes to pipe shells, reverse shells and zigzags. They are at their best, however, when used to pipe curved forms.

AT LEFT, the tubes are pictured in actual size. Below are some of the forms the curved ribbon tubes can pipe, also pictured in actual size. On the opposite page is a sampling of borders.

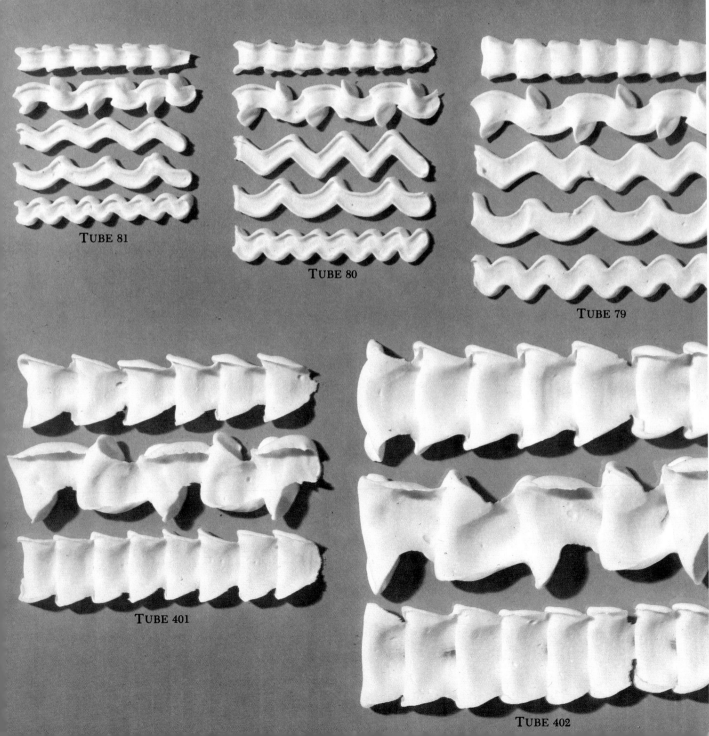

TUBE 81

TUBE 80

TUBE 79

TUBE 401

TUBE 402

ANGLED BORDER. Pipe two parallel zigzags with tube 80, fill in with tube 15, repeat with tube 3.

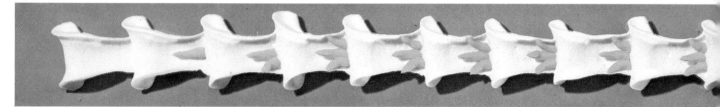

SHELL-MOTION BORDER is piped with tube 401 and trimmed with tube 3 in contrasting color.

SWIRLED BORDER. Pipe sweeping curves with tube 401, repeat the curves with tube 13.

SCALLOPED BORDER. Pipe a row of scallops with tube 401, trim with tube 13 curves and string.

FIGUREHEAD BORDER starts with tube 401 curves, adds tube 80 "C" and "S" curves.

Some of the loveliest flowers that ever bloomed are piped with the curved ribbon tubes. Their crescent-shaped openings give lifelike curves to the petals.

THE POETIC WATER LILY

This is the lotus of ancient times—the symbol of purity and life renewed.

FOR A LARGE FLOWER, use tube 401, a number 7 flower nail and royal icing. Pipe a circle of six green petals, lying flat on the nail. Add a row of six pastel petals more upstanding, then a row of five petals with tube held at a 45° angle. Dust your fingertips with cornstarch and pinch tips of petals to a point. Finally pipe four cupped petals in the center, tube held vertically. Pull out a cluster of tube 1 stamens in the center. For a smaller flower, use tube 80.

FOR LARGE LEAVES, use a number 7 nail and tube 127. Hold tube flat to nail and turn to pipe almost a full circle. Vein with a damp artist's brush. Use tube 104 to pipe smaller leaves.

THE PHILIPPINE DAISY

Make many of these flowers in the fast Philippine way. See a beautiful wedding anniversary cake trimmed with them on page 319.

INSERT THE END of a 6″ length of florists' wire into a tube fitted with tube 7 and filled with royal icing. Squeeze lightly as you pull out to form pistil. Dry. Cover top half of pistil with many tube 1 stamens, starting at top.

HOLD FLOWER UPSIDE DOWN by the wire and touch tube 81 to pistil, squeeze lightly and pull away. Continue to form a circle of petals. Make a hook at end of wire and hang to dry upside down. (Weight a cake rack at one end, letting most of it extend beyond table. Hook flowers on it to dry.)

LILY OF THE VALLEY

Pipe this delicate bloom directly on the cake with a small curved ribbon tube.

TOUCH THE CURVED SIDE of tube 80 to surface and squeeze out a tiny curve of icing. Without stopping, continue pressure and move tube in a circular fashion. Stop pressure and move away. For a variation in size, use tube 79 or 81.

DECORATE A HEART CAKE
WITH LILY OF THE VALLEY SPRAYS

One of the prettiest cakes you could trim to present to someone very dear.

TUBE 401 WATER LILY, TUBE 127 LEAF

TUBE 80 WATER LILY, TUBE 104 LEAF

DAISY PETALS PIPED WITH TUBE 81

BAKE AND FILL a two-layer 9″ heart cake. Also bake a little heart in a heart cupcake pan. Ice both cakes in buttercream, cover with poured fondant and set large heart on heart-shaped cake board. Secure small heart to top. Pipe name on small heart with tube 1, then edge with tube 2 beading.

PIPE A GRACEFUL LONG LEAF on both sides of small heart with tube 113. Make sure icing is thinned to flow smoothly. Pipe sprays of tube 2 stems curving onto small heart, then pipe lilies with tube 80, just as described at left.

PIPE BOTTOM BORDER of sharply curved bulbs with tube 6. At point of heart, pipe tube 70 leaves, tube 2 stems and tube 81 lilies of the valley. Serve this enchanting cake to twelve.

A FIESTA DOLL FOR A BON VOYAGE PARTY

First pipe royal icing drop flowers with tube 25 and dry. Use Wilton Way III pattern to cut banner from rolled gum paste. Dry over pencils, pipe tube 1 greeting and attach to a toothpick.

BAKE THE CAKE IN A WONDER MOLD PAN. Ice half a marshmallow to top of cake to extend waist, then insert doll pick. Place arms of doll straight out and ice entire cake, filling in waistline with icing. Mark a line around cake just below waist. Divide base of cake into twelfths and mark vertical lines from base to marked line. Now mark the triangular opening in skirt and divide into five stripes. Define stripes with tube 2 strings.

FILL IN STRIPES with tube 14 stars. Do skirt with scallops, starting at the top at marked line and using picture as guide. First pipe six rows of orange scallops and seven rows of yellow scallops with tube 81. Change to tube 80 for six rows of pink and five rows of orange. Finish skirt to hem with six rows of yellow piped with tube 79.

Pipe a tube 401 fluted ruffle at base of striped area. Starting at center back, pipe a tube 401 ruffle around hem, curving up, then down, striped area. Fill bodice area with tube 14 stars, place doll's arms in position and pipe a tube 401 collar. Attach banner and flowers to hands and serve to twelve.

280

CURVED PETAL TUBES FEATHER A YELLOW CHICK

The children will adore this whimsical yellow chicken—it will cheer lots of grown-ups too! Make it just for fun for an impromptu party.

BAKE AND FILL a 6″ ball cake and bake a cupcake. Trim off the base of the ball cake to steady it and set on 3″ cake circle. Attach cupcake to ball cake with toothpicks, rounded top facing front. Ice the assembled cake, filling in at neck. Set on serving tray. Mark a line around ball, 3½″ up from base and a second line below neck. Pipe red topknot in royal icing with tube 401 on a square of wax paper. Dry within curved surface.

WORKING FROM THE BOTTOM, pipe rows of tube 401

feathers, touching tube to surface and pulling down. When you reach marked line, pipe two rows of tube 14 orange stars. Fill in with yellow stars above them, then at upper mark, two rows of orange stars. Pipe spaced feathers over starred area with tube 402. Start at base of feather and move up, then pinch upper tip to a point.

Pipe a circle of tube 14 red stars, then cover head with yellow stars. Pipe eyes with tube 7 balls, flatten with a fingertip and surround with tube 2 dots. Pull out beak with tube 7 and attach topknot with icing. Serve this cute treat to twelve, presenting the head to a lucky child.

A GARDEN POOL CROWNS A SHEET CAKE FOR AN ANNIVERSARY

If their anniversary is in July, decorate this lovely cake for them. It features July's flowers, water lilies, afloat on a garden pool. Curved ribbon tubes pipe the flowers and graceful borders, too. This cake is just as pretty for a birthday.

MAKE TRIMS AHEAD. Pipe royal icing water lilies with tube 79 as described on page 279. Pipe leaves with tube 124.

For gum paste molded trims, follow directions that come with the molds. Mold cupid figure in the five-year-old People Mold, wings in Baroque Angelica mold. When dry, attach wings to cupid with balls of wet gum paste brushed with egg white. Mold two-piece pedestal in Baroque molds, using shell sections from Classic Shell and Regalia molds. Use Wilton Way III pattern

282

to cut banner from rolled gum paste. Lay dried cupid figure on his back, drape wet banner over hands and dry. Pipe tube 1s names.

Assemble pedestal with small balls of wet gum paste brushed with egg white. Attach feet of cupid to shell the same way.

BAKE, FILL AND ICE a 9″ x 13″ two-layer cake. Lightly mark oval on top with a 9″ x 7″ oval pan, then outline oval with a tube 6 line. Pipe message on side of cake with tube 3.

AT BASE OF CAKE, pipe a tube 13 fleur-de-lis in center. Use a cone striped with green icing. Now pipe border with tube 401, using a shell motion. Fill in curves with tube 13 fleurs-de-lis. Border on sides of cake is the same as the Swirled Border on page 277, piped with tubes 401 and 13.

Pipe a curved shell top border with tube 79. Swirl piping gel in oval area and edge oval with tube 79 and a shell motion. Line bottom of pedestal with clear plastic and set on edge of pool, then float the water lilies and leaves. Serve to 24 party guests. Cupid on his pedestal is a gift to the anniversary couple.

FRESH NEW BORDERS FEATURING CURVED RIBBON TUBES

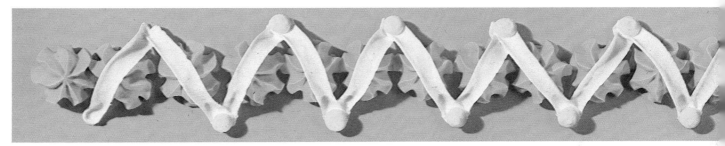

SPRINGTIME. Pipe tube 18 stars, center with tube 3 balls, add tube 80 petals to every other one.

ROOF TOP. Cover a row of tube 18 stars with tube 80 diagonal lines. Trim with tube 3 balls.

FLOWER FRAME. Pipe a row of tube 3 spaced balls. Add tube 80 petals and scallops, tube 3 bulbs.

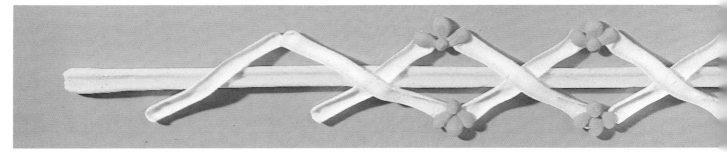

CRISSCROSS a tube 320 line with tube 80 diagonals. Add half-flowers piped with tube 3.

283

CHAPTER SEVENTEEN

Giant Tubes Create Dramatic Trims

These fascinating tubes are different from all the other tubes because of their heroic size. But there are similarities with tubes of more modest size. Within the group of giant tubes you'll find a petal tube, ribbon tubes, open and closed star tubes, round and leaf tubes. The giant tubes pipe forms just like those done with their smaller cousins, but very much more dramatic.

Use the giant tubes to decorate really big show cakes or to add drama to smaller cakes. And don't overlook some of the chief uses of these extra-large tubes. They give style and elegance to many foods, from hors d'oeuvres to desserts.

Leaf through this chapter to see some of the bold decorative uses of the giant tubes. We suggest you use a 16″ or 18″ coated fabric decorating bag when piping with these tubes. Meringue boiled icing is ideal to flow easily through the large openings.

LULLABY ... ALMOST AS LOVELY AS THE NEW BABY

Decorate this spectacular showpiece to celebrate a christening or for an elegant shower party. Roses in the most delicate tints are heaped around the ruffled tiers. At the top, a butterfly spreads its glittering wings to bring in the baby figure in its petalled cradle.

To PIPE THE ROSE CRADLE, fit a large decorating bag with tube 127R, the giant rose tube. Fill with a mixture of half royal, half boiled icing made with meringue powder. Prepare a flower nail for the big blossom. Cover a 6″ corrugated cardboard cake circle with wax paper or clear plastic wrap. Tape the underside securely to a number 13 flower nail.

Now pipe the rose in the usual manner, but pipe only the last two rows of petals. After petals are piped, remove center cone with a scissors and smooth middle area. Stick the nail in a block of styrofoam to dry.

PLEASE TURN TO PAGE 300 for Lullaby directions.

THE GIANT PETAL TUBE, actual size

THE GIANT CURVED RIBBON TUBE, actual size

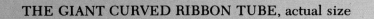

THE GIANT STRAIGHT RIBBON TUBES, actual size

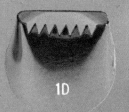

Tube 789 can be used to ice sides of tiers

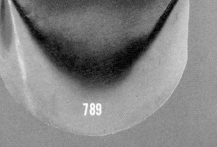

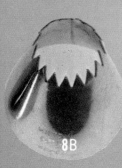

MORE GIANT CLOSED STAR TUBES in actual size

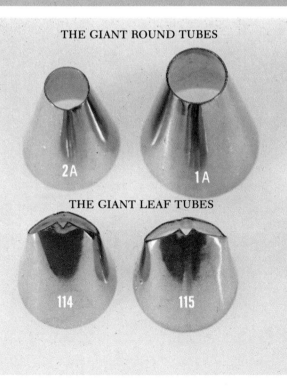

THE GIANT ROUND TUBES

THE GIANT LEAF TUBES

THE GIANT CLOSED STAR TUBES

These big tubes pipe stars, rosettes, shell and reverse shell borders and many other decorative motifs, just as do their smaller cousins shown on page 165. Because of their deeply cut teeth, the forms they produce are especially sculptural and clear cut. Another use of all six of these giant tubes is to pipe the showiest of drop flowers. See them in this role on pages 234 and 239.

THE GIANT ROUND AND LEAF TUBES

THE GIANT ROUND TUBES, tubes 2A and 1A, pipe simple strings, dots and bulbs as shown on page 52, but in super size. They are indispensable for figure piping as Chapters Six and Seven show. Use them too for piping uniformly sized cream puffs, cookies, meringues, and eclairs, and to neatly fill tarts or tiny cream puffs with whipped cream or pastry cream.

THE GIANT LEAF TUBES, tubes 114 and 115, pipe out-size leaves, ruffly or smooth, as shown on page 251. They'll also pipe very pretty shapes in whipped cream or spritz cookie dough.

289

Four towering tiers, lush red roses and a sparkling fountain come together in this spectacular masterpiece. After all the symbolic trims are prepared, giant tubes make quick work of piping the ruffled garlands and lavish borders.

PIPE ROSES IN ROYAL ICING with tubes 127, 126, 125, 124 and 104. Use a deeper tint of icing for the centers of the flowers. Pipe a few tiny 101s roses to place in the hand of the bride figure. Pipe royal icing spikes on backs of twelve larger roses and buds to attach to sides of base tier.

PAINT FILIGREE for frame to surround fountain with pink thinned royal icing. Cut a 7″ circle from center of a 10″ x 3″ styrofoam cake dummy. Cut a notch at base for wire. Ice with royal icing. Attach filigree to frame with royal icing.

Paint bases of six Cherub Concerto figures with pink thinned icing. Trim six petite ornament plates with hearts piped with tube 1 and red piping gel. Secure cherub figures to plates.

MODIFY BRIDE AND GROOM ORNAMENT. Remove white tulle from bride's figure and paint dress pink. Gather pink tulle and glue over skirt, then attach tiny roses to hand. Add red piping gel "jewelry" and dots on double ring. Trim plate with piping gel hearts piped with tube 1.

REMOVE ARTIFICIAL FLOWERS and white tulle from pink Bridal Bells ornament. Replace with pink tulle and add "ruby" trim with piping gel.

DECORATE THE CAKE

BAKE AND FILL FOUR TIERS. Base tier is composed of four three-layer 12″ square cakes. Each layer should be about 2″ high. Assemble these cakes, before icing, on a 28″ square plywood cake board. Ice assembled cakes. The completed tier should be at least 6″ high and 24″ square.

Second tier is a two-layer 16″ round, each layer 2″ high. Third tier is a two-layer 12″ round, each layer about 1¾″ high. Fourth, or top, tier is a two-layer 8″ round, each layer 1½″ high. Ice the tiers and assemble with the Arched Pillar tier set above base tier. Use 12″ separator plates and 7½″ Corinthian pillars above 16″ tier. Set fountain on Arched Pillar base plate and place filigree-trimmed frame over it.

Mark base tier at top edge 3½″ in from corners on all sides. Leave front empty, but divide spaces within marks on other three sides in thirds and mark on top edge for garlands. Drop string guidelines. Leave a 5″ space in center of side of 16″ tier empty and print design on rest of tier with a pattern press. Divide 12″ tier in

eighths, mark midway on side and drop string guidelines for garlands.

DECORATE BASE TIER. Pipe scroll on side with three curves of giant tube 789. Do base border with tube 403. Pipe deeply ruffled garlands at each corner with tube 1C. Fill in with triple garlands on three sides with tube 1B and add reverse shell top border with tube 195. Edge separator plate with tube 18.

ON 16″ TIER, pipe fluted base border with tube 402. Pipe the number "40", as well as side designs and top border with tube 18.

On 12″ tier, pipe a shell border at base with tube 18. Do side garlands with tube 508, fleurs-de-lis with tube 4B and top border with tube 18.

On top tier, pipe base border with tube 402, top border with tube 18.

ADD FINAL TRIMS. Pipe "ruby" piping gel trims on base border, scroll and "40" with tube 1. Set cherub figures around fountain and ornaments within 7½″ pillars and on top tier. Arrange roses on mounds of icing and trim with tube 114 leaves. Cut into 488 wedding cake-sized pieces.

GIANT TUBES GIVE A PROFESSIONAL FINISH TO GOURMET DESSERTS

LEFT TO RIGHT: *Chocolate Mousse, Schwarzwälder Kirschtorte, Charlotte Russe*

292

293

USE GIANT TUBES TO MAKE YOUR DESSERTS LOOK AS GOOD AS THEY TASTE

Make one of these elegant desserts as the finale for a formal dinner, or prepare a group of them to take their place on a lavish sweet table for a reception. Their outstanding flavors are enhanced by simple but beautiful trims done with giant tubes. All recipes are from *The Wilton Book of Classic Desserts*.

CHOCOLATE MOUSSE

¼ ounce unflavored gelatine (1 envelope)
1 cup milk
½ cup sugar, divided
⅛ teaspoon salt
2 eggs, separated
6 ounces semi-sweet chocolate morsels
½ teaspoon vanilla
1 cup heavy cream, whipped
½ recipe Crème Chantilly for Decorating
   Shaved Chocolate

Sprinkle gelatin over milk in small saucepan. Add ¼ cup of sugar, salt, egg yolks and chocolate morsels and stir until thoroughly mixed. Place over low heat, stirring constantly, until gelatin is completely dissolved and chocolate is melted. Remove from heat and beat until chocolate is blended. Stir in vanilla and chill, stirring occasionally, until the mixture mounds slightly when it is dropped from a spoon.
Beat egg whites until stiff and gradually add remaining ¼ cup of sugar. Beat until very stiff and then fold into chocolate mixture. Next fold in whipped cream. Turn into a one-quart oiled mold and refrigerate several hours, until firm.

To DECORATE, crown top of mousse with curved shells and a puffy star piped with the Crème Chantilly and tube 8B. Pipe puffy stars around base with the same tube. Garnish with candied cherries and shaved chocolate.

CRÈME CHANTILLY FOR DECORATING

Add 1 teaspoon gelatin to 2 tablespoons cold water in a metal or pyrex cup. Set in a small pan of boiling water and heat until gelatin dissolves and looks clear. Do not stir. Beat this mixture into 1 cup heavy cream just as the cream thickens. Add two tablespoons sugar and flavoring

SHAVED CHOCOLATE AND CHOCOLATE CURLS

CHOCOLATE SHAVINGS. Melt 3 ounces of semi-sweet chocolate over hot water, stir until smooth and pour onto a flat platter or marble slab. Spread to a 6″ circle. Cool until firm. Draw the sharp edge of the blade of a knife, held parallel to platter, across the chocolate, to form shavings.

CHOCOLATE CURLS. Spread the melted chocolate on a marble or a flat platter in a strip about 3″ wide. When firm, mark into a neat rectangle with a knife. Draw the blade of a large knife or sharp pancake turner across the rectangle to peel off the chocolate in uniform curls.

SCHWARZWÄLDER KIRSCHTORTE
(*Black Forest Cherry Cake*)

1 recipe Chocolate Sponge Sheet
⅓ cup Kirsch
½ recipe Continental Butter Cream,
   chocolate flavored
2 cups pitted black sweet cherries, cut in
   half (fresh or canned)
1 recipe Crème Chantilly for Decorating,
   flavored with Kirsch
Chocolate Curls

Bake the sponge sheet in two 8″ or 9″ layers. Cool slightly and sprinkle each layer with the Kirsch. Cool completely. Spread one layer with Chocolate Butter Cream, and press 1½ cups of the cherries into the cream. Top with the second layer. Spread Crème Chantilly on top of the cake.

To DECORATE, pipe vertical stripes around side of cake with tube 1D and the Crème Chantilly. Edge base with tube 1G shells and top with tube 4B shells. Press chocolate curls into side of cake and arrange cherries on top. Brush Currant Glaze over cherries. Refrigerate until serving time.

CHOCOLATE SPONGE SHEET

¼ cup flour
¼ cup dark cocoa
6 eggs, separated, room temperature
¼ teaspoon salt
½ cup sugar
1 teaspoon vanilla

Sift flour and cocoa together. Beat the egg whites with the salt until they stand in soft peaks. Add 4 tablespoons of the sugar, one tablespoon at a time, and continue beating until meringue is very stiff. In a separate bowl beat the egg yolks with the remaining sugar and vanilla until fluffy.
   Gently fold about one-fourth of the meringue into the egg yolk mixture, then pour back into the

bowl of meringue. Sprinkle with 2 tablespoons of flour-cocoa mixture and fold together. Repeat until all the flour-cocoa mixture is blended. Do not over-mix. Pour into two 8″ or 9″ round pans lined with buttered wax paper. Bake 10 to 12 minutes in a 400°F oven until done. Remove from pan immediately to cool on a rack.

CONTINENTAL BUTTER CREAM

⅔ cup sugar
⅓ cup water
⅛ teaspoon cream of tartar
5 egg yolks
1 cup soft butter

Mix sugar, water and cream of tartar in a saucepan. Stir over low heat until sugar is completely dissolved. Raise heat and boil without stirring until syrup tests 238°F.

Meanwhile, beat the egg yolks in a bowl until they are fluffy. Then pour the hot syrup in a thin stream into the yolks, beating constantly. The mixture will become thick and light as it cools from the beating. Set aside until completely cooled. Beat in softened butter, a little at a time. Flavor to your taste.

Makes 2 cups. Butter Cream may be kept in the refrigerator for a week or two and brought to room temperature and re-beaten before being used for piping or spreading.

CHOCOLATE BUTTER CREAM. Beat three ounces melted, cooled, unsweetened chocolate and three tablespoons of cognac into the finished Continental Butter Cream.

CURRANT GLAZE

Use this to glaze any red fruit. Put one cup of Currant Jelly through a sieve and heat to boiling. Remove from heat and stir in two to four tablespoons of Kirsch. Brush on while hot.

CHARLOTTE RUSSE

Here is the recipe created by the master-chef Carême to please Czar Alexander I.

30 or more lady fingers
1 recipe Bavarian cream
½ recipe Crème Chantilly for Decorating

Line a straight-sided Charlotte mold with wax paper, then with lady fingers, cutting them in diamond shapes to line the bottom of the mold in the shape of a flower, and setting them upright all around the sides. Fill the mold with the Bavarian Cream. Chill several hours, or overnight,

and unmold on a serving tray.

TO DECORATE, pipe curved shells around base of Charlotte with tube 4B. Pipe shells on top and center with a rosette. Garnish with candied or well-drained maraschino cherries.

BAVARIAN CREAM

¼ ounce gelatin (1 envelope)
¼ cup cold water
1 cup milk
1 inch piece vanilla bean
⅜ cup sugar
4 egg yolks
pinch of salt
1 cup heavy cream, stiffly whipped

Soak the gelatin in cold water. Mix the milk with the sugar in the top of a double boiler, add the vanilla bean and scald. Beat the egg yolks and salt in a large bowl until thick.

Pour a little of the hot milk into the beaten yolks, stir quickly and pour gradually into the hot milk mixture, stirring constantly. Cook over 1″ of simmering water about 10 minutes, stirring constantly, or until the mixture coats the spoon.

Pour into a large bowl, discard vanilla bean, add gelatin and stir until gelatin is dissolved and mixture is cool. Chill until custard starts to thicken. Gently fold in cream. Pour into lined Charlotte mold. Chill several hours or overnight.

SHERRY JELLY

½ ounce gelatin (2 envelopes)
½ cup cold water
1 cup boiling water
¾ cup sugar
¼ teaspoon salt
½ cup orange juice
2 tablespoons lemon juice
1½ cups sherry (use a medium-sweet, gold-colored sherry)
½ recipe Crème Chantilly for Decorating
Fresh mint leaves for garnish

Soften gelatin in cold water. Add boiling water, sugar and salt. Stir till dissolved. Add fruit juices and sherry. Pour into a one-quart mold and chill in refrigerator till set.

TO DECORATE, press mint leaves against side of mold at base. Pipe tube 172 puffed shells on leaves with the Crème Chantilly. Add a tube 172 rosette at top and serve immediately.

Continued on next page

VACHERIN CHANTILLY

Vacherin is French for a meringue "bowl".

2 recipes Meringue Suisse
1 recipe Continental Butter Cream,
   tinted pink, flavored with Kirsch
1 cup heavy cream, whipped and sweetened
   with two tablespoons sugar
2 cups fresh raspberries
2 tablespoons Kirsch
2 tablespoons sugar

Trace four 8″ circles on buttered and floured baking sheets. Fill one circle with a spiral of meringue piped with tube 1A, starting in center.

Pipe two rows of meringue around edges of other three circles. Pipe tube 4B puffed stars with remaining meringue. Bake all meringues as directed in Meringue Suisse recipe.

Place circle of meringue on serving plate. Pipe a tube 2A line around edge with Butter Cream. Set one ring of meringue on icing, pipe a Butter Cream line around it and top with second ring. Attach third ring the same way.

Sprinkle the berries with the Kirsch and fold in the sugar, being careful not to bruise the berries. Refrigerate one-half hour to blend flavors.

TO COMPLETE AND DECORATE, ice side of Vacherin with Butter Cream. Pipe tube 4B shells at base and fleurs-de-lis on side with Butter Cream. Add tube 508 shells at top and press in the tube 4B meringue stars.

An hour before serving, fold one cup of the berries into the whipped cream. Pile into the Vacherin. Heap remaining berries on top. Refrigerate until serving time.

MERINGUE SUISSE
(Swiss meringue)

5 egg whites, at room temperature
¼ teaspoon cream of tartar
¼ teaspoon salt
1 teaspoon vanilla
1¼ cups sugar

The secret of crisp tender meringues is in the baking—they should be dried, rather than baked, so they become just the palest off-white, and do not become tough. Set the oven at 200°F before beating the egg whites.

Put the egg whites, cream of tartar, vanilla and salt in a large bowl and beat at medium speed with an electric mixer until the mixture holds soft peaks. Add one-half the sugar, a tablespoon at a time, as you continue beating. Continue beating until the meringue is stiff and dull, and until a bit rubbed between the fingers is smooth, not grainy. It should be stiff enough to hold its shape when formed with a pastry tube. Fold in the remaining sugar.

Form the meringue as directed for the particular recipe on a well-buttered, lightly-floured baking sheet. Put in the preheated oven for 15 minutes. Then turn off the heat and allow the meringues to stay in the oven for at least 4 or 5 hours—overnight is better.

Meringues can be stored in a dry, airy place (not tightly covered) for several weeks.

INDIVIDUAL STRAWBERRY MERINGUES

1 recipe Meringue Suisse
1 recipe Crème Pâtissière
½ recipe Crème Chantilly for Decorating
1 quart fresh strawberries,
   small to medium-size
½ recipe Currant Glaze

Butter and flour a baking sheet. Mark circles on it, 1″ apart, with a 2½″ cookie cutter. Using tube 195, fill the circles with the meringue, piping in a spiral fashion. With the same tube, pipe a rim around each circle, then a second rim. Bake as directed in Meringue Suisse recipe. Makes about 18 individual meringue shells. Wash and hull the strawberries, then cut in thin slices.

TO COMPLETE AND DECORATE, fill the baked shells with the Crème Pâtissière. A neat way to do this is to fill a pastry bag fitted with tube 1A with the Crème, then pipe it into the shells. Set slices of berries against the sides of the shells, brush with glaze. Pipe a tube 172 puffed star in the center of each meringue with the Crème Chantilly. Top with a berry slice or a small berry.

CRÈME PÂTISSIÈRE *(Pastry Cream)*

A rich, delicate filling for continental cakes, meringues and tarts.

3 tablespoons flour
⅛ teaspoon salt
⅜ cup sugar
1 cup light cream
4 egg yolks, slightly beaten
1 teaspoon vanilla

Mix the flour, salt and sugar in a heavy saucepan, blend in a little of the cream and place on medium heat, stirring constantly. Add the rest of the cream and continue stirring until the mixture becomes as thick as a medium cream sauce.

Stir a little of the heated sauce into the egg yolks, then pour the egg yolks into the sugar-flour-cream mixture. Return to low heat and cook for a few more minutes till thickened. Do not boil. Add vanilla and cool as quickly as possible.

To prevent a skin from forming over the cream, brush with melted butter. Stir briefly before using. Fills a 9″ tart shell or 18 small meringues.

LEMON TARTS

1 recipe Rich Tart Pastry
1 recipe English Lemon Curd
½ recipe Crème Chantilly for Decorating
Candied citron peel for garnish

Bake the tarts as recipe directs, then fill with the Lemon Curd. Do this by fitting a pastry bag with tube 4B or 1A and pressing the filling into tarts.

To DECORATE, pipe a puffed star on each tart with the Crème Chantilly and tube 6B. Thinly slice the citron and make a tiny fan on each tart.

RICH TART PASTRY

This is the crisp, delicious pastry that is the base for subtly-flavored European tarts, tartlets and barquettes. The cook who has mastered the art of making tart pastry will find it easy to turn out many spectacular desserts, so it is a worthwhile project to practice on until perfect. This recipe will make two 8-inch tart shells or more than a dozen small tarts.

3 cups sifted flour
¾ cup sugar
⅛ teaspoon salt
¼ cup butter, firm but not hard
3 eggs
2 teaspoons grated lemon rind

Mix the flour with the sugar and salt and sift it onto a mixing board, or into a large bowl. Make a well in the center and into it put the butter (cut in large flakes) the eggs and the lemon rind. Make a paste of the ingredients with your finger tips, gradually working in the flour mixture, until a smooth firm dough is formed. Work quickly so the butter does not become oily. When the board (or sides of the bowl) is clean, wrap the dough in wax paper and chill until firm.

Roll out the chilled dough between sheets of waxed paper to a thickness of less than ¼″. Cut the dough into 4″ circles with a cookie cutter, line tartlet pans and prick well with a fork. Freeze for 1½ hours. Bake in a pre-heated 350°F oven on middle shelf about 10 or 12 minutes, or until golden.

ENGLISH LEMON CURD

2 large lemons, juice and grated rind
5 egg yolks
½ cup sugar
¼ cup butter

Grate the lemon peel, then squeeze out the juice and strain. Combine egg yolks and sugar in the top of a double boiler. Add lemon juice and grated peel, then butter, little by little. Stir constantly until thick. This will keep in a covered jar in the refrigerator for months.

GIANT TUBES GIVE ELEGANCE TO MANY FOODS

Even a serving of butter looks beautiful when it's been put through giant tubes to form a bouquet of flowers and leaves. Cream the butter, then use tubes 1G, 1E and 4B to press out drop flowers and tube 114 to pipe ruffled leaves on wax paper. Freeze, then arrange on serving plate and center flowers with pimento circles cut with tube 12.

Use your imagination and giant tubes to give glamor and form to many dishes. Pipe puffy stars of mashed potatoes around a meat or chicken stew and brown in the oven. Set a steak on a fireproof platter, pipe mashed potatoes around it, brown under the broiler and garnish with parsley and cherry tomatoes for a mouthwatering presentation. Accent a molded vegetable salad with seasoned mayonnaise rosettes. Fill onion or spiced apple cups with mashed sweet potatoes put through a giant tube. Set the cups around a roast turkey or pork roast. Pipe hard sauce in decorative rosettes and freeze to accompany a hot steamed pudding.

Use any of the larger giant star tubes for piping foods. You'll gain a reputation as a gourmet cook.

GIANT TUBES SHAPE DECORATIVE COOKIES

The quickest and easiest way to an impressive tray of beautifully formed cookies is to press them out with giant tubes! The recipes used for these cookies are all from *The Wilton Book of Classic Desserts*.

SWISS BROYAGE

3 egg whites, room temperature	1 teaspoon vanilla
	¾ cup sugar
⅛ teaspoon cream of tartar	¼ cup ground almonds
dash of salt	⅓ cup cornstarch

Combine egg whites, cream of tartar, salt and vanilla in a large bowl. Beat with an electric mixer at medium speed until soft peaks form. Add ½ cup sugar, a tablespoon at a time, beating constantly until dull and firm. Combine the almonds, sifted cornstarch and remaining sugar and fold into the egg white mixture.

TO SHAPE THE COOKIES, press out tube 8B curved shells on a well-buttered, lightly floured baking sheet. Or use tube 172 to form fleurs-de-lis. Bake in a preheated 200°F oven for 15 minutes. Turn oven off and allow the cookies to remain in the oven four or five hours or overnight. Trim with tube 1 and chocolate buttercream.

CHRISTMAS COOKIES *(a spritz cookie)*

1 pound butter	½ teaspoon vanilla
1½ cups sugar	About 5 cups flour
2 eggs	

Cream butter, add sugar, a little at a time, beat till fluffy. Add vanilla, mix well. Add eggs, one at a time, beating well after each addition. Mix in enough flour to bring to piping consistency. Divide dough in three portions. Tint one portion pink, a second green, by kneading in a few drops of food color. Leave one portion untinted. Keep well wrapped in plastic until ready to pipe.

TO SHAPE THE COOKIES, press them out on a buttered baking sheet. Use tube 6B, 1E or 1B for flowers, tube 114 for leaves, tube 4B for shells. Use bits of candied fruit to center the flowers. Bake in a 375°F oven about eight minutes.

AMARETTI *(Macaroons)*

½ pound almond paste	3 egg whites
1 cup sugar	½ teaspoon vanilla

Stir the almond paste to soften it and work in two-thirds of the cup of sugar alternately with the egg whites. Add vanilla. The consistency should be a little softer than that of mashed potatoes.

TO SHAPE THE COOKIES, cover a cookie sheet with white letter paper, and pipe with a giant tube. Sprinkle with the rest of the sugar. Use tube 1D for bars, about 2″ long, tube 195 for puffy stars. Bake in a preheated 300°F oven for about 20 minutes. When they are taken out of the oven, cover a cake rack with a damp towel and slide the paper containing the macaroons onto it. In a few minutes they may be easily removed.

Dip the bars in melted semi-sweet chocolate, then in chopped almonds and dry on wax paper. Pipe a tube 1 spiral of chocolate buttercream on the puffs. Store in a covered container.

GIANT TUBES TURN OUT A DAZZLING HORS D'OEUVRES TRAY

The simplest of foods, well seasoned and piped in dainty shapes create these tempting appetizers. These little morsels appear elaborate, but they're quickly put together with the help of the giant tubes.

CHICKEN SALAD PUFFS. To two cups of finely diced cooked chicken, add ¼ cup diced green pepper, two tablespoons well-drained diced pimento, four or five drops of onion juice, two tablespoons of chopped black olives, enough mayonnaise to bind together and salt to taste. Fill tiny cream puffs (recipe at right) with a teaspoon.

CUCUMBER SANDWICHES. Scrub cucumbers, score with a fork, slice and lay slices on paper towels. Sprinkle with salt. Whip two tablespoons of cream cheese and mix with one cup of mayonnaise and one tablespoon of finely chopped fresh dill weed. Cut 2″ rounds from thinly sliced white bread with a biscuit cutter and spread with softened butter. Lay a cucumber slice on each round, press out a flower with tube 1G and the mayonnaise mixture and garnish with a slice of stuffed olive. Crisp and delicious!

CREAM CHEESE CANAPÉS. Whip cream cheese, season well with tabasco, onion juice and salt, and tint with food color. Pipe stars of this mixture on crisp crackers with tube 508 and garnish with triangles of green pepper and slices of ripe olive.

PATÉ SHELLS. Mix crumbled paté, canned or your own, with enough mayonnaise to bring to piping consistency. Spread small slices of rye bread with softened butter and pipe curved shells with tube 6B. Trim with sprigs of parsley and slices of olives or sweet pickle.

DEVILED EGGS. Boil six eggs. Mash the yolks with one teaspoon dry mustard, four drops of onion juice, one teaspoon Worcestershire sauce, salt to taste and a tablespoon of mayonnaise. Fill the egg whites with this mixture piped with tube 4B. Add fanciful trims with pimento strips, capers, olive or pickle slices and parsley.

PÂTÉ Â CHOU (Cream puff paste)

For guaranteed foolproof results have all the ingredients at room temperature, and make sure of an accurate oven temperature.

1 cup water	¼ teaspoon salt
½ cup butter	4 eggs
1 cup sifted flour	

Bring water and butter to a boil. Lower the heat, add the flour and salt all at once and continue to cook, stirring constantly until the mixture leaves the sides of the pan and forms a ball. Remove from the heat and add the eggs, one at a time, blending well before adding the next.

Press out tube 2A mounds on a buttered baking sheet. Allow 1″ between the mounds. Bake in a preheated 400°F oven for 20 to 25 minutes until golden and no beads of moisture show. Turn off heat and leave the puffs in a closed oven for ten minutes more. Cool slightly, then cut in two with a sharp knife and cool completely.

After piping the rose cradle (page 285), continue to prepare all trims in advance.

MAKE THE BUTTERFLY. Roll out gum paste to 1/16″ thickness and cut two wing shapes from Wilton Way III patterns. Dry on flat surface, then transfer designs to wings and outline with tube 000 and white royal icing thinned with piping gel. Tint gel in pastels of pink, peach and yellow and fill in areas with touching dots piped with tube 000. Dry both wings, turn over and outline and fill in again. Dry.

Lay an 8″ length of stiff, cloth-covered florists' wire on wax paper. Tape one end to secure and pipe a body about 2¼″ long on other end of wire. Use tube 7 and a back and forth movement. While icing is still wet, insert wings into body in open position. Prop to dry. Also insert two fine wires for antennae. When thoroughly dry, stick stiff wire into a block of styrofoam and reinforce butterfly by piping lines of icing where wings join body on both sides. Set aside to dry.

MAKE BABY FIGURE. Form a ⅝″ ball of gum paste for head and groove below forehead. Form gum paste into a cone shape for body about 2″ long, ½″ in diameter at widest point. While body and head are still wet, secure head to wider end of cone by brushing with egg white. Dry

thoroughly with head and upper body propped up. Roll out gum paste thinly and cut into a 2″ square for blanket. Brush a ¼″ stripe of egg white diagonally across blanket while still wet. Lay baby figure on it, point above head, and wrap two other corners of blanket around body. Secure with egg white.

When dry, paint features with thinned food coloring, pipe a tube 1s nose, and edge blanket with tube 1s beading. Dry again.

PIPE ROSES AND BUDS in varied tints and sizes. Use royal icing and tubes 104, 118, 124 and 127. Set aside to dry.

DECORATE THE CAKE

BAKE AND FILL TWO-LAYER TIERS, one 12″ round, the other a 9″ oval. Ice and assemble on an oval cake board or tray about 13″ x 22″. Divide both tiers in eighths and mark at top edge and midway on sides as picture shows. Drop string guidelines for ruffles.

AT BASE OF 12″ TIER pipe small scallops with tube 104. Within each scallop pipe a tube 22 star. Following guidelines, pipe tube 104 double ruffles on side of tier. Add tube 2 beading and bows. Pipe a tube 13 top shell border.

AT BASE OF OVAL TIER, pipe a border similar to one

on 12″ tier. Use tube 103 for scallops, tube 20 for stars. Pipe double ruffle with tube 103, add tube 2 beading and a tube 13 top shell border.

PUT IT ALL TOGETHER

Wrap end of wire extending from butterfly with clear plastic wrap, and insert in top tier near edge. Attach giant rose to a 5½″ separator plate with icing. Secure baby figure within rose and set on top tier. Use royal icing to attach two lengths of narrow ribbon under petals of rose extending to body of butterfly.

Arrange roses on lower tier and on tray at ends of cake. Trim all roses with tubes 70 and 66 leaves. Before serving, lift rose cradle and butterfly off cake, and present roses on tray to guests. Serve to 34 guests.

GIANT TUBES MAKE A BIRTHDAY CAKE QUICK TO DECORATE

Don't reserve your super-size tubes just for big cakes. Try trimming a cake of modest size with them. See how the bold forms they pipe give drama to the simplest design, and complete the decorating in a hurry.

BAKE TWO LAYERS in 12″ round pans, each layer about 2″ high. Fill and ice and set on cake board. Divide into tenths and mark midway on side of cake and at top edge. Drop string guidelines for garlands. Mark a circle on top of cake by gently pressing with an 8″ cake circle.

DO ALL DECORATING IN BUTTERCREAM right on the cake. Edge base and top with tube 16 shells. Following guidelines, use giant tube 508 for the showy ruffly garlands. Start each garland with light pressure, increase pressure and lift tube as you near the center, then relax pressure as you near the end. Pipe tube 6 balls at points of garlands. Accent the curves with tube 3 string in green. Pipe ten ruffled leaves on side of cake with giant tube 114.

PIPE MESSAGE in center of cake top with tube 2. From marked circle, pipe ten tube 114 leaves, tips meeting tips of leaves on side of cake. Add a second series of leaves piped between the first. Pipe ten drop flowers with giant tube 1F and push a birthday candle into each. Pipe tube 1F drop flowers on side of cake between leaves and center with tube 233. Light the candles and serve to 22 guests.

CHAPTER EIGHTEEN

Specialty Tubes Pipe Unique Forms

In this chapter we present a dozen unusual tubes that are completely different from those in the other tube families. Each has a personality all its own. Some will create attractive effects much faster than other tubes.

Every decorator will find it worthwhile to become familiar with all the specialty tubes. The unique forms they pipe will broaden and enrich your decorating skills.

Leaf through this chapter to see just a sampling of the work these tubes perform. Experiment with them to discover many more beautiful uses.

YELLOW ROSEBUD

This dainty and pristine little bridal cake is decorated very quickly with the specialty tubes. Even the yellow rosebuds are made with just one quick motion of tube 63.

Prepare the ornament ahead of time. Glue a small filigree heart to the plate from a petite ornament base. Add a froth of yellow tulle and figures of the bridal couple.

STEP ONE. Bake and fill the tiers. Base tier is two 12″ round layers, each 2″ high. Upper tier is two 9″ heart-shaped layers, each layer 1½″ high. Ice smoothly in buttercream and assemble on a ruffle-edged cake board. Divide lower tier in twelfths and mark about 1½″ down from top edge. Drop string guidelines for garlands. Divide each side of heart tier in sixths, mark on top edge and drop guidelines.

STEP TWO. Decorate base tier. Pipe a bottom border of deeply curved shells with tube 100. This tube produces an interesting, grooved form. Curve two shells from every other garland guideline with tube 339. Pipe the textured garlands with the same tube, lifting tube and increasing pressure in the center to let the form build up. Finish the tier with a tube 100 curved shell top border.

Trim for the top tier echoes that of the lower tier. Pipe bottom and top curved shell borders with tube 99 and do garlands with same tube.

STEP THREE. Finish the cake with the surprising little rosebuds. Pipe tube 1 stems in clusters on sides of tiers and in a spray on top of cake. Use tube 63 to pipe quick shells right on the cake. The serrated edge on this tube gives the effect of unfolding petals. Trim with tube 65 leaves. Trim the ornament with rosebuds too. Serve the lower tier of Yellow Rosebud to 68, upper tier to 28.

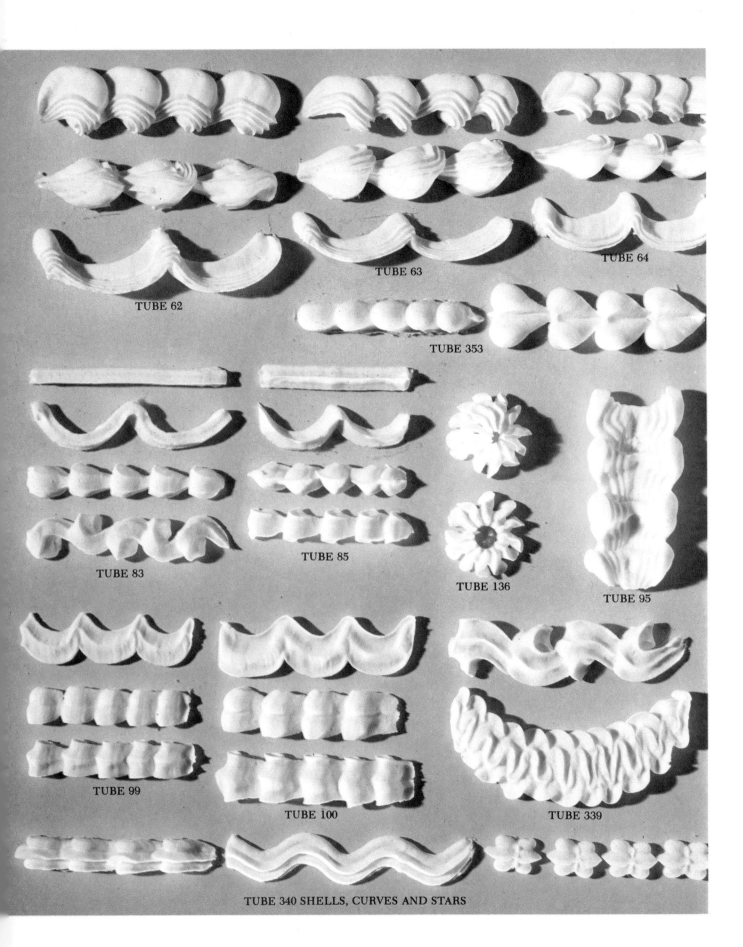

TUBE 62

TUBE 63

TUBE 64

TUBE 353

TUBE 83

TUBE 85

TUBE 136

TUBE 95

TUBE 99

TUBE 100

TUBE 339

TUBE 340 SHELLS, CURVES AND STARS

THE TWELVE SPECIALTY TUBES

Study the opposite page for actual size samples of what these tubes do. Tubes 62, 63 and 64 are a sub-family, pipe shells in variety, curves and intricate ruffled garlands. For some of the effects, *work from right to left with these tubes.*

Use tube 353 for upstanding borders or plump heart shapes. Tubes 83 and 85 are the square and triangle tubes. Tube 136 pipes just one form—a candle holder!

Tube 95, the French plume tube, pipes lavish double ruffles. Tubes 99 and 100 pipe interesting grooved shapes, tube 339, more deeply grooved forms. Tube 340 does tailored, textured borders and decorative stars.

BELOW: SOME OF DECORATIVE MOTIFS you can pipe with the specialty tubes. Pipe them quickly on the tops and sides of pretty cakes, then compose some specialty trims of your own.

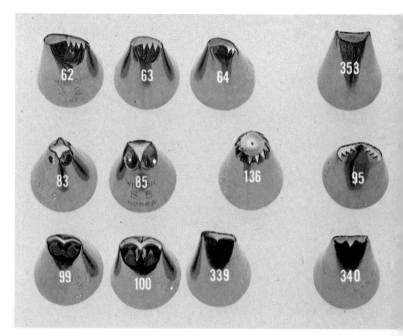

TUBE 83 FLEURS-DE-LIS FORM A SQUARE

TUBE 2 STEMS AND LEAVES, TUBE 63 PETALS

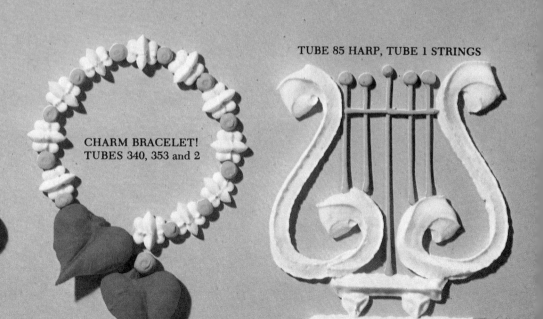

TUBES 353 and 340 PIPE A
QUAINT FLOWER. TUBE 1 STEMS

CHARM BRACELET!
TUBES 340, 353 and 2

TUBE 85 HARP, TUBE 1 STRINGS

NEAT TAILOR-MADE BORDERS. Pipe tube 340 stars on a tube 2B ribbon, add tube 2 string.

BLOSSOM BORDER. Tuck tube 225 flowers, tube 65 leaves in the curves of tube 100 shells.

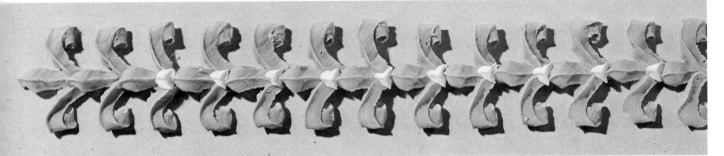

FLAMBOYANT BORDER. Trim tube 85 deeply curved shells with tube 85 stars.

SURPRISE BORDER. Pipe tube 85 stars in tube 62 shells, trim with tubes 85 and 2.

FLUFFY RUFFLES with tube 62! Start with tube 199, trim with tube 2 dots and strings.

306

PIPE IMAGINATIVE BORDERS WITH THE
SPECIALTY TUBES . . . CREATE UNIQUE TRIMS

Unusual forms piped with these tubes make even the simplest borders look exciting! Curves piped with tubes 62, 63 and 64 end in a crisp "pleated" look. Tube 340 stars have a "jewelry" effect. The angular cut of tubes 83 and 85 give interesting shapes to curved and upright shells. Study the borders on the opposite page, then go on to invent new specialty tube trims. Note: pipe the tube 62 ruffles at the bottom of page 306 *from right to left.*

DECORATE A CAKE WITH THE "FRENCH PLUME" TUBE
FOR A LAVISH CONTINENTAL LOOK

It takes just a few minutes and tube 95 to turn out a confection that looks like it had been done by a French pastry chef!

Slice an 8″ loaf cake into four layers and fill with your favorite filling, or variously flavored buttercream. (The Continental Butter Cream, page 295, or Creme Patissiere, page 296, are appropriate and especially delicious.)

If you would like your dessert to have a true European flavor, use the recipe for Chocolate Sponge Sheet, page 294, for the cake. Bake it in an 11″ x 17″ pan. Chill, then cut in 5½″ x 8½″ pieces. Assemble with the filling of your choice, then ice the cake.

Ice the assembled cake in Continental Butter Cream and press sliced toasted almonds into the sides. Pipe three rows of double ruffles on the top with tube 95, using a back-and-forth motion. Pipe bottom shell border with tube 362. Fill a decorating cone with jelly and cut a tiny opening in the tip. Use this to fill the center areas of the ruffles. Serves eight very lavishly.

Tube 95 can be used for a fancy ruffled border at the base of a cake, too. After you've piped the fluffy double ruffle, fill the center area with dots, stars or drop flowers in a contrasting pastel tint. The result is a lavish looking border, very quickly done.

LIGHT UP A 21st BIRTHDAY
WITH A CHOCOLATE MINT CAKE
(at left)

Specialty tubes do all the decorating on this handsome confection!

BAKE AND FILL a two-layer 9″ heart cake. Ice sides in chocolate buttercream, top in white buttercream. Starting 1″ away from point of heart, divide each side into tenths and mark on top and bottom edges. Transfer Wilton Way III message pattern to cake top or make your own.

PIPE 21 GARLANDS around base of cake with tube 340. This tube makes a fluffy, strongly textured garland. Frame garlands with tube 339. Pipe message and scrolls on cake top with tube 85. Do top garlands with tube 340, then add tube 136 stars and insert candles. Serve to twelve.

TRIM A PETAL CAKE
WITH HEARTS AND SCALLOPS
(above)

Specialty tubes give the hearts and scalloped curves on this cake a raised, sculptural look.

BAKE, FILL AND ICE a two-layer 12″ petal cake. Lightly mark curves to define scallops on side of cake and about 1″ in on top. Mark a 4½″ circle in the center of the cake top.

PIPE SHELL BORDERS on base and top edges with tube 63. Pipe tube 353 hearts in center of each "petal" on cake side. Do scallops and fleurs-de-lis with tube 85. On top of cake, print name in center of marked circle with tube 85. Letters are about 1¼″ high. Add scallops and fleurs-de-lis with the same tube. Finish the cake-top trim with tube 353 hearts. Serve to 26.

CHAPTER NINETEEN

Decorating Icings
and Their Characteristics

by Norman Wilton

Icing is the basic material used by the decorator. Therefore it is important to understand the various icings and their characteristics—how they are made, whether they dry hard or stay soft, which is the best for a certain purpose. With this knowledge you can use your own judgement in choosing icings to cover and decorate a cake, perhaps changing from a written direction to substitute your own choice.

There are basically three types of icing—boiled, royal and buttercream. Get to know all of them, then feel free to make your own choices for decorating beautiful cakes.

THE BOILED ICINGS

There are two kinds of boiled icing, one made with egg whites, the other with meringue powder. Let's discuss the advantages and disadvantages of each.

Egg white boiled icing. A boiled icing is just like an angel food cake—even a little bit of grease will flatten out the icing and it won't whip up lightly. So be sure your bowls and all your tools are absolutely grease-free. While the sugar, water and cream of tartar are heating to 238° or 240° F, dip a pastry brush in hot water and wash down the sides of the pan five or six times. Otherwise, granules of sugar will form and make the finished icing gritty. Meanwhile, while the syrup is cooking, beat the egg whites with an electric beater. Remember, separate the whites and the yolks, then let the egg whites come to room temperature before beating. They'll whip to a higher volume. After the hot syrup is com-

bined with the whipped egg whites, powdered sugar is added to give the icing body. This fluffy icing is similar to Seven Minute Icing.

Among the advantages of egg white boiled icing are its good taste and the fact that egg whites are readily available. It remains soft and therefore is fine for icing a cake.

However, egg white boiled icing has several limitations. It is not particularly good for decorating. After it is made you must use it at once, for it cannot be stored and rebeaten.

Boiled icing made with meringue powder is put together almost the same way as egg white boiled icing. One big advantage is that this icing does not need refrigerating and can be rebeaten to its original consistency. I've been gone for as long as ten days on a trip to give demonstrations on decorating to groups of people. I take along meringue powder boiled icing packed in plastic bags. When I'm ready to demonstrate, I just squeeze the icing into a mixing bowl and whip it back into its original consistency.

I like to use it for most flowers and borders, but it tastes too tart for icing a cake. I prefer a cake to be iced in buttercream or covered with rolled or poured fondant, then do the decorating in boiled icing made with meringue powder.

A disadvantage is that this icing tends to crust up in the winter time or in dry weather. When you cut it, it will chip, almost like royal icing. To keep it tender, add a little glycerin. When I was doing a lot of cakes, I would add nulomoline (available at bakery supply houses) as well as

Continued on next page

glycerin. To a ten quart batch I would add two tablespoons of glycerin and a half-cup of nulomoline. You'll need to experiment a little because it all depends on the weather and how dry your house is. For just a small batch, glycerin alone is sufficient. Keep it well covered with a damp towel in dry weather.

Boiled Icing made with meringue is surely my preference for decorating.

ROYAL ICINGS

Use royal icing when you want your decorations to dry very hard. It's the best icing for delicate flowers, lattice, filigree and some figure piping. It will dry as hard as a mint lozenge.

One of the biggest advantages of royal icing is that you can pipe flowers with it well ahead of time. Then on a busy decorating day you can quickly arrange the flowers on your cakes.

If you've ever decorated a cake with a beautiful spray of flowers on it, you know that people want to save that beauty, not cut through it. So make your flowers of royal icing. Then you can lift them off and give them as souvenirs.

ONLY ROYAL ICING FLOWERS are strong enough to mount on wire stems to make a bouquet. You can use this icing to pipe leaves right on the end of a length of florists' wire to fill out your bouquet. If you want to attach a heavy flower to the side of a cake, pipe a spike of royal icing on the back. After it's dry, you can push the spike right into the cake and the flower will stay there securely.

ROYAL ICING MAKES A STRONG "CEMENT" to secure one part of a decoration to another. I use it for sugar molds, lattice ornaments to top wedding cakes, even to put together a gingerbread house.

MIX ROYAL ICING AND BOILED ICING together, half and half, for piping roses, pansies and other strong flowers. This mixture will pipe a well-shaped flower and is much easier to squeeze out of the cone or bag than straight royal icing.

DON'T OVER-WHIP royal icing. The more you beat it, the more air cells you're putting in the icing. It can become so light and aerated it's just like boiled icing. Then it becomes less durable. You can take a big rose made with aerated royal icing, and after it's dry, just squeeze it slightly and it will go into powder, because the icing has become just a series of air cells. Especially for lattice and fine lace you want your icing to be as strong as possible, so don't over-beat.

EGG WHITE AND MERINGUE POWDER royal icings are used for the same purposes—the egg white icing is even a little stronger. Be sure to store the egg white royal in the refrigerator, otherwise it will spoil. Both icings need to be kept covered with a damp towel, since they dry out quickly. Of course, you'd never ice a cake with royal icing— it dries too hard—but it's perfect for a dummy display cake you'd like to keep a long time.

BUTTERCREAM ICINGS

There are various recipes for buttercream but they all contain powdered sugar, some liquid and either shortening or butter. The shortening or butter keeps the icing soft so it cuts easily and is the most popular icing for covering the cake. It also has a better flavor than most other icings. If you whip it up, it becomes very light and fluffy.

YOU CAN PIPE FLOWERS with buttercream, but first you must stiffen the icing with additional powdered sugar. You can air-dry or freeze the flowers, and then arrange them on a cake top, but boiled or royal flowers are easier to handle.

THERE ARE SOME LIMITATIONS to buttercream. Some people do all their decorating, including flowers and borders, with it, but I find that much buttercream too rich. I prefer to have the cake iced in buttercream, then decorated with meringue boiled icing. Buttercream is a little difficult to work with, too, in hot humid weather because the shortening tends to soften.

TESTED RECIPES FOR DECORATING ICINGS

All of these recipes have been tested and re-tested by the Wilton Book Division staff—each is excellent for its own purposes. Most cakes in this book are iced in buttercream, then decorated with meringue powder boiled icing, but experiment with all these recipes, then use your own judgement as to which is best for the task at hand. All recipes produce an icing of medium consistency, ideal for most uses.

TO PREPARE A CAKE OR TIER for icing, first chill it, brush off all loose crumbs, fill and set on a corru-gated cardboard cake circle the same size and shape. To keep the icing crumb-free, brush the cake with hot apricot glaze. Heat apricot preserves to boiling, strain and use immediately. This glaze will dry in just a few minutes, helps to keep the cake fresh and moist and adds a touch of tangy flavor. You may prefer to cover the cake with a thin coat of buttercream, and let it set before the final icing with buttercream.

IT IS NECESSARY TO THIN THE ICING for piping leaves, stringwork or lettering. Do this by adding a small amount of piping gel to any icing except Color Flow icing. The amount varies according to humidity. Start with one teaspoon per recipe, then add more as needed. Corn syrup will also thin icings satisfactorily. *For Color Flow* icing, thin with water. *For royal icing,* a few drops of lemon juice may be used.

To STIFFEN ICING for piping most flowers, add confectioners' sugar to the basic recipe. This will help to make petals stand up in natural fashion.

A HEAVY-DUTY ELECTRIC MIXER IS IDEAL for mixing icing, but a standard mixer may be used when the recipe yields four cups or less. Do not use a hand-held mixer.

WILTON BOILED ICING—EGG WHITE

A good-tasting snow-white icing for covering the cake. Do not use for flowers or borders. Any trace of grease will break it down.

    2 cups granulated sugar
    ½ cup water
    ¼ teaspoon cream of tartar
    4 egg whites (room temperature)
    1½ cups confectioners' sugar,
        measured then sifted

Boil granulated sugar, water and cream of tartar to 240°F. Brush sides of pan with warm water five or six times while syrup is heating to prevent crystals from forming. Do not stir. Meanwhile, whip egg whites seven minutes at high speed. Add boiled sugar mixture slowly, beat three minutes at high speed. Turn to second speed, gradually add confectioners' sugar, beat seven minutes more at high speed. Rebeating will not restore the texture of the icing. Yield: 3½ cups.

WILTON BOILED ICING—MERINGUE

Excellent for piping borders and flowers, but not suitable for covering the cake. Grease will break this icing down.

    2 cups granulated sugar
    1 cup warm water
    ¼ teaspoon cream of tartar
    4 level tablespoons meringue powder
    3½ cups sifted confectioners' sugar

Boil granulated sugar, ½ cup water and cream of tartar to 240°F. Brush side of pan with warm water and a pastry brush to keep crystals from forming. Meanwhile, mix meringue powder with ½ cup water, beat seven minutes at high speed. Turn to low speed, add confectioners' sugar, beat four minutes at high speed. Slowly add boiled sugar mixture, beat five minutes at high speed. Store tightly covered in the re-

frigerator. Rebeat before using again. Yield for this recipe: 6 cups.

WILTON ROYAL ICING—MERINGUE

This is a very durable, hard-drying icing and should not be used for covering the cake. It is perfect for piping long-lasting flowers and for "cementing" sections of trim.

    3 level tablespoons meringue powder
    1 pound confectioners' sugar, sifted
    3½ ounces warm water
    ½ teaspoon cream of tartar

Combine ingredients, mixing slowly, then beat at high speed for seven to ten minutes. Be sure all utensils are completely grease-free. Keep covered with a damp cloth, icing dries quickly. To restore texture, rebeat. Yield: 3½ cups.

WILTON ROYAL ICING—EGG WHITE

This icing dries even harder than meringue royal icing. It is used for the same purpose as that icing and also for piping lace, fine stringwork and lattice. Be sure all utensils are free of grease.

    3 egg whites (room temperature)
    1 pound confectioners' sugar, sifted
    ¼ teaspoon cream of tartar

Combine ingredients and beat at high speed for seven to ten minutes. Dries quickly—keep covered with a damp cloth. Rebeating will not restore texture. Yield: 3 cups.

WILTON SNOW-WHITE BUTTERCREAM

A pure white icing with a fine flavor. It covers the cake well, tints to clear and true colors (these will match the hues of royal icing flowers) and pipes precise borders and flowers for the cake top.

    ⅔ cup water
    4 tablespoons meringue powder
    1¼ cups solid white vegetable shortening,
        room temperature
    ¾ teaspoon salt
    ¼ teaspoon butter flavoring
    ½ teaspoon almond flavoring
    ½ teaspoon clear vanilla
    11½ cups sifted confectioners' sugar

Combine water and meringue powder and whip at high speed until peaks form. Add four cups sugar, one cup at a time, beating at low speed after each addition. Alternately add shortening and remainder of sugar. Add salt and flavorings and beat at low speed until smooth. This icing may be stored, well-covered, in the refrigerator for several weeks, then brought to room temperature and rebeaten. Yield: 8 cups. Recipe may be cut in half or doubled.

WILTON CHOCOLATE BUTTERCREAM

This is an exceptionally good-tasting icing. Fine for covering the cake and for piping cake-top flowers. Flowers can be piped in advance and air-dried or they can be frozen if the weather is warm and humid. Place them on the cake top right from the freezer just before serving.

⅓ cup butter
⅓ cup solid, white vegetable shortening
½ cup cocoa
½ cup milk
1 teaspoon vanilla
⅛ teaspoon salt
1 pound confectioners' sugar, sifted
5 tablespoons cool milk or cream

Cream butter and shortening together with an electric mixer. Mix together the cocoa and ½ cup of milk and add to creamed mixture. Beat in sugar, one cup at a time, blending well after each addition and scraping sides and bottom of bowl with a spatula frequently. Add the cool milk, vanilla and salt and beat at high speed until it becomes light and fluffy. Keep icing covered with a lid or damp cloth and store in the refrigerator. Bring to room temperature and rebeat to use again. For a very dark color, add one or two drops of brown food coloring. Yield: 3⅔ cups.

FIGURE PIPING ICING

1½ cups granulated sugar
⅓ cup water
¼ teaspoon cream of tartar
2 tablespoons meringue powder
⅓ cup lukewarm water
⅝ cup sifted confectioners' sugar

Cook the first three ingredients to 236°F. While this mixture is cooking, beat meringue powder with lukewarm water until it peaks. Add confectioners' sugar slowly, then beat at medium speed until blended. Now pour the cooked mixture into meringue mixture and continue beating at medium speed until peaks form. Wrap the bowl with towels wrung out of cold water to cool the icing while you are beating. The quicker the icing is cooled, the better it is. (A heavy duty mixer is needed.) Use immediately. Yield: 4 cups.

ROLLED FONDANT

This is the rolled icing that gives a perfectly smooth decorating surface.

½ ounce gelatin
¼ cup water
2 tablespoons solid white shortening
½ cup glucose
¾ ounce glycerine

2 pounds confectioners' sugar, sieved three times
2 or 3 drops clear flavoring

Put gelatin and water in a small pan and heat gently until just dissolved. Add shortening, glucose and glycerine and heat until shortening is just melted. Mix well. Put sieved sugar in a large bowl and make a well in the center. Pour warm liquid mixture into well and mix with your hands to a dough-like consistency. Transfer to a smooth surface covered with non-stick pan release and lightly dusted with cornstarch. Knead until smooth and pliable. Add flavoring while kneading. If too stiff, add a few drops of boiling water.

Use immediately or store in an airtight container at room temperature for up to a week. Knead again before rolling out. If storing longer, refrigerate and bring to room temperature before kneading and rolling out. Recipe will cover an 8″ x 3″ square or a 9″ x 3″ round cake.

To COVER A CAKE with rolled fondant, bake a fruitcake or pound cake. Set on matching cake circle, fill any cracks or holes with marzipan and brush with apricot glaze. Roll out marzipan to a circle large enough to cover cake. Smooth over entire cake and trim off excess at base. Brush with glaze again, roll out fondant and cover and trim cake just as you did with marzipan.

MARZIPAN

1 cup almond paste (8-ounce can)
2 egg whites, unbeaten
3 cups confectioners' sugar
½ teaspoon vanilla or rum flavor

Knead almond paste by hand in a bowl. Add egg whites and mix well. Continue kneading as you add sugar, one cup at a time, and flavoring, until the marzipan feels like heavy pie dough. Cover with plastic wrap, then place in a tightly covered container in the refrigerator to keep for months. To tint marzipan, knead in liquid food coloring, one drop at a time, until you reach the shade you desire. To glaze, combine ½ cup corn syrup and one cup of water, heat to boiling and brush on with a small artist's brush. This gives a soft shine. For a high gloss, use just one or two tablespoons water with ½ cup corn syrup. To attach marzipan pieces, brush with egg white and press together.

To ROLL OUT MARZIPAN, dust work surface with confectioners' sugar and roll out to ¼″ thickness.

To COVER A CAKE IN THE ENGLISH MANNER, fill holes or cracks with marzipan and set on matching cake circle. Brush top with apricot glaze and set upside down on a circle of rolled marzipan. Trim with a sharp knife. Shape remaining marzipan in a long cylinder and flatten with a rolling pin. Lay a ruler on strip and trim one side to a straight edge. Brush side of cake with apricot glaze and set on strip, bottom on straight edge. Roll like a wheel to cover side. Trim top edge and butt seam. Pat to smooth and let harden 48 hours before icing with two thin coats of royal icing.

WILTON QUICK POURED FONDANT

This icing for covering the cake gives a smooth, shiny finish that is perfect for decorating.

6 cups confectioners' sugar
4½ ounces water
2 tablespoons corn syrup
1 teaspoon almond flavoring

Combine water and corn syrup. Add to sugar in a saucepan and stir over low heat until well-mixed and heated until lukewarm. Fondant must be thick enough so it won't run off the cake but thin enough to be poured. Stir in flavor and liquid food color if desired.

TO COVER A CAKE with poured fondant, ice the cake thinly with buttercream. Place the cake on a cooling rack with a pan or cookie sheet beneath it. Pour fondant over the iced cake, flowing from the center and moving out in a circular motion. Fondant that drips onto the sheet can be reheated and poured again. Yields four cups—enough fondant to cover an 8″ cake.

CHOCOLATE QUICK POURED FONDANT

Follow the recipe for Quick Poured Fondant, but increase the amount of water by 1 ounce. After it is heated, stir in 3 ounces of melted, unsweetened chocolate, then add flavoring.

COLOR FLOW ICING

1 pound confectioners' sugar
2 level tablespoons Color Flow mix
3 ounces water

Combine sugar and Color Flow mix, then add water. Set electric mixer at low speed and mix for five minutes. Too high a speed will beat air into the icing and the finished work may have bubbles. Use at once for outlining areas. Keep bowl covered with a damp cloth while working—icing dries quickly.

To thin icing for filling in areas, place a portion in a small bowl and stir in water, a few drops at a time. *Never beat.* Icing is of proper consistency when a spoonful dropped back into bowl disappears at the count of ten.

GUM PASTE

Baroque trims, flowers that look like fresh-cut blooms and lifelike little figures are all achievable with this pliable substance.

1 tablespoon Gum-tex™ or tragacanth gum
1 heaping tablespoon glucose
3 tablespoons warm water
1 pound confectioners' sugar (or more)

Heat glucose and water till just warm. Mix Gum-tex with 1 cup of the sugar and add to glucose mixture. Mix well. Gradually knead in enough sugar until you have used about ¾ pound.

Gum paste handles best when aged, so store in a plastic bag at least overnight, then break off a piece and work in more sugar until pliable but not sticky. Always keep well-covered.

To store for a length of time, place gum paste in a plastic bag and then in a covered container to prevent drying. It will keep several months.

To tint, add color directly to the gum paste by applying a small amount of paste food color with a toothpick. Knead to spread tint.

TO ROLL OUT GUM PASTE, dust your work surface well with cornstarch. Work a small piece of gum paste and roll it out with a small rolling pin, also dusted with cornstarch.

TO MOLD GUM PASTE, follow the directions that come with the molds.

CHAPTER TWENTY

Tubes in Variety Create Showpieces

FAMILIARITY WITH ALL THE TUBES and what they can do will free your talent to work quickly, creatively, enjoyably. Leaf through this parade of pretty cakes to see how the use of well-chosen tubes can produce decorating effects of real beauty and originality.

THREE SIMPLY BEAUTIFUL CAKES

A cake needn't be elaborate to be appealing! These three charmers show how simple designs piped with the proper tubes can produce cakes of distinction, very quickly decorated.

THE "QUILT" PATTERN on the cake above looks intricate, but is quick to do. Make your own pattern for the squares—each is 2″, space between each is ¼″. See a closeup on page 305. Transfer it to a two-layer 10″ square cake iced in buttercream. Tube 83 does all the decorating. Pipe reverse shell top and bottom borders. Pipe a fleur-de-lis on each corner of each marked square and add dots in center. Color contrast brings out the pretty design. Serves 16 generously.

THE DAINTY BIRTHDAY CAKE at left starts with two 10″ round layers covered with poured fondant. Divide the cake in tenths to mark the scalloped top design, use a 2″ cookie cutter for the circles on the side. Press a 6″ cake circle on the top to define the message. Do all the decorating with round tubes, tube 8 for base border, tube 2 for lettering, tube 1 for the tiny scallops. The flowers are piped with tube 96. Serves 14.

THE IRISH CAKE at left, is a two-layer 8″ square, covered again with poured fondant. Mark a 5″ circle on top and pipe harp with tube 85. (See page 305.) Add tube 2 strings. The shamrocks almost pipe themselves with tube 353. Use this tube for the base border too. Serve to twelve.

317

FLOWERS TRIM ROMANTIC CAKES

VIOLETS MEAN FAITHFUL LOVE in the language of flowers. Here they're heaped on a shower cake topped by a lacy piped parasol. Make the flowers ahead in royal icing with petal tube 101. The parasol is piped on a greased 4½" ball mold in tube 13 scrolls. Use Wilton Way III pattern and royal icing. Remove from the ball when dry and attach a cocktail stirrer with icing for handle.

Assemble the two-layer tiers, a 12" x 4" and an 8" x 3" round. The trim is all piped with stellar tube 502. Arrange the violets, add tube 65 leaves and serve to 32.

THE DAISY MEANS "I SHARE YOUR LOVE" so it is an appropriate trim for this exquisite cake for a wedding anniversary. Pipe the flowers on wire stems in the Philippine manner described on page 279. Also make some sampaquita sprays.

Pipe tube 59° petals directly on 8" lengths of fine florists' wire. Start with a three-petal bud at the tip and gradually add more petals to make rose-like flowers as you move down. Form four sprays to insert in Flower Spikes.

Glue a plastic filigree heart to an ornament plate, then attach flowers. Paint 9" separator plates with pink thinned royal icing and insert pink tulle into iridescent pillars and bells.

Assemble two-layer tiers, 14" and 8" round. Hang the bells with invisibile thread taped to the underside of the separator plate. Mark Wilton Way III patterns on tiers, then cover them with tube 1 cornelli up to the marked areas. All borders and scrolls are piped with closed star tubes. Trim the cake with flowers and add the names of the happy couple. Serve to 46 party guests.

A RUFFLED CAKE FOR THE FIRST ANNIVERSARY

Cascades of sweet peas give color to this winsome cake with a single candle to light up the first wedding anniversary. Star-cut tube 87 makes quick work of all the ruffled garlands and lavish borders.

Ice and assemble a two-layer 9″ x 13″ tier and a single-layer 6″ round. Mark heart shapes with a 2″ heart cutter and edge with a ruffle. Pipe curved shell borders and ruffled garlands. Make the unique ornament by gluing a filigree heart to a petite ornament plate. Add a little winged angel and tiny tube 101s sweet peas. Pipe tube 103 sweet peas and form the lavish cascades. Finish with tube 65 leaves, two angel musicians and the single taper. Light it and serve the cake to 27 party guests.

A FLOWER CART HEAPED WITH GARDEN ZINNIAS

That's the feature of this charming cake. Here's a different way to pipe the brilliant zinnias in royal icing. Pipe a tube 7 ball on rounded flower nail number 2 and flatten with your fingertip. Starting at outer edge of ball, pipe rows of tube 101 petals, lifting each row a little higher. Add a tube 13 star and tube 1s dots in the center.

Make the cart in rolled gum paste using Wilton Way III pattern. Pipe the wheels in royal icing with tube 5 and trim the cart with tube 2.

Assemble a 9″ x 13″ two-layer tier and a single-layer 9″ oval tier. The fence effect is piped with ribbon tubes 48 and 47. Shell borders are done with graduated sizes of the Stellar tubes. Arrange the zinnias, then trim with tube 66 leaves. Serve this summertime treat to 30.

Petal tubes make the beautiful flowers that trim these cakes—rich color enhances their beauty.

CHOCOLATE ROSES FOR DAD

Pipe luscious chocolate buttercream roses and buds with tube 124 and arrange a spray on a sheet cake. Dad will be delighted!

Ice the top of a two-layer 9″ x 13″ cake white, sides chocolate. Transfer Wilton Way III pattern and do message in fill-in method described on page 117. Fill in with piping gel. Cover sides of cake with ribbon tube 48 and edge with tube 21 shell borders. Pipe stems with tube 6, arrange flowers and trim with tube 68 leaves. Serve to 24.

POPPIES FOR AN ANNIVERSARY

If they were married in August, the spectacular poppy is their flower. Pipe the double ruffled petals on nail number 8 with tubes 104 and 103 for two sizes. Pipe a tube 8 green ball in the center. Top with a tube 27 star and surround with tube 1 yellow dots. Pipe a few tube 101 tiny poppies for ornament.

BAKE, FILL AND ICE three two-layer tiers—a 14″ round, 4″ high, an 8″ x 3″ square and a 6″ x 3″ round. Set the square tier on a 9″ square separator plate and place on base tier. Use a 7″ round separator plate and clear pillars to support the top tier. Decorate plastic numerals and glue to a popsicle stick to insert in square tier.

FINELY CUT STAR TUBES are featured in the beautiful borders. Pipe tube 199 hearts, and tube 364 stars at the base of the bottom tier and trim with tube 4 balls. A tube 364 garland trimmed with tube 4 edges the top of the tier. Add tube 4 stringwork and dots.

On base of middle tier pipe tube 364 hearts and stars, tube 4 trim. Use tube 363 to pipe hearts and daisy shapes on top of tier with tube 3 trim and dropped stringwork.

Edge base of top tier with tube 363 hearts and stars, and use the same tube for the top border. Trim with tube 3.

Set a cherub figure on the cake top and attach all the beautiful flowers. Pipe the names with tube 3. Serve to 54 party guests.

323

A TINY TUBE PIPES DELICATE TRACERIES ON WEDDING CAKES

A small round tube and the fine line technique pipe designs as fragile as the finest lace on these breathtaking cakes. Use Wilton Way III patterns as guides, but the designs must be done freehand. Review the information on page 97, and measure and mark the cakes carefully.

A CAKE FOR THE BRIDE

Bake and fill the petite tiers—a two-layer 12" round and a two-layer 6" square. Cover with poured fondant in the palest tint of pink. Assemble with 5" Corinthian pillars and 7" square plates. Divide lower tier in eighths and mark just the main points of the pattern. Transfer the main points of side pattern to upper tier. Press a 2" heart cookie cutter in each corner of the top of the upper tier to guide the piping.

Using patterns as guides, pipe all designs with tube 1s and thinned royal icing. Edge separator plate with tube 3, then outline with a fine line border. Use tube 7 for ball border on lower tier, tube 5 for upper tier. Add cupid figures and ribbon bows at tops of pillars. Base tier serves 68, upper tier 18 wedding guests.

A CAKE FOR THE GROOM

Precisely trimmed with fine line piping, this confection makes beautiful harmony with the dainty bridal cake.

Mix four tablespoons of cocoa with the poured fondant recipe and cover a two-layer 8" round cake. Fold a 7" paper circle into thirty-seconds and use it to mark points of scallops on top of cake. Press cake with 2½" round cookie cutter to define center motif.

Use tube 1s and thinned royal icing for all decorating. First pipe the center motif, then the scallops on cake top. Use scallops as guide to drop strings extending to side of cake. Add hearts, fleurs-de-lis and dots. Using upper border as guide, pipe hearts connected with curves on side of cake. Finish with dropped strings and dots. Pipe a tube 6 ball border at base of cake and it's ready to take its place on the reception table. Serve wedding cake-sized pieces to 30.

325

TUBES SHOWN IN THIS BOOK IN NUMERICAL ORDER

All 180 of the tubes readily available to American decorators are pictured in actual size in this book. With these tubes you can achieve an amazing variety of effects in the Wilton-American style of decorating. They also can be used to decorate in any of the foreign methods.

tube number	page shown	tube number	page shown	tube number	page shown
000	53	44	265	112	250
00L	68	45	265	113	250
0L	68	46	265	114	250, 289
1	53	47	265	115	250, 289
1A	53, 289	48	265	116	15
1B	238, 288	49	221, 235	118	15
1C	238, 288	50	221	119	15
1D	265, 286	51	221	121	15
1E	238, 289	52	221	122	15
1F	238, 289	53	221	123	15
1G	238, 288	54	221, 235	124	10
1L	68	55	150	125	10
1s	53	57	150	126	10
2	53	59	15	127	10
2A	53, 289	59s	15	127R	286
2B	265	60	15	129	236
2C	238	61	15	131	236
2D	238	62	305	132	165, 235
2E	238	63	305	133	165
2F	238	64	305	134	150
2L	68	65	248	135	236
3	53	65s	248	136	305
4	53	66	248	140	236
4B	287	67	248	150	265
5	53	68	248	172	287
6	53	69	248	177	236
6B	287	70	248	190	236
7	53	71	224	191	236
8	53	72	224	193	236
8B	287	73	224	194	238
9	53	74	224	195	287
10	53	75	224	199	163
11	53	76	224	217	236
12	53	77	221, 235	220	236
13	160	78	221	224	236
14	160	79	276	225	236
15	160, 235	80	276	233	150
16	160	81	276	234	150
17	160, 235	83	305	320	223, 235
18	160	85	305	326	248
19	160	87	223	327	265
20	160, 235	88	223	339	305
21	160	89	150	340	305
22	160	95	305	347	223
23	165, 235	96	223, 235	349	248
24	165	97	15	352	248
25	165	98	223	353	305
26	165	99	305	355	248
27	165, 235	100	305	362	163
28	165	101	10	363	163
29	165, 235	101s	10	364	163
30	165	102	10	401	276
31	165, 235	103	10	402	276
32	163	104	10	403	286
33	165, 235	105	223	501	162, 235
34	165	106	236	502	162, 235
35	165, 235	107	236	504	162, 235
41	150	108	236	506	162, 235
42	150	109	236	508	162, 235, 288
43	150	110	223	789	286

INDEX